CLOSE QUARTERS

NEIL HARMAN

CLOSE QUARTERS

An Extraordinary Season on the Brink

First published by Pitch Publishing, 2020

Pitch Publishing
A2 Yeoman Gate
Yeoman Way
Worthing
Sussex
BN13 3QZ
www.pitchpublishing.co.uk
info@pitchpublishing.co.uk

ISBN 978 1 78531 717 0

Typesetting and origination by Pitch Publishing
Printed and bound by TJ International, Padstow, UK

Contents

Introduction

IT had to be a team that wore blue. Nothing political, mind. I had been that odd one out in my road, at school and on the local playing fields, wearing the Manchester City kit of the 60s, imagining myself as Colin Bell or Francis Lee. There was something about the colouring that was so distinct.

I was lucky enough to report on my home-town club Southend United – 'the Blues' – and cover Billericay Town when they won the FA Vase in 1976 and 1977 wearing blue. A career graduation offered the opportunity to become the Blues writer on the *Sports Argus*, delivering a full page every weekend on Birmingham City in the days of the beloved Frank Worthington, Colin Todd and Archie Gemmill. Then I moved to Manchester, where Maine Road was a regular work stop and I got to meet Colin Bell and Francis Lee.

At that time, Trevor Francis, the first £1m English player, had moved to City and manager John Bond regularly dispensed champagne at press conferences before the club entered another of its twilight zones. Bond resigned, City were relegated and I befriended the new boss Billy McNeill, a hero forever in my eyes. Green became a second-favourite colour.

It was when I was collaborating on a book with Harry Findlay, the gambler, who regaled me with stories about how much supporting Wycombe Wanderers had played a part in his teenage years that an idea sprung into my head. It wasn't a novel one. Hunter Davies wrote the acclaimed *The Glory Game,* spending a season with Tottenham Hotspur in the 1970s and, contemporarily, my old pal Michael Calvin had done the same with Millwall when he penned the excellent *Family.*

Wycombe Wanderers, though. Would anyone care? Could it be a sell? I'd met Gareth Ainsworth the manager a few times, chatting sport and stuff. We lived 15 minutes apart and would see each other in church or at the local Caffe Nero. He definitely wasn't your archetypal football manager.

I checked on the club and it was clear they had something disarming about it. A proud non-league history, an FA Cup semi-final in 2001 when they lost to Liverpool, a cup tie a few years back at Tottenham Hotspur when they should have won but lost deep into injury time and what seemed like an annual flirtation with either promotion or relegation.

There was the penalty shootout loss in the 2015 League Two play-off final at Wembley against my Southend. Wycombe didn't appear to do plain sailing. They were also skint.

Martin O'Neill had managed them, so too had John Gregory, John Gorman, Peter Taylor, Paul Lambert, Lawrie Sanchez , Tony Adams and Gary Waddock, which was a pretty esteemed list. I chatted with O'Neill before setting out. 'I loved it, absolutely loved it,' he said of his five years in charge. 'I was actually late with my application and the job had been offered to Kenny Swain who was at Crewe at the time. But he changed his mind, I was interviewed and took the job.'

O'Neill was 37 when he was appointed, led the club back to the Football League from the old Conference, and then into Division Two (now League One) after winning the Division Three (League Two) play off final at Wembley against Preston North End. O'Neill's side also won the FA Trophy twice, in 1991, his first full season as the manager, and 1993.

'Brian Clough used to say that it didn't matter what trophy it was, it could be the Anglo-Scottish Cup or the European Cup, it meant you had won *something*. All the Wycombe teams I managed had a special bond.

'From a distance, I sense Gareth has the same rapport with his squad I had. He has excellent charisma. He may not look like your average manager but what he's done has been absolutely terrific. He's been able to attract players while working under a real handicap. Players want to play for Wycombe and I'm sure it's because they want to play for him. And it is a lovely club.'

The fear in starting something like this was that nothing would happen, the team would be average, the season free of incident, the players failed to engage, the storylines were few and far between and the writer would have to overindulge in imagination. Trust me, I didn't. There were occasions though when there was a distinct blurring between non-fiction and fiction.

I am indebted to Jane from Pitch Publishing for coming on board with the concept, who helped shape its structure and prodded me along. Andy Rowland of Prime Media Images has provided most of the pictures, the others I took with my iPhone. Thanks, of course, to Duncan Olner who designed the cover, Michelle Grainger who edited the book and Graham Hales who organised the picture section.

Along the way I have met and become great mates with so many terrific people. Matt Cecil and Conor Shaw from the club's media department were exceptional from the word go and I have forgiven their insistence on keeping me abreast of the goal flashes from Roots Hall rather too smugly for my liking.

These introductions are inevitably tricky in case you miss someone out, so could I please thank with the utmost sincerity the staff, management, executive and matchday volunteers at Wycombe Wanderers FC for going out of their way every day to make what was an historic and unforgettable season that bit more special.

As for the players, manager, the coaching staff and all at the training ground that became a second home (a special shout out to chef extraordinaire Ahmed Maaref) there's little I can say about them that they didn't say for themselves. They are a truly remarkable bunch of people who, in the year I was side by side with them, did truly remarkable things.

Wycombe is, indeed, a lovely club.

Neil Harman,
31 July 2020

The Madness Awaits

THE morning of Thursday, 25 July 2019 had broken and found the United Kingdom in a similarly shattered state. For three years the old country had been up to its nostrils in divisive angst and days like this compounded both misery and the loss of a common sense of direction.

A deep blue British sky was usually to be cherished but the heat was becoming too oppressive. The mercury this day would near 100°F, causing overhead railway cables to crackle, lines buckle, points fail and thus services were cancelled, concourses choked, thoroughfares clogged and buses rammed.

Queues formed everywhere. One of the longest was outside a London lido where even if you were patient enough to make it through the throng, stripped off and entered the cooling waters, there was only enough elbow room to bob up and down as if you were impersonating a buoy.

Rather than acknowledge that this shared keeping of heads above water was necessary to contend with the Brexit mayhem ahead, Boris Johnson was characteristically late to the Downing Street podium and welcomed his first full day as Prime Minister as the herald of ambrosia for all the UK's citizens.

This cuffing of reality was to become a common theme in the months ahead, on the football field almost more than in the corrosive chamber of politics. Particularly on one football field in Buckinghamshire.

The day's bananas football news was topped by manic scenes from north London where a couple of knife-wielding car thieves attempted to steal the £90,000 Mercedes SUV of Arsenal's Mesut Ozil (with him still in it) before his team-mate Sead Kolasinac leapt from the passenger seat and took them on with his fists as a quivering Ozil sought sanctuary in a nearby Turkish restaurant.

Nothing quite that exciting was happening in High Wycombe, although there was a bit of a buzz developing. An animated group of young men in light and dark blue football kit filed into a room of balsa walls and splintered window frames where the shade was provided by brown-striped curtains that once hung in a household 20 miles away.

Gareth Ainsworth, the manager of League One Wycombe Wanderers, grew weary of complaints that his players couldn't be expected to work on deployment of forces if they couldn't see what was being explained to them. Any early afternoon sunlight fell directly onto the flat screen at the end of the room, rendering it impossible to define shapes and forms.

Ainsworth's request for spend on curtains was met with the Old Mother Hubbard shoulder shrug that had become the cash-starved Wycombe board's go-to response to housekeeping requests. They said 'No' and insisted this was prudent control of the club's listing state.

The manager drove home, took a pair of cutters to the drapes in his living room and fashioned them into a size that would fit the training ground windows. Now his team would see. He ordered new ones for the house.

On this midsummer murder of a day there was not a spare seat in the refreshingly dark common room that marked quite a transformation at the football club.

A month earlier, Wycombe's supporters had been reduced to squinting at the resources Ainsworth could summon to begin preparations for a second consecutive season in the third tier of English professional football. The count was a meagre seven outfield players and two goalkeepers, and the prevailing mood was one of hopelessness.

The debate that wake-up call of a morning was on the essentials: a lick of paint for the posts and crossbars – 'to make it look to the lads as if we've got some new goals' – additional clips to secure the nets properly to the goal frames and tidying up the unsightly waste at the back of a tin-plated building that had seen better days.

'Come on boys,' Ainsworth implored his five-man staff, assistant manager Richard Dobson, goalkeeping coach Andy Fairman, head of sports science Dave Wates, head of medicine Cian O'Doherty and analyst Josh Hart. 'The chairman's on his way and we need to get these signed off.' I naively wondered if the discussion with Trevor Stroud might incorporate player recruitment. I had plenty to learn about Wycombe Wanderers.

Ainsworth swept his hair behind his ears and scoured the gym floor to see what resources he'd be working with on this first day of pre-season when summer's cobwebs clung to more than just the masonry. The manager wanted to appear his usual energised self – he rarely entered any room without a whoop of enthused delight – but his stomach felt as empty as the landscape one floor down.

A knot of players were being nursed back to health in O'Doherty's department while others were disconnected – centre-half Anthony Stewart had just become engaged and his partner was six months pregnant, and Joe Jacobson, the full-back, had recently returned from his honeymoon. Adebayo Akinfenwa – the face and physique of the team – had been given leave for extra time in Los Angeles where his million followers on Instagram were fed regular updates of hedonism on Sunset Boulevard.

Akinfenwa was pictured with a ridiculously muscled arm across the contrastingly puny shoulders of Jordan Henderson for an image that received a slew of irrepressible comment. 'Bayo' had long been a committed Liverpool fan. Steven Gerrard wrote a glowing foreword to Akinfenwa's autobiography *The Beast* and to stumble across a second Reds' Champions League-winning captain in the flesh was, well, a beautiful thing.

One doubted – given the backdrop of Hollywood Hills – that a conversation between the two men broadened to the state of Wycombe's playing budget for the new season. Had Henderson learned it was a measly £1.15m (his gross wages for a couple of months if the national press were to be believed) he may have been temporarily shaken from his post-Madrid transcendental state.

Two divisions separated Liverpool and Wycombe in pure on-paper terms, but the truth was that unless something nuclear happened to their respective finances the clubs were heading inexorably in opposite directions.

On the back of bounteous American investment and with their worldwide fandom bursting at the seams, Liverpool were able to plunge millions into an aspiration for Premier League supremacy that would be celebrated even more wildly than their 2019 European Cup glory.

Wycombe, largely unheralded beyond junction four of the M40, had long been straining every fiscal sinew for simple, sustainable self-sufficiency. These were now stretched to snapping point. By any conceivable marker the two clubs would be a long way further apart come the following May.

Everywhere you looked, discrepancies were as wide as a sea. A Premier League manager didn't often soil his own hands with the upkeep of the training ground. I may have been wrong but couldn't picture Jurgen Klopp heaving mighty hoses across his shoulders to water its bare spots, shovelling sand where rabbits had left their calling cards, distributing and stacking mannequins, dragging full-sized goals around by the rigging and arguing the finer points of worm infestation.

Ainsworth was as much groundsman as he was manager. Back and forth he ploughed barelegged into knee-high nettles that bordered the training ground to recover ball after ball that missed its target – his players were terribly rusty – and never moaned that this drudgery was beneath him. 'I wouldn't ask anyone to do anything I wouldn't do myself.'

All Ainsworth really wanted was decent player numbers to build a team that could win enough matches to keep Wycombe in League One, not an extravagant dream for a professional football manager but one that was squashed when he was handed his wiggle room for the 2019/20 season.

Then, a few days into rehearsals and with the real thing a month away, there appeared an angel from New Orleans that landed on the manager's shoulder and whispered 'do not fear' or something to that effect. This bringer of news of great joy went by the name of Rob Couhig.

A septuagenarian lawyer with zero experience of English football was promising to sprinkle the magic dust of real, spendable dollars. If he came through, Wycombe might have a shot at survival and at the very least be sportingly competitive. This unexpected gesture from the USA's deep south had encouraged a perceptible bounce in the step of the players, old and new, as they converged for a mandated gathering.

Ainsworth had been able to invest a fraction of Couhig's benevolence as a benefit-in-kind so there were now 23 faces in the group, more than double the count-on-the-fingers-of-one-hand opening day of pre-season.

This was nirvana around these parts. Not only was there a healthy quota of players but the entire football staff were summoned with Kelly Francis, the secretary without whom nothing at the club functioned. These were the trusted few in front of whom the manager could say anything and know it would be kept within the four non-soundproofed walls.

* * *

A reverential hush descended on the group. The pool table cleared. Ainsworth said a few words of introduction and stood aside. The speaker today was not the manager but his irreplaceable second-in-command of seven years Richard 'Dobbo' Dobson. The kernel of his talk was what it meant to be a Wycombe Wanderer.

Dobson bore the appearance of a substitute teacher, the one the bad boys at the back of the class delighted in poking fun at. The 43-year-old had a slender frame, close-shaved fair hair, wore a freshly minted, grey Wycombe training kit and had flip-flops for footwear (well it was beach weather).

For those who had heard him speak many times on his specialised subject and others listening for the first time, it was worth hanging onto every syllable. There was a gravitas to each word. They all counted.

'The gaffer and I spoke about this when we started our journey in 2012. We wanted it to be that every player who joined us stayed with us or came through us, when they moved on would say that the best time in his career was when he was at Wycombe. That we had the best dressing room with the best bunch of people. It started with the characters we have brought into the building.'

He flipped the chart on an easel in a corner of the room. It highlighted the words 'technical', 'tactical', 'social' and 'physical' all directed to a central reference point: 'psychological'. 'What does psychologically strong mean? Resilience has seven factors so you have to dig deeper than that. Every successful team builds on a psychology.

'The best team may not have been the best technical team, the tactical side was our [the coaches'] job, though you could sometimes get away with not being tactically the best. You didn't always have to have the quickest or strongest players but this [pointing to psychological] was what we had in abundance.

'If you got into this building, you'd done well, because all the time you'd been out there on the training pitch, let me tell you new recruits, you had been stalked like you wouldn't believe, on social media, your phone calls, the background checks and so on. You could have had the best trial in the world but, believe me, if you were the wrong type, you wouldn't be in here today.

'How would we know if someone had a good or a bad culture? Txiki Begiristain [Manchester City's director of football] once said that talent would get you into the dressing room but how you behaved within the culture would determine how long you stayed there.

'It wasn't a surprise that people stayed here for long periods of time. Within the space of a couple of years at many clubs, 90 per cent of the squad had turned over but a lot of lads stayed five years, or 15 in Matt Bloomfield's case. Many left and wished they hadn't. A lot came back. This was more than football.'

Dobson would leave favoured quotes and sayings scrawled on boards around the training ground. He was especially fond of the sage words of Frank Dick, the former head coach for UK Athletics, who said 'A coach at some point will have rough diamonds in his team. If being a rough diamond hurts a player it's his choice, if they hurt you it's your choice, if they hurt the team, it's no choice.'

'If it hurts a player, it is his choice, think of that. The standards we set here, if somebody doesn't hit them he is killing himself because he stands out. At some clubs the first player in the gym in the morning will be the only one there and looked on as abnormal. Here if you're not in the gym first thing in the morning and stretching you stand out a mile. What is culture then boys?' The responses came slowly at first, then everyone chipped in – 'beliefs', 'standards', 'way of life', 'routine'.

'Everything you say, everything you do when you come into this club has to align and contribute to the culture every word and every action. If a single person slips by walking into our dressing room before a match with a frappuccino then the whole lot slips. That's where the rest of you say to anyone who falls below what we expect "Hey, this doesn't happen here."

'It doesn't have to be a bollocking but just a simple "these are the standards we set and we don't fall below them as a group".

The social and psychological side are the things that make us because we do them particularly well.'

The perfectly shaded video screen flickered into life to show the New Zealand rugby union team with captain Richie McCaw at its head shaped like the reds at the break of a frame of snooker performing the Haka, the Maori exhortation with its call to work in harmony as one. 'All together!'

Dobson was not advocating that Adam El-Abd – Wycombe's central defender who possessed the build of an openside flanker – lead a display of tongue-poking, eye-popping and thigh-slapping against the forces of Bolton Wanderers on the opening day of the season, much though it would have made a few hairs stand on end.

'What are you seeing boys?' to which responses came from them thick and fast: 'Intensity, passion, union, preparation, pride, fearlessness, respect, commitment to heritage.'

'Those are absolutely right. But culture is not something that you turn on and off like a tap. You can't excel at the training ground then go home and behave like a bloody idiot. This culture has to be within you, always, in terms of excellence. Look at the All Blacks' togetherness. Would the Haka have the same effect if there were three guys doing it in one corner, four in another, five in another?

'The first thing that hit me is that the psychological gains are already mounting against your opponent. When we leave the dressing room, if we do it in dribs and drabs and are still putting our shin pads on in the hallway, what message does that send, as opposed to we all stand there, we wait, and when the captain say it's time, we all walk out together.

'We're saying that we're organised and we're ready. We will leave the dressing room this season when the last person is there. Look at the words you've used watching that clip, they scream "culture" and this is what we're all about. Next I want you to study the intensity of this performance. Everyone knows Pavarotti.'

Scott Kashket broke the contemplative mood by asking, presumably tongue-in-cheek, what team he played for. The ribbing rose and fell quickly. 'Pavarotti has sung this song thousands of times but see the intensity in his face at the end when he knows he's nailed it. This has to be our intensity.'

The final exhilarating chord of Puccini's 'Nessun Dorma' – the BBC's 1990 World Cup anthem – stirred the room. The light in Luciano Pavarotti's eyes at the precision of the last note was that of someone who knew he had given it all that he had in his soul and voicebox. The song was replayed with its volume reduced as Dobson impactfully voiced over.

'This is what will get you to the top. We have to strive for excellence. If you strive for perfection you can't get there. Nobody is perfect. We're going to lose matches. We'll take them on the chin and keep striving for what we're focussing on.

'Now we should talk about first impressions. Whenever anyone walks in, these are vital. I was at the Chelsea training ground a couple of years ago with Steve Holland when he was first-team coach [now the assistant to Gareth Southgate with the England national team]. John Terry was helping himself to lunch. He put down his tray, walked over and introduced himself. I knew who he was. But his actions said a lot about the place for me and you do that a lot now.

'Phones. Phones. I've seen more phones at the training ground already this week than in an EE store. Boys, this is work. We understand life and the world is changing. You take a photograph of yourself on a Saturday night when you're out and you send it to your mates. We get that.

'When we're working, when we're stretching, let's not have phones with us. If the American investors walk through the door and people are on their phones, imagine the impression that sets. I'm not going to police you. I leave that down to you now. That's trust.

'Dress code boys. I thought we were better last season, not walking into service stations wearing flip-flops. For home matches, it's a suit and tie and away we wear club colours. Headphones. I remember watching Arsenal on TV one match last season and every one of the players walked into an away ground with headphones on. It looked terrible. Let's be smart in every way.'

* * *

The final preparatory match of the season set Wycombe against Maidenhead United of the National League eight days before they plunged into ten months of full-on competition. This was the third year in succession the clubs had met in a friendly and Matt Cecil, Wycombe's head of media and a living, breathing encyclopaedia, said it had been a perennially testy occasion.

As a new season neared, so nerve-ends were exposed and tempers easily frayed. At the height of expectancy for the 2018/19 season, Wycombe supporters en route to York Road learned that Luke O'Nien, a highly favoured midfield player for the best part of three years, had been sold to Sunderland for a reported £135,000, which helped pay a bill or ten.

On this appropriately unsettled evening, the reigning supporters' player of the season Jason McCarthy failed to appear on the team sheet. Familiar emotions had been aroused. He was whispered to be heading to Championship club Millwall.

Three previous friendlies had been against buff non-league opposition – firstly Barnet, managed by Darren Currie, who had been Wycombe's £200,000 joint-record signing from the Hertfordshire club in 2001 and who went on to score 14 goals in 126 appearances. How many professional clubs had made its most expensive signing almost two decades ago?

From Barnet, there were contests against Woking – where in the Wycombe team trialists outnumbered official players – and Wealdstone. Half-an-hour before the kick-off at Woking, Adebayo Akinfenwa was having his massive thighs massaged on a leather-trimmed table by the side of the pitch, which looked like something out of a 1950s biblical classic but without the Hedy Lamarr love interest.

When Brentford of the Championship arrived for the one rehearsal at Adams Park, it felt as if something tangible was happening around the ground. Talk of potential American interest in the club was fizzing through the lounges and kiosks and some of Wycombe's football matched the mood of bridled optimism.

They led 2-0 after a first half of imposing intent encapsulated by Northern Irishman Paul Smyth, signed on a year's loan from Queens Park Rangers and truly something out of the blue – an old-fashioned pocket dynamo who ran straight at his defender and lifted bums from seats. We cried out for these players at whatever level we watched the game.

Michael Kenny, the matchday announcer, declared (not over the public address system) that he'd be leaving his girlfriend for Smyth if he kept this up. The second half was far less dramatic. Brentford hauled two goals back, Smyth was substituted and a delicate conversation avoided in the Kenny household.

After the match a knot of Wycombe players mingled in a hospitality lounge with the 500 Club members who had dipped into their pockets to provide the funds necessary so Ainsworth could at least contemplate a summer offer or two.

Alex Pattison, a young midfielder from an exciting but since fractured generation at Middlesbrough, had been the first confirmed new face, due in no small measure to the £20 notes the 500 Clubbers transferred to the club's account to keep things ticking over.

Patto seemed particularly reserved and nervous. I put it down to his age – 21 – and being among strangers and only truly appreciated his reticence when I learned that his mother, Alison, had passed away a few weeks earlier from a recurring brain tumour.

Alex had spent an unfulfilled time on loan to Yeovil from Middlesbrough, returned to his parent club to sign a few statutory forms and walked into his family's home on Teesside to find his mum lying on the floor. He tried to resuscitate her, called an ambulance but knew in his heart of hearts that she had gone.

He was still traumatised, had made up his mind to quit football and try his hand at something else when he took a call from Ainsworth and was given a chance he hadn't expected. 'I talked it over with my nana and dad and they said I should give it a go. It was a League One side after all.' It was a season when he would have to come to terms with such a deep loss and learn how to truly express himself again.

The manager unexpectedly appeared in the suite and marched up to the stage. 'You guys have put your hands in your pockets and said you weren't going to let our club fade away after what happened last year. That enabled me to sign players and determine targets. Alex Pattison is your man, we were confident we could get Dominic Gape to sign for another year and you saw how Paul Smyth tore it up in the first half [loud cheers].

'Since then we've had the introduction of Rob Couhig, Pete, his nephew, and consultant Mark Palmer who we hope are coming in to help out. The feeling around the club is spectacular, so positive, and there's an ambition to build it in the right way. Please don't get carried away and think everything is going to be superb and there's plenty of money so we'll get promoted. That is unreal.

'What is realistic is improving on last year and see if we can do that the year after and the year after that. If we can build in this league, the next target is something special. To think about it is spine-tingling. But for now, let's finish above 17th in League One this season.'

* * *

Six weeks before he uttered those words, Gareth Ainsworth had never heard the name Couhig. In far-off Louisiana, Rob was secret squirrelling into as many elements of Ainsworth

– manager and more importantly man – as he could lay his hands on.

Like any conscientious trial lawyer, Rob pored over the evidence required to construct his case. It was precisely the forensic attention to detail Ainsworth and Richard Dobson used when they were attracted to a player.

A responsible investor dipping his toe into the perilous mire of English football needed to do his due diligence and Rob was sharpening focus on the club in his sights, especially the man who had kept the team's head above the foam. The deeper Couhig dug the more he believed Wycombe Wanderers were the club for him – but only so long as they kept the present occupant in the managerial chair.

This was not a given in their current plight. Having assured Wycombe's survival with 53 points on the last weekend of the previous season – though it would have needed an absurd correlation of results that day to send them down – Ainsworth discovered he would have to make an even better job of patchwork quilting the team next time around.

From the bonus he earned for keeping Wycombe up, he was personally subsidising the pay rise the Supporters' Trust that had run the club for seven years had refused for Dobson. Then he discovered the club hadn't kept up the payments on his health insurance so he had to make good on that shortfall as well.

Wycombe paid the lowest wages in League One and much of League Two. £1,200 a week was the very height of extravagance. One or two took home £1,500+ but they were a significant exception. They had fewer player numbers than any club in direct competition and the hours Ainsworth spent on his knees in his local catholic church could become very useful when negotiating with any player who considered relocating to Adams Park.

He was about to celebrate seven years in his job – only Jim Bentley of League Two Morecambe had currently served one club longer across the four professional leagues – but lack of sustainable hope meant both an acute sense of demoralisation and an ever-increasing susceptibility to itchy feet.

Ainsworth had spent ten days of the summer working flat out to acquire a League Managers' Association diploma, a course on which the pupils were schooled in mental toughness and resilience, transformational leadership, health and well-being and football finance. He could have role-reversed on the last subject. Ainsworth knew so much about shopping on a tight budget he'd have been the perfect face of Poundstretcher.

Wycombe were in dire fiscal straits, more than their most ardent supporters realised. The status as a fans' trust had long been fought for, fiercely protected and admirably principled based on a simple motive to do what they believed best- protected the club. Fans would never let the side down, well not deliberately.

The downside was that in the wacky world of football finance even those supporters with genuine business acumen were wrestling with a sport where the normal rules didn't exist. Being fans once they got into positions of influence, they tended either to become institutional tightwads or no expense spared dream chasers.

Now the Wycombe trust were at their wit's end. The money had run out. The balance sheet simply refused to balance. The manager needed to know what the future held and when he asked the trust leaders what happened next they stared at their feet.

The board of directors of Wycombe Wanderers FC consisted of Trevor Stroud, the chairman, his deputy David Cook and former chairman, now president, Ivor Beeks MBE, JP, who had seen most things come and go (largely go) at the club for half a century; the trust board numbered 11 and all had a say in how Wycombe was run. That was a lot of snouts in a rapidly emptying trough.

* * *

Rob Couhig was not the first American with a glint in his eye to show his hand at Adams Park. From the midpoint of the 2018/19 season, Seaport Capital, a New York City-based private equity company owned by Jim Collis and Bill Luby, was in constructive dialogue with the Trust and its proposal to take control of the club appeared watertight.

Luby had been a member of the consortium that purchased Derby County in January 2008 with the club on the way to relegation from the Premier League. Manager Paul Jewell was given funds in that transfer window and the following summer as 16 players joined and 12 departed, but the team struggled to gel.

Jewell left midway through the following season and was replaced by Nigel Clough, son of Brian, who was such an heroic figure at the club in the 1970s. Derby was said to have played 'austerity football' under Clough Jnr but their finances stabilised. Once that happened Luby's group looked to extricate themselves with a bit in it for them.

Pumped by Wycombe fans eager for intelligence on how it had fared under the alliance, one County contributor wrote that if Collis and Luby became involved 'they'll be all business, hard but professional, probably try to get you up a league and then if a good offer comes will sell. They shrewdly rescued a sinking ship here and stopped a crisis on the field become a crisis off it.'

Collis and Luby had presented to the Wycombe board and the sums added up to the extent the trust were very tempted. Conversations went back and forth for the best part of nine months. Then a former Wanderers player, Andrew Harman, emerged with an offer that skewed hope of a smooth transition.

The Buckinghamshire businessman called a meeting at the Holiday Inn in January 2019, where he proposed an investment of £2m and the construction of an academy bearing his name. There was much debate about whether Harman was on a vanity project and his proposal was rejected ten to one by the trust board. He upped his offer by £500,000 but the margin of opposition remained the same and he stepped away.

That would not have been so bad had Collis and Luby not decided to move on too. They cited investor fatigue brought on by waiting so long for their offer to be accepted and the extent to which the gloss had gone off the entire project for them.

They had a full diary of business interests back in the States that demanded the personal touch and didn't much relish being arm's length owners, saying that was neither fair on them nor the club. They departed leaving a tab for £500,000 they had loaned Wycombe so it could stay afloat while discussions were ongoing. That was another debt that would need settling.

Wycombe were back to square one in the game of chance on a board that contained plenty of snakes and no ladders. Trevor Stroud, chairman of both football club and trust boards, told Ainsworth that in the circumstances drastic cuts were required. The manager was desolate.

He knew players currently on the books would delay signing contract extensions and how could he bargain for new blood when he could offer a mere trifle compared to those clubs who dangled £5,000-a-week cherries on top of sponge-cake salaries?

The minute agents asked what he had in mind for wages, Ainsworth could just imagine the cackling laughter and clicks on the line.

* * *

Through Mark Palmer's network of contacts, the Couhigs had initially been ready to invest in Yeovil, the Somerset club that climbed to the Championship in 2013 then slid down the leagues like a toboggan whose brakes had failed.

A forensic assessment concluded – with sound evidential logic – that Yeovil had long fought a losing battle with their balance sheet. The family thought they had a deal agreed but the Yeovil board suddenly, ungraciously, rejected them. Rob Couhig never did find out why.

'I was very disappointed the way we were treated there. People said we backed out because they got relegated but nothing could have been further from the truth. We put up our money, we had the feeling we were getting ready to take over, it got to the day where Yeovil had to put up or shut up and the people there said, "We don't want to do it." That was their right and things tended to work out for a purpose.'

Rob was in New Orleans with his wife Missy when the Yeovil deal fell through and over dinner that night they discussed dropping the thought of getting involved in English football. But Rob couldn't quite let go. A week later his phone rang and Palmer was back on to offer a new opportunity. Rob was already working on one of his own.

'It was difficult for me to get rid of the itch so I rang the guy at Bury. That was an interesting conversation.' Steve Dale was the owner of the Lancashire club who purchased it for £1 from previous owner Stewart Day in December 2018. The air had since been thick with the scent of dodgy dealings, subterfuge, investigations, inquiries, political interventions and fan revolution.

'He [Dale] and I talked for a bit and then I put my nephew Pete on the phone because he did our due diligence work. Pete immediately said to me that the guy was a screwball. I had asked Dale, "How much do you want?" and he couldn't give me an answer. He said he wanted to clean up the debt and do this and that and I said, "Assuming you do that, how much do you need?" He couldn't tell me.' The line went dead and the club soon followed.

Then came the call from Palmer asking Rob to take a look at Grimsby Town of League Two. 'I went there and I say this delicately but it was not a place I thought my wife and I would want to come to one week every month. It was freezing in late May. Driving away from there I was debating whether to go to Bury and try that again when the phone rang and I was asked if I wanted to meet the Wycombe people. I looked at my map, it was near Heathrow airport and so I thought, "Why wouldn't I?"

'I met Trevor [Stroud] and thought he was a guy who cared desperately for his club and was looking for a solution to a big problem. He was playing his cards pretty close to his chest as to how big the problem was so I said I'd be interested and please let me know. A week later he called and said, "We've selected you," which was quite amusing. I said I'd do it and what did he need? He said, "Half a million pounds."

'That's when I knew I'd lost my mind because I'm not an overly rich person but I sent him the money and went home and told my wife.'

* * *

There were plenty of hurdles ahead but within 12 hours of the start of his negotiations with Wycombe, Rob Couhig was on board a plane from Louisiana to London and arrived without ostentation at the training ground with Missy to meet the scratchings of the first-team squad.

At first sight, he reminded me of a corner-store owner right out of *The Waltons* rather than a highly respected trial lawyer who had twice run unsuccessfully for mayor of New Orleans. There was both a charm in his manner and a lack of trapping that I suspected would suit the environment into which he wanted to move.

Wycombe's trust members converged on a suite (more a depressingly cold area with a bar on one side) at Adams Park on Thursday, 11 July to meet Rob, Pete and Palmer to get a sense of them as people and the depth of their intent if not yet their pockets. Gareth Ainsworth chose to stay away, fearing he'd be expected to cheerlead for the potential owners. He shouldn't have to make up people's minds for them.

Trevor Stroud spoke of credible offers of investment, emphasising that Wycombe had not been flaunting itself. All discussions emanated from those showing an interest, not by the club going around with a begging bowl, though they probably had one handy.

Collis and Luby had come and gone, many doubted Harman was a credible alternative, there were soundings here and there that hadn't amounted to anything realistic and fresh funding was absolutely imperative.

Stroud – initially a fan of Tottenham Hotspur – had been a Wycombe apostle for 30 years, emerged from putting his hand up for trust membership to the elected leader of the pack, had kept former chairman Andrew Howard's five-year plan for sustainable EFL survival on track and was amazed he still oversaw a League One club.

Months of trying to balance hope and reality was taking a toll. 'It has been very stressful and expensive because I haven't been able to do my day job. I'm down to one client. I keep waiting for the phone to ring from him. But once I get into something I'm dogged, whatever it is. If it's finding the cheapest litre of fuel, I won't be beaten. Somehow, through it all here, I managed to remain married and vaguely sane.'

The chairman had done nothing more upsetting in his term of office than telling Ainsworth his budget had to be savaged. He craved happier times new investment should bring. 'If they [the legacy members] don't take it [the offer], I'll say, "You can have your keys back, I've done all I can."'

He was looking out at a sea of friends who might not all accept what he was about to say. The trust remained trusted though, and in Stroud's mind this was a case of Wycombe surviving or going under, which is what would have happened had it lost to Torquay United on the final day of the 2013/14 season and been relegated to the National League.

A decent proportion of those in the room were among the Wycombe 929 at Plainmoor that day to witness the most daring of their remarkable acts of escapology. This wasn't a placard-waving, unseemly crowd given its average age, but there was a noticeable tension in the room. The defining moment in Stroud's chairmanship had arrived. He took a swig from an enormous water bottle.

He said the deal agreed – in principle – was for Rob Couhig to acquire a 75 per cent shareholding, requiring the same percentage of legacy members to vote in favour given the constitution that tied the club to such restrictive numbers. Until that vote was taken – most signs pointed to the spring of 2020 – Wycombe Wanderers would remain 100 per cent owned by the trust.

That said, Couhig had agreed to fund the club in the interim to an agreed sum (not revealed) that Stroud said, 'allowed us to re-instate the playing budget of 2018/19, which I'd reduced by 30 per cent, a decision that had broken my heart and Gareth's.'

Stroud affirmed that all Wycombe's outstanding club and trust debt – he stopped short of specifics – would be cleansed on the successful completion of a deal. On the basis that the required 75 per cent of legacy members nodded him through, Wycombe would become Couhig's to own, with the trust taking on a quarter shareholding. Its voice would be heard but more faintly than before.

Rob Couhig was introduced. The greeting was diffident, though appreciative. His dialect seemed more Brooklyn barstool than Louisiana bar and he was a polished public speaker. But this was a very different jury to the ones he was used to trying – and more often than not succeeding – to persuade.

How would an advocate from howdy-doody land go down with an audience better suited to a Conservative Party hustings? These were dyed-in-the-wool season-ticket main stand dwellers, not the drumbeat of the terraces.

'Why am I here? Why I am interested in this team? I've been fortunate in my life to be able to do certain things, to take risks, some of which have turned out fine, others not so much, but we move on and we learn. About three years ago, having had great success with baseball we [his family] began to look at what else we could do that would be a challenge at this stage in our lives.

'I fixated on English football. I began to look for the right opportunity and was fortunate to meet Mark Palmer who consults with over a dozen clubs, and we wanted to embrace the Wycombe way, to make it better and deliver the product we want for everyone. It is tough to find the right team because I insisted upon something a lot of people in football don't appear to be interested in – building an economic model that made sense.

'I am not so rich, nor does it make good sense, to pour money into a team so I can have five years parading myself around, saying "look at me". In everything I've done my interest has been to build a culture and institution for success. This place has that. I went through a few clubs, some of which I liked, some of which I didn't like. We got pretty close in Yeovil. Then a few weeks ago Mark called and said, "Why don't we go and see Wycombe?"

'The goal is to have an engagement, just as before a marriage. When I first talked to Trevor, I said, "I don't know you and you don't know me," but I believe if we do things right, people will want us to be part of a marriage going forward. Candidly, I don't want to be any part of someone who doesn't want me. Trevor drove a hard bargain. I said, "Well I'm in for some money so what level of interest rate will I get?" He looked at me as if I was mad.

'We finally came up with this deal. My nephew Pete, a tremendous analytics guy, will spend as much time here as the immigration people will allow, even though he has kids in school back in New Orleans.

'You should all be aware of my philosophy. I'm not interested in mediocrity, either on the pitch or off it. What I want is that when fans come to a game, they have a good time. I can't guarantee success on the field but shame on me if the place isn't clean, the ladies go the ladies' room and aren't embarrassed by its state. If you can't get a good cold beer, a [hot] dog, and a decent pie, that's our responsibility because we know how to deliver that.

'Obviously, having a good football team is vital. We are among the most fortunate clubs because we have the right manager at the right time, he is assembling the right players and I know he can take us to where we need to be.

'I've known lots of people in his position in various sports and I couldn't name on the fingers of one hand people with as much maturity, integrity and devotion to getting the job done as we have here with Gareth.

'Y'all can contact me any time. I'm not saying I'll be able to reply at that moment but I'll respond within 24 hours, because that's the way I like to operate. It's your club and mine. We will fulfil our goals together and the premier goal is to be a financially sound institution that will last forever and that we'll put a great team on the field.'

Pete Couhig, Rob's high-spirited nephew, was to be the go-between, linking the operational and football sides of the club on a day-to-day basis, once he had sorted out his family affairs back home. 'Our job is to create as much money as we can for Gareth to bring young quality players to the club so it can grow naturally while we try to get the ship straightened financially.'

Pete's curriculum vitae suggested he was impressively sound at raising capital. 'Three years in business with a company I co-founded called RES US (Resource Environmental Solutions, pioneers in ecological restoration across the United States), it was the 399th fastest growing company in the whole of North America.

'We went from zero to boom and over ten years had a great time, the family was an active investor and now we have the opportunity to take all that experience and apply it to this business and see where we can go.

'Typically you find the lawyer is the detail person and the business guy is the entrepreneur with the crazy ideas. It is exactly the opposite with Rob and I. The respect I have for his craziness is through the roof. In years of investing and starting businesses, I've become very practical about what works and we'll be applying that here to increase revenues and become very efficient at spending. You'll get sick of me saying "cost benefit analysis".

'We need to be efficient in all we do so we can create the capital for Gareth to spend on the squad, that we can spend on stadium improvements, and on everything that everyone in this room knows what it takes to become a successful club. Let me tell you guys something about Rob, he's like a dog with a bone. When he wants something he gets it.'

His uncle asked for the microphone back. 'I think you now realise that we are confident in our own minds that we are capable of doing what you're going to want us to do. You don't have to worry about that. Everyone who comes into a business has a tendency to say, "We can do what these guys have been doing better and let's get them out of the way." In this case, that's not so.

'Yes, this club has been held together with string and twine, they lost £400,000 two years ago and £700,000 last year. That said, the staff have done a wonderful job and just because we know what we're doing doesn't mean they didn't know what they were doing.'

One wondered if this could all be true or was Rob Couhig simply saying nice things to keep the die-hards onside? The club had, indeed, been haemorrhaging money for months, and without the injection of funds already wired from his account to the football club without a second's hesitation Wycombe would have foundered.

As it was, the family regarded the club's financial situation as insane, bordering on irreparable. Indeed, someone whispered to me that night that if the Couhigs had not come along when they did and already invested a few dollars in the enterprise, Wycombe Wanderers were truly up a Louisiana shit creek without a paddle.

* * *

Ten days after Rob Couhig's inaugural address and on the back of an initial trickle of investment, Wycombe's squad began to flower. Paul Smyth, a sprightly forward from Belfast with two Northern Ireland caps, arrived from QPR thanks to Ainsworth's association with the club where he'd been a rampaging forward across 141 appearances from 2003 to 2010.

The reaction from QPR supporters suggested that its old player had engaged in a sleight of hand that would have made Fagin blush.

Inside 72 hours four more dressing-room hooks had new names attached. Right-back Jack Grimmer, a free agent after 53 appearances for Coventry City, joined on a two-year deal. The former captain of Scotland's under-16s, who scored at Wembley in the 2018 play-off final to secure Coventry's promotion to League One, lost his place the following season to Dujon Sterling, on loan from Chelsea. He was demoralised, released, spent a couple of days keeping fit with Notts County and was desperate for a new home.

Ainsworth couldn't conceal his glee at acquiring such quality, especially as Jason McCarthy had packed his suitcases for Millwall and Sido Jombati, a long-time defensive servant, wasn't expected to recover from a metatarsal injury for two months. Grimmer was an unexpected and hugely welcome tick in the box.

Jacob Gardiner-Smith – the son of Labour's international development spokesman Barry Gardiner – had played for Russia's Zenit St Petersburg and the not-quite-so-remote outposts of Hendon and St Albans. Jacob had been recommended to Ainsworth by Luke O'Nien, the former Wanderer now at Sunderland, and signed for a year. It was hoped that, unlike his father, he wouldn't appear to be permanently attached to a bench.

Next was Giles Phillips, a central-defender from QPR in whom Ainsworth saw definite potential. Chicago-born Phillips was tall, elegant and assured, as if he'd never had a rough edge.

League One might come as a bit of a shock. The manager felt he could mould the 21-year-old into a defender of real substance and a loan for the season was mutually perfect.

Jamie Mascoll followed, a left-back released by Charlton after their promotion to the Championship, on a one-year contract. Mascoll had once worked for extra pocket money in the kiosks serving food and drink on match days at The Valley before being taken onto the playing staff. He was clearly not afraid of hard graft and was described by his new manager as 'my pet project.'

Wycombe had had to draft in members of the football staff for a semi-decent five-a-side in the first couple of weeks of pre-season. Now, they would have an entire first team and full substitutes' bench for the season's curtain-raiser against Bolton Wanderers.

There was an awful lot of pinching of skin in the coaches' room.

* * *

Gareth Ainsworth walked into the Caffe Nero in Wokingham one June morning in 2019 and we took a window table. The idea of sketching a season with Wycombe had been forming for a while and I broached the possibility to him. There was a long pause.

He was wrestling with the perilous nature of the club's finances, the looming sense that he would be unable to perform one more miracle – 'we're really screwed Neil' – and how the first relegation of his managerial career might be an unwelcome blot on his CV.

He mulled over the pros and cons for ten minutes then said, 'To hell with it,' determined to give it another season and accept whatever consequence befell him. And why not let the public that looked at football's finances with utter incredulity appreciate what it took to manage a League One club that didn't have a pot to piss in?

Imagine his transformative mood as new jerseys embroidered with new names and numbers started to roll off the production line. Yet an onset of light-headedness provoked a different set of concerns. How would the manager deal with the strain of selecting the right team from an ever-enlarging collection of egos?

Ainsworth had a team of generals, Adam El-Abd, Matt Bloomfield, Joe Jacobson and Adebayo Akinfenwa, the senior pros he trusted each to mentor a group of players, watch them like surrogate parents, to cajole and console – the management's eyes and ears. But what if one of these had to be left out? Ainsworth said that in dealing with these differing circumstances, he'd need to acquire a new skill set. All these thoughts had begun to pre-occupy many of his waking moments and several non-waking ones as well.

'I love my squad – they're black, white, nice background, not so nice a background, some with money, most with very little money. When they train together, listen to the noise. They're all in, relishing each other's company.

'It's how it was when I played for John Beck at Cambridge, Lincoln and Preston. He told me to run, pass, head, shoot and if he said I needed to run up the steps of the stand ten times after training, I would do that too. These lads would do the same for me.

'I couldn't afford any weak links. I often recounted *The Nail* by former US President Benjamin Franklin: "For the want of a nail the shoe was lost; for the want of a shoe the horse was lost; for the want of a horse the rider was lost; for the want of a rider the battle was lost; for the want of a battle the kingdom was lost; and all for the want of a nail." These boys all have to be nails but if we lose one nail, we can lose the kingdom.'

There were a number of hard as nails players on view for the final pre-season friendly. Maidenhead was not for the aesthetes, but exactly the robust challenge Ainsworth expected. The National League side was managed by Alan Devonshire, once a darling of West Ham United, and across all positions they were an average of two inches taller than their League One opposition.

My sense was that Wycombe would require guile, accuracy of passing, shrewd use of alternating tactics and great group togetherness if they were to be consistently at this height and strength disadvantage during the season proper.

At least a little time was on Wycombe's side. For the opening day opponents, Bolton Wanderers and their Lancashire neighbours Bury, the sands had been slipping inexorably into the lower compartment of the hourglass. Their futures were in dire peril.

Debbie Jevans, the interim chairman of the EFL, assured me on Sunday, 28 July, 'If the players and other creditors haven't been paid in full five days before the season opens there is no way I'll allow either team to play.' That deadline fell the following day.

* * *

The photoshoot for the official 2019/20 Wycombe squad picture was at 2pm on Monday, 29 July precisely as the EFL convened a conference call to discuss the impoverished states of Bolton and Bury. The clubs had been given until five that evening to demonstrate that their finances were sound enough for their opening fixtures to be sanctioned.

It was a glorious afternoon at Adams Park, the players parading first in the new daffodil-yellow second-choice kit before switching to the famed shades of blue. Pete Couhig was enamoured by the quaintness of the custom but was bemused by its timing, especially as Fred Onyedinma was at that moment taking the medical that would secure his second return to Wycombe from Millwall as Jason McCarthy made the opposite track.

The arrangement had added complexity because Championship-club Barnsley were due a sell-on fee for McCarthy that had to be confirmed and signed off by the trust. There was much to-ing and fro-ing before the deal was completed. 'We'll be taking these again in a month [the day the League One and Two transfer windows closed] won't we?' Couhig said. 'This is just stupid shit.'

Maybe so, but for those individuals, firms and families who sponsored players, had their names on the front of the shirts, supplied the mattresses, the expensive gym equipment and sound systems at the training ground, who provided goodwill and any spare change they could for the players' fund, this was a day in the sun. The club wouldn't be here without such generosity of spirit and hard cash.

By later that evening, all debate about team photographs was froth and bubble. The EFL decreed that Bolton were allowed to fulfil their fixture at Wycombe but Bury's game at MK Dons was suspended and, unless there was a dramatic change of circumstance, their following match against Accrington Stanley would go the same way.

This was only a month after Bury could have been sold to Rob Couhig had the owner been able to give a straight answer to his request for exactly how much he wanted to dig him out of the shit he was in. It was not long before #FucktheEFL became a trending hashtag on Twitter, in the north of England especially. #FuckDale (Steve, not Rochdale) was rather popular too.

In Buckinghamshire the arrivals continued. Onyedinma put pen to paper on a three-year contract and David Wheeler, admired at MK Dons and Exeter City for his resolution in attack and midfield, signed for three years on a free transfer from QPR – fast becoming an unofficial feeder club. The first thing I noticed about Wheeler was his classical first-day-back-at-school haircut.

Trevor Stroud's lightened mood was demonstrated by a mic-drop confirming Onyedinma's return. The chairman posed as if to speak, dropped the microphone, stepped aside and Fred was behind him, arms folded, trying hard to look serious. In four seconds of Twitter magic the sea change in the club's standing was clear, even if, in Stroud's words, 'I only did what I was told.'

Josh Parker, a striker who had 26 caps for Antigua and Barbuda and was still trying to come to terms with a wild and terrifying experience at Red Star Belgrade, was the confirmed ninth new entry after he had been released by Charlton Athletic. He immediately opened a coffee shop in the town named TONE – The Old New Experience.

Ainsworth was having one himself. He decided that was that in terms of new faces and ran his fingers across the tactics board in the coaching room where a thumbnail of each player's face was attached to an adhesive counter. He drew all the forward faces into one penalty area.

'We could go full Keegan,' a reference to the former England striker's period as manager of Newcastle United in the 1990s, when his team perfected reckless abandon. 'Fuck me look at that attacking strength. Has any side in our league got that variety?'

* * *

Indeed, Smyth, Wheeler, Parker and Onyedinma, in addition to Adebayo Akinfenwa, Alex Samuel, Nick Freeman and Scott Kashket, offered a surfeit of positive options, whether Ainsworth played three forwards, a diamond or a more resolute 4-4–2. He was right that this was a display of riches not afforded many managers in League One and allowed himself a cheery whistle as he contemplated his resources.

We moved to the common room with another message to drill home. 'Wycombe Identity' was the mantra. 'If you don't live to our standards, you're going to be living somewhere else. Here, no one thinks they're bigger than anyone. Of course, a player may be better at certain things than someone else, but no one is *better* than anyone else.

'Here it is give, give, give. On the coaching side, we need to improve every day. You have to respect what every single person brings to the party. You cannot do your job without the help of someone else's attributes and strengths. Here, you back your mates. You accept and own everything you do.

'If you make a mistake it's yours as much as it is when you make a good pass, score a goal or save a penalty. We are all part of the jigsaw. One day that jigsaw may be complete but it's a long way from that today, even with all the new boys arriving.'

Certain shapes, styles and pieces were intrinsic to Wycombe's approach. Ainsworth continuously impressed on his players the need to adhere to his ten-yard rule – to quickly stultify an opposition player's time to look up and measure his options. That ten yards of space had to be engulfed without delay. His midfield would thus require engines that didn't break down, at least not often.

The manager's probable preference for 4-3–3 meant that in the initial stages of the season Matt Bloomfield, Alex Pattison and Dominic Gape would need to form an alliance marked by feverish momentum.

Gape was a protégé of the vaunted Southampton academy system, working with far-sighted coaches on the south coast from the age of seven, and he captained the team from a young corps labelled a golden generation. He had grown up with Luke Shaw, Calum Chambers, James Ward-Prowse, Jordan Turnbull, Harrison Reed and Sam McQueen, an intelligentsia of talents.

Many managers would have rejected him on size alone. At 5ft 7in he was Tom Thumb in a football kit. Ainsworth often said had Gape been a few inches taller he would have been a Championship regular no doubt about it.

There had been an opportunity to move in the summer – 'sideways rather than upwards' – but when he learned of decent investment on the way Gape signed for an extra year, as had Akinfenwa, somewhat at the opposite end of the physical spectrum and 13 years his team-mate's elder.

Wycombe's fans cherished both men for the extremes they brought to the team. Bayo was now 37, a one-man rolling maul, offering a presence and substance no other club in the league possessed with his 16 stone of solid, unremitting bulk. The leadership he delivered by virtue of his physical strength and force of personality made him stand out in every possible way. He was one of a special kind.

Akinfenwa could lift Gape from the floor with one sweep of his arm and wanted to do so often since the penultimate weekend of the 2017/18 season when Gape's winner at Chesterfield guaranteed Wycombe's automatic promotion to League One and hero status at Adams Park. But Gape was much more to the club than a single, history-defining shot. He was a pivot, a secure base, the marshal of so many moves.

'I knew my strengths, which was important for a footballer, and I stuck to them. I wasn't a player who was going to pick the ball up, dribble past ten players and score, that wasn't me. The team were best off when I didn't have the ball too long.

'If I had a picture in my head of where everyone was on the pitch, I saw my winger had a one v one chance, my next thought was, "How can I manipulate the ball to him?" I knew I was playing well when I had clear pictures.

'Did I get to play lots of sexy passes and do lots of things that I'd like to do? Not really. You could be the best passer in the world but if you weren't winning second balls, headers, tackles and getting stuck in, your range of passing was irrelevant. Especially the way Wycombe set up, as a high-paced counter attacking team, I might only get one opportunity a game and I had to be able to execute that pass otherwise I was a waste.

'You wouldn't see many games in our league when a midfielder played hundreds of passes. What I'd be doing for the most part was fight for second balls, compete for headers, try to intercept, to turn the play over and defence into attack.'

And bloody good he was at all of those elements of football without the trimmings on which much of League One was based. He never appeared out of breath or flustered, a tribute to his powers of endurance and technical ability given the demands Ainsworth and Dobson placed on the midfield players.

Gape was very much the heartbeat of the Wycombe way. Football at its most selfless and intense. The little man battling against the odds.

*　*　*

Those odds were unambiguous and unanimous. The club was a certainty to be relegated, a veritable lamb to the slaughter. Even Bolton Wanderers, starting with the 12-point deduction for falling into administration in May, were quoted by some bookmakers with better odds of survival than the upstarts from the pretty, field-speckled end of a Buckinghamshire industrial estate.

The football staff shrugged their shoulders, girded their loins and gathered their thoughts.

Six weeks before the season, the entire edifice had been built on quicksand that was slowly sucking Wycombe under. There was now the potential for a solid structure. A second League One campaign in succession had arrived with the sun on the team's back.

There was something curiously distinct about the club that the staff inspired with such passion. They in turn had grown into its identity over a decade of campaigns and without their leadership Wycombe would almost certainly have foundered as a full-time professional club.

Those who played in the famous quarters did so on less than the average League One wage, were shorter in numbers and physical stature than every club they were to compete against and had long accepted being written off by the neutrals and even some of their own.

Yet the bond this devout, diverse squad had forged in a month led one to believe that when they emerged together for the first day of the season – and with the bit of luck every team required once in a while – they wouldn't be the whipping boys roundly predicted.

The Boys from Bolton

IT was 11.30am, three and a half hours before the whistle sounded on another League One season. What was left of Bolton Wanderers were summoned to a conference room at the Holiday Inn, High Wycombe, where the previous night's struggle for sleep reflected neither the quality of the mattresses nor the décor of its guest rooms.

Most of the lads had endured an uncomfortable few hours, the hope of rest not helped by another swathe of humid summer air invading the south of England. The morning brought with it conflicting senses of awe and dread.

It was hard for Bolton's boys to digest even the healthiest of breakfast options as their stomachs seemed strangely detached from the rest of their bodies.

Those meeting and greeting in the foyer for lunch that August morning could have been forgiven for assuming a local junior club was preparing for a trophy presentation as track suited kids mingled with hotel guests. Instead, for a handful of these untainted freshmen, a professional football debut and all that it could mean was just a few hours away.

This ought to have been the preparation for an occasion to savour, one of hope and adventure, the grass newly laid, lines and posts gleaming white, shirts a perfect fit, hearts a-flutter and everywhere around them a shared eagerness to burst from the traps. A few aspired to become a legend in the manner of Nat Lofthouse, Tommy Banks or Youri Djorkaeff.

The Adams Park pitch was a pretty picture and – free from the clutter of a sponsor's name – the kit was crisp and white. Bolton almost looked like Bolton. Except that this became a head down, dash from the coach, smell the fear, don't make eye contact with the autograph hunters (who wouldn't recognise you anyway) and hope you didn't shit yourself kind of occasion.

Before the morning summons, whispers were that the match might still be voided. Into this unhappy vacuum walked Sharon Brittan of Football Ventures, who didn't at first glance strike the room's occupants as saviour material.

Bespectacled, dressed appropriately in black, hair tied back in a bun, Brittan could have been the last character you suspected of wielding the killer instrument in an episode of *Midsomer Murders* rather than being on the threshold of owning a football club once among the virtuous pride of the English game.

But there was an effervescence about her that recent negotiations had not completely drained. Despite all the shocking discoveries about Bolton's finances in eight months of head-banging, the fact she'd rescued the club from the brink of liquidation gave her confidence it would survive long term.

A shaft of hope had materialised. The administrators said she was the preferred (only credible) bidder. Brittan lived in Beaconsfield – a hop, skip and jump down the M40 – and her elder son Toby was an avid Chairboy, which gave the fixture an even deeper resonance.

There had been so many conflicting messages in the past few months of the Bolton saga that distinguishing fact from fiction induced a migraine. Brittan's assurance that the match would be played allowed manager Phil Parkinson to formulate some kind of team plan.

His over-riding dilemma was how many untested kids he could toss into the deep-end and keep the score within a limit that would not destroy their confidence.

A few miles across town, the Bolton supporters who'd set off at sunrise were enjoying Wycombe's hospitality and hoping a trip to the Rebellion beer tent – home of Marlow's finest brew – might dull the senses of betrayal and bewilderment matched only by those players they hoped to identify when they took to the field.

With the EFL's grace, Bolton had registered three players the previous afternoon, James Weir, formerly of Manchester United and Hull City, Josh Earl, on loan from Preston North End, and local lad Harry Brockbank, who had spent the summer being tempted by offers to move but remained loyal to his home-town club.

Bolton's team doctor David Humphreys had not been paid for months but drove to Wycombe fearing that the younger players riding high on adrenalin and without a care for their developing bodies might suffer adverse reactions.

If there was not a manager in the country who would have swapped places with Parkinson, Gareth Ainsworth was not particularly revelling in his first team talk of the campaign. For six weeks he had swayed back and forth between fearfulness of a season, where talk of relegation was an unshakeable companion, to possession of a squad capable of more than 'better than 17th' that was the limit of his public pronouncements.

Neither manager had the slightest clue how Bolton would play. That was hard enough for its own gaffer but equally it sorely tested one charged with finding a way to beat them. Both knew that Bolton's players would run, but for how long and in which direction?

Josh Hart was the tactical analyst critical to Wycombe's planning. He was 23 and bounded around the place like a lamb offered first sight of an empty field. Ainsworth was twice his age and thrived on Josh's boundless energy and tactical appreciation. There was absolute trust between them.

Josh had managed to acquire a bit of footage of Bolton's behind-closed-doors friendly against Bradford, though it wasn't much to go on. Players who hadn't been paid for weeks were hardly likely to run their bollocks off in a friendly in front of, well, nobody.

'I reminded my boys that they were 18 once and if this opportunity had been presented to them to make their debut they'd be desperate to impress,' Ainsworth said. 'We simply couldn't underestimate anyone.

'We'd have to match their eagerness first and foremost, and once the game opened up I felt sure we would do what was required.'

Nothing prepared Parkinson for this doomsday scenario. His career at Colchester United, Charlton Athletic, Hull City and Bradford City had encompassed the regular diet of triumph and disaster, play-off heartbreak, sackings, the periods when your team lost and there was had no reason why, the momentary elations and the incredible sinking feelings, the disturbed nights brought on by heart-pounding stress.

But never, surely, had he been unable to plan beyond the next cup of coffee or been told not to speak to anyone outside his club lest he make a bad situation worse. Worse? Padlocks had been placed on the training ground gates and staff members, unpaid for weeks, had been making the best of a bad job with donations from local food banks.

Parkinson's life had descended into absurdity. In the 24 hours before his kids were sent to the wolves, he had to deal with a player mutiny, endure a six-hour wait at a service station because the coach company refused to carry the team unless an outstanding debt was paid, oversaw three signings, and now had to dig deep into his man-management resource to come up with some novelties.

He did not strike me as a paint-stripping type and would need to be to make himself heard over the din emanating from Bolton's dressing room. The young players were clearly trying to blot out the conversation inside their heads by playing rap music so loud it drowned out everything else.

In fact, Parkinson preferred solitude which may not have been a bad thing. At 2.15pm he was still wandering the concourse, eyeglasses perched on his nose, a jumble of notes in one hand and mobile phone in the other. Home supporters watched, nudged and pointed. I asked how he was faring. He used the word 'crazy' twice, and not without feeling, for this was indeed some crazy shit.

On the Betfair exchanges Wycombe were backed from an opening show of 1.50 to 1.22, settling at 1.24 by kick-off. According to Harry Findlay, a great sport gambler who happened to have been raised as a Wycombe fan, 'this was without doubt the shortest price any team outside the Premier League had started on the opening day of a season.'

* * *

Adams Park was fresh and bright for the occasion. It was an unprepossessing ground without any hint of pretence, tucked away at the end of an ugly street full of potholes and soulless offices on which giant lorries parked with total disdain for any other traffic that might want to move.

The view from the front-office side across the pitch was almost entirely taken up by the imposing Frank Adams Stand and trees upon a steep hill. If you transferred and looked back the other way, from behind the single-tiered main stand rose fields beyond where dogs were walked, horses ridden and, on a sunny day like this one, you could lose yourself in the tranquillity. It could have been a Constable scene were it not for a couple of giant electricity pylons in the eyeline.

My first impression was that the place itself could do with a lick of paint and some rust-preventative coating. The manager may have enjoyed a bit of heavy metal but the ground appeared to have been designed by someone who had a lot of it he wanted to get rid of.

The staff were unfailingly nice. The green-jacketed greetings were warm, and rather than just point you in the direction you needed to head they accompanied you to make sure you didn't go somewhere you ought not. The lady with the trolley – Hazel, I later learnt – delivered the food to the press room, returned every five minutes to ask if we'd eaten yet and fussed around us lovingly.

It was clear that hospitality was in the Wycombe genes. The club set their heart on being a perfect host and this was powerfully evident before and during the first match of the season.

In the days preceding the fixture Wycombe had taken on the role of service provider as Bolton's administrators refused to let the club's staff do anything other than breathe. Ticket information and distribution was arranged by Wycombe, travel arrangements were provided by Wycombe and the welcome was in the fan-first manner of American sports, which was as new to Wycombe and it was an eye-opener for Bolton's travellers.

One reported that he thought nine quid was steep for a beer, only for the server to call him back and apologise for charging for two bottles rather than one. It was remarkable how honesty was seen as something to applaud, though, given the rape of Bolton by gluttonous recent owners, maybe this was not a surprise.

Bolton's supporters got honesty on the pitch too. It was all that they asked and for 90 minutes it was what they received. The cause wasn't helped when Earl, a previous-day signing, over-stretched trying to keep Paul Smyth from bursting onto a pass and was helped off the pitch. Joe White became a seventh debutant. Only 20 minutes had gone. Parkinson's face was steadily accumulating lines.

The common purpose of Bolton's defending – built around a remarkably assured Yoan Zouma, the gangling 20-year-old younger brother of Chelsea's Kurt – denied Wycombe a first-half breakthrough. Ainsworth was sure that if his side scored the game would open and Bolton's initial discipline would bend and break.

Ten minutes into the second half, centre-back Anthony Stewart was plugged near the touchline by two attackers, where he swivelled, produced a drag back that wouldn't have shamed Paolo Maldini and delivered a 30-yard pass to Smyth who was off, haring past Brockbank. Goalkeeper Remi Matthews dashed from his area but Smyth was a pace too quick, swerved around the red-misted, red-shirted keeper and rolled the ball in from 20 yards.

It was precisely the kind of goal in precisely the style Ainsworth signed Smyth to score. His back flip was a trademark topping of the cake. After 68 minutes he was withdrawn for an equally pacey Fred Onyedinma. Bolton – metaphorically at least – had their socks around their ankles.

Fred was firing, Alex Pattison burst through the middle and a third substitute, Nick Freeman, twisted and turned the leggy youngsters. From an 81st minute-Joe Jacobson corner, Akinfenwa headed across goal and Onyedinma outleapt the defence to nod over the line. A goal from inside the six-yard box – Ainsworth and Dobson loved those.

As the match neared its climax, Wycombe's management pair demonstrated why they placed so much emphasis on match momentum – either as a positive force for their own side or the need to kill it should the opposition be enjoying a decent spell of control.

Bolton had regained their composure after the first goal and linked together a few composed moves. The crowd grew edgy. Ainsworth planned to introduce David Wheeler but the moment had to be right.

It was pointless bringing him on at any old time for the sake of freshness. Wycombe won a corner on the left and the defence was jockeying for position to resist what they feared would be a customarily cunning delivery from Joe Jacobson. This generally amounted to how many bodies it required to stop the ball reaching Akinfenwa.

Wheeler had been on his feet for a minute, the fourth official was poised but Ainsworth asked him to hold his horses. Matt Bloomfield jogged slowly from the field applauding all sections. A corner that should have taken 30 seconds had now been a four-minute affair, enough for Bolton to reboot defensive options with a perceptible waning of precision. Who was supposed to be picking up whom again?

The little momentum Bolton gained had evaporated. Opposition supporters agitated by Wycombe's stymying approach in past seasons – they could be a rotten side to play against – would not be surprised to learn that wilful time-wasting formed part of the cunning plan. A few minutes later they had made the match safe with Onyedinma's header.

The second goal sucked the legs and life from Bolton. The players started to cramp as Doc Humphreys feared. When the fourth official told Parkinson there were four added minutes he cursed, not in the forlorn hope his side could score twice in that time but that they might concede a couple more. But for Matthews, they would have done. A total of 25 shots meant that Wycombe had had more than any other club in the EFL on the opening day.

Parkinson dutifully fulfilled his post-match duties. It was a release to have the chance to talk. He shuffled from one microphone to the next, asked over and again to sift through the terrible complexity of being a manager at a loss to know what he was expected to manage.

There was a faraway look in his eyes. Bolton, 12 points worse off than every other side in League One bar fellow sad case Bury at 3pm, were now 15 adrift of Wycombe and a slew of others. From whichever side of the story you stood, this was a developing tragedy.

'If I'd got the team I wanted on the pitch I believe we'd have won. The club and the town deserve better than they've had to put up with. It's been draining for all of us. I want to try to help this club regain its credibility. We can only hope the takeover comes soon and we can move forward together.'

There was a definite sense of 'there but for the grace of God go I' as clubs in the lower reaches of the Football League watched the stories of Bolton and Bury unravel. Accrington Stanley's owner Andy Holt never held back on Twitter, especially where football's egregious financial state impacted his club.

Accrington lost at newly promoted Lincoln on the opening day and its subsequent fixture against Bury was suspended on the grounds that its opponent wasn't able to provide sufficient proof of funds. Holt tweeted: 'We were beaten by a good @ LincolnCity_FC side yesterday fair and square. A similar team to us @wwfcofficial had a bye taking on a load of kids from @OfficialBWFC. We had a bye next week in my view [when Accrington was due to face Bury].'

How much of the match between Wycombe and Bolton Holt had seen we could not be sure, but talk of a bye was unworthy. Pete Couhig quickly responded. 'It didn't feel like a bye to us. Those Bolton lads gave their all and did the shirt proud under extremely trying circumstances.'

In the coaches' room at Wycombe's training ground on Monday there was incredulity at Holt's tweet. Richard Dobson was eager to point out the times in the past his club had had to field seriously weakened teams but, 'because it was little old Wycombe no one really gave a toss.'

* * *

Across at Adams Park an intense debrief of the first weekend was underway. The Couhigs and Mark Palmer were determined that each part of the operation should be alert to the good, the acceptable or the inadequate in their performance.

There had been a few cock ups. The promise of a free beer for fans who signed up to the Wycombe app became a frustrating exercise because the scanners went missing, leaving people queuing for ages and searching for their names on a nonalphabetical list when they reached the head of the line. Most simply turned away, thirst unquenched.

In the club shop, a tiny nook, potential purchasers were replacing merchandise on the shelves because the crush took an intolerable time to clear. The official matchday programme sales were a disappointment – too many team sheets had been given away to supporters who should have purchased a magazine. The sellers were boarding up their wooden kiosks 15 minutes from kick-off to make sure they were in their seats for the start of the match, leaving behind a stockpile of unsold material. At £3.50 a throw that added up to quite a loss.

It was important that points were made to the staff but not in a way that alienated them. The Couhigs were only interim custodians and needed to stay on the right side of employees, full- and part-time, while pointing out any shortcomings.

This was a balancing act – overdoing the heavy-handedness and support for the cause might wane; not raising pertinent points and improving standards meant nothing would change and one of the prime pillars of their promise to supporters crumbled.

The same was true of ticketing policy. The second home fixture was a Carabao Cup tie against Reading, a Championship opponent from ten miles down the road who would bring bus-loads of supporters for a Tuesday-night match. With that, of course, came the potential for enhanced ticket sales, greater trouble and the need for increased stewarding.

How many seats in the main stand should be granted to the away side? It was decided Wycombe should make as much booty from a derby fixture as they could. If pieces needed to be picked up later, it was a price worth paying.

Pete Couhig was going to be a noise, one which staff, management and players might find jarring. He wanted to get his feet under the table, drive enhancements and encourage people to step up. He talked loudly and quickly, called everyone 'dude', high-fived the tunnel stewards Tom and Josh (the look on their faces was a hoot) and breezed through the corridors with an invigorating gusto.

The night before Pete headed home to Louisiana to see his family after six weeks at the takeover's sharp end, Wycombe suffered a loss on penalties to Reading. He was gutted, especially as he had spent the first part of the day trailed by a team from Goalhanger productions who had been invited inside to produce a sizzle that might be commissioned for a season-long documentary on the club.

These had become a popular genre. Manchester City, Leeds United and Sunderland figured in recent exposes but a club like Wycombe offered something appealingly different and aligned to the true nature of professional football in England where most clubs were borderline survivors. This was real football rather than the reality kind.

The management was happy to concede dressing-room access. 'We're confident in our message and our skills,' Ainsworth said. Once he'd given the okay, the players fell into line. Indeed, the production boys were astonished to be so warmly greeted.

Adam El-Abd and Matt Bloomfield, two of the senior pros, went out of their way to make the crew welcome. The Goalhanger boys collected their images, shook us by the hand, left and never set foot on the premises again.

* * *

As the opening few weeks unfolded, Bolton's plight became increasingly depressing. The team Parkinson put out for the first home fixture against Coventry City was the youngest in the club's history and squeezed out a goalless draw greeted with the acclaim usually reserved for someone who had sailed around the world single-handed.

On Saturday, 17 August Bolton were trounced 5-0 at Tranmere and at midday on Monday took the unilateral decision to void against Doncaster Rovers, a match scheduled for the following night. Their defence was a need to protect young bodies and minds from further punishment. Doncaster were enraged, the EFL spluttered and severe sanctions would likely follow.

In the background the protagonists were still bickering over the ownership of the club and the adjacent hotel – two separate administration cases interminably inter-linked and entrenched. Time was running out.

Before the end of August Phil Parkinson had resigned, driven to the brink of despair by the dire circumstances he had tried so hard to overcome. In an individual study that encapsulated football's crazy times we had a first – an unemployed manager looking forward to a decent night's sleep.

The Life of Darius

'THERE must be a chapter in that match alone eh Neil?' Adam El-Abd had been a non-playing central-defender at the end of Wycombe's frenetic first month of the season. Being a spectator hadn't seemed to dull his mood even if, to mark the absurdity of the current week, he'd gone for a walk one evening and strained his calf muscle.

The contest that left El-Abd in breezy form was a last-minute winner, three penalties awarded, wildly unharnessed 3-2 victory over MK Dons the sub-title for which was, 'What Trevor Kettle did next'. What were the corniest clichés the press boys could come up with about the referee? Kettle blows a fuse? Full steam ahead for Kettle? Is Kettle on pot? (that was mine).

The referee was five months from his 53rd birthday and should probably have retired a few years back. Leagues One and Two were repositories for part-time officials, the newbies, has-beens, those who couldn't count to ten at free kicks, vaguely understood what constituted a foul, saw things that weren't there and didn't consider that a personalised number plate parked in the officials' bay was an open invitation to a brick through the windscreen.

They had become an ever-more secretive society. I fondly recalled the days not far distant when the match programme informed you where the referee lived – Wootton Bassett, Barling Magna, Poulton-le-Fylde, Newton Abbot – and something about them: was a basket-weaver, collected Lego, worked mornings as a lollipop man, was married to the daughter of the EFL referees' appointments secretary, that sort of thing.

All we knew now was how many times they'd officiated matches involving the home side and their grand total of yellow and red cards (i.e. the matches they'd ruined).

In the space of seven days Wycombe had been bounced from Paul Marsden, who had not refereed a League One match before and denied them a blatant penalty at Bristol Rovers, to Kettle giving them out like a leaflet provider at a political party conference.

Of course it was easy to malign the man in black, green, blue, yellow, pink or red (in Kettle's case) because they couldn't answer back and I found it troubling that press room conversation before the Buckinghamshire bunfight centred solely on how many cock-ups this referee would make in 90 minutes. I formed this terrible image of him being put in charge of a VAR machine and electrocuting everyone in the studio.

Kettle had awarded four penalties at Gillingham in the Carabao Cup against Newport the previous Tuesday, so three at Adams Park was a decent stab at consistency. It was not as if we hadn't seen enough of them already.

Wycombe had been eliminated from the cup by Reading in a penalty shoot-out that same night. Ryan Allsop took the brunt and accepted his lot. I ran into him sitting alone in the canteen the next morning and wondered if I should offer a consoling word.

He was nibbling at a slice of toast and we briefly chatted. I asked him about the penalties and said from my angle I doubted he had a chance with any of the four that bowed the netting behind him. He tried to be nice but gave me that 'would you mind sitting over there' kind of look.

I was carrying a book for Paul Smyth. *Forever Young* by a former colleague on *The Times*, Oliver Kay, told the beguiling story of Smyth's fellow Northern Irishman Adrian Doherty, a beautiful talent once on the books of Manchester United who had walked away from football, became an itinerant musician and whose body was later discovered at the bottom of a canal in Amsterdam. How or why he got there no one would ever know.

Allsop asked to see it and wondered if I'd read the book on Robert Enke, the Hanover goalkeeper who committed suicide in 2009 by throwing himself in front of a train. Enke was 32, a husband, father and international goalkeeper. The morning after the ball repeatedly flashed past Allsop felt like a ghoulish moment to mention it, but I told him I'd read it and found it profoundly moving.

Enke's close friend Ronald Reng wrote a haunting book from which one quote from the goalkeeper's father Dirk had always stuck with me, 'Robert had a way of thinking that if he wasn't the best he had to be the worst.'

Allsop had skimmed a few chapters but couldn't finish it. He said when his mum read it she wanted him to stop being a goalkeeper but it was too late. He'd tried to play outfield when he was 15 but was overly excitable, was sent off twice and ached to go back in goal.

At that, a holler came for a resumption of the grind with Cameron Yates, the number-two keeper, and Andy Fairman, the goalkeeping coach. The trio retreated to the corner of the training establishment reserved particularly for the practice of their specialist dark art.

* * *

The training ground was often a repository of shadows for all its instinctive joviality and comradeship. A location of work, eager minds and strong bodies – but for those hurrying to return to full fitness who watched forlornly as the fitter, stronger players made their way out to train it felt like a prison cell.

The quiet spaces doubled as confessionals where anyone with a doubt or dilemma might confide in a team-mate or, if the situation had become really difficult, to seek out the manager or Richard Dobson. Their door was always open.

On the second day of pre-season Darius Charles was sitting on his own next to the artificial playing surface and was noticeably pensive. I had never met the man and didn't feel it was my place then to ask how he was.

Alex Samuel walked across to Charles and was doing *all* the talking. I managed to contain my nosiness and not butt in. In the week preceding the season, Gareth Ainsworth handed the tactical debrief to Dobson and walked Charles around the training pitch for 20 minutes, deep in conversation.

When the time was right – the central defender signed a six-month contract extension the day after the Reading defeat – I asked on what he was ruminating that morning in July. He said he was trying to come to terms with the fact that the previous November a surgeon told him he should retire because of a damaged, now arthritic, left hip. Though he rebuffed that advice, life had begun to get on top of him.

He had been in a toxic personal relationship that prompted him to visit a therapist – 'and that's not what a black person, a black man, a black footballer does, we don't do therapy,' he said with a searing openness. People of his colour and in his occupation were supposed to suck it up uncomplainingly.

'When I first went [to the therapist] I'd lost my love for football. I'd found love in a woman and because I didn't have a focus or love for football, we sped through things and it blew up in my face. I thought I'd found the woman I was going to spend the rest of my life with but instead I was holding on to a relationship that was bad. I'd lost football and I couldn't lose this as well. It was a real scarcity mind set.

'I was completely broken without control of my emotions, my thoughts, my feelings. That's what the conversation with the gaffer was about. He affirmed how incredible I was and there's a real lesson and blessing there. The first couple of sessions with the therapist were helping me get over the relationship I was still dealing with. The next two were the correlation between my childhood and why I behaved the way I did.

'Yesterday's visit was celebratory because I'd signed my contract. The beauty of these meetings was that the therapist acted as a sounding board. I said whatever I wanted without judgement and the most she did was drop an idea in. I'm a firm believer in God, the universe and that anything you need you have and she said, "Yes, you have everything you need."

'She prompted thoughts to rise to the surface that were so deep down in my sub-conscious. I had to learn to be kinder to myself, to be okay with the fact that when I was in pain or upset those emotions were perfectly normal.'

Charles was born and raised in Ealing, West London. His father left the family home and moved to South Africa when he was three and his mother took on all the parenting duties. He kicked a ball like most kids in the area. There were plenty of green spaces around. Brentford, the local professional club, chose to stage a football tournament to assess the local talent. A ten-year-old Darius excelled and was asked if he'd attend an advanced camp. He ran all the way home and dragged his mum back to sign the forms.

From a football graduate he would make 37 first-team appearances for Brentford while spending time on loan at Thurrock, Staines, Yeading and finally Ebbsfleet, who he formally joined in January 2009, the first player in the history of the English game to be signed by club members, MyFootballFirst. The group rallied the following year when York City made a £10,000 offer for Charles and voted 98 per cent to reject it.

They were unable to see off the next interested club so Charles joined fledgling League Two side Stevenage, helping them to a place in League One via the 2011 play-offs where he set up the winning goal at Manchester United's Old Trafford against Torquay United. But by now, injuries were commonplace and taking a huge mental toll.

He ruptured ankle ligaments and broke his leg at Stevenage, who decided to release him to Burton Albion in 2015. Charles didn't play a match for the Midland side before returning south to join AFC Wimbledon initially on loan and then for a year on permanent terms. When that expired, he signed for Wycombe on a one-year deal following their promotion to League One in 2018. Six months later, he was written off.

'There was still fluid on my hip when I came to Wycombe and I had issues with it three months before that. I was told it wasn't anything serious, a lot of players had latent tears, most of them were asymptomatic. I was suffering in pre-season, only played seven games and then completely broke down. I went back to see the surgeon and he advised me it was best if I retired.

'He'd injected the hip before and said I should stay away from surgery because in general it was unreliable. The success rate was below 50 per cent. A lot of people who had surgery tended to turn out worse off and came back for another hip replacement. Those were only available three times, so by the time I was in my 60s I could be in a wheelchair.

'That was a lot to think about when I had a son of nine, I wanted more children and I might not be mobile enough to kick a football around in a park. I didn't comprehend how huge and devastating it actually was and there were times during last season when I found it very, very, very difficult.

'Watching was tortuous. Coming in every day, on the bikes, being part of the group until 10.15am and then the lads went out and you were inside, catching the odd bit of the session. In my head I decided I was retiring. I was going through the motions. It was death by a thousand cuts. It was always difficult to go to home games, you were part of it but you weren't.

'I know the gaffer would say I played an incredibly huge part in the success we had last season and I agreed there was a role to play irrespective of whether I was on the pitch or not but I wanted to be on the pitch. That was what I was here to do.'

Such was the 31-year-old Charles's importance to Ainsworth as a character, with his humble and gracious manner, the empathic element to his personality vital to the squad structure and the wellbeing of the people in it, the manager wanted to see his face every day. He might play a few matches too, which would be a distinct help.

Ainsworth had only once gone against the advice of Cian O'Doherty, the club's medical chief, when it came to a player's roadworthiness. O'Doherty counselled against signing Charles, noting the egregious state of his hip. 'But I knew Darius had something to offer, so we shortened the contract from two years to a year. In that year, he played five games. I did wonder if I'd done the right thing.' There was something about Darius that Ainsworth didn't want to lose.

'If I couldn't give it physically, I had to double down on emotional support,' Charles said. 'There were days when I didn't want to be around the boys. I had to come in and fake it. I couldn't allow myself to grieve. I'd wake up every morning and feel like rubbish. I was always reminded of how my hips felt because putting on my socks was painful, a real chore.

'I read an article about Andy Murray who had the same injury as me and spoke about his difficulty with dressing and I said, "Yeah, that's me." No matter how good I felt in the morning as soon as I bent down it was, "Oh there it is again." That is what life had become.

'The medical boys Cian and Isaac [Leckie] didn't sugar coat anything, there was no softening of the blow. They said I had two options, try to manage it and get through that way or have an operation. But if I did that there was no going back. It was an option later in life but it would be invasive, they'd go in, shave something down or take something out or put something in. Footballers were accustomed to having an injury and someone saying "oh we'll operate on that" and you come back and you're better.'

It was while he was in the midst of this clutch of smothering emotions, his head hurting from all the turmoil, that I had initially seen Charles in silent contemplation at the training ground.

'I couldn't see the forest for the trees that day, and for several days. Once I made the decision I wasn't going to retire and would try to come back I wholeheartedly threw myself into it, but there was no safety net so I had to give my all, and if it didn't work out I didn't know what I'd do.

'God knows what kind of depression I may have fallen into. I'd let myself go, essentially. Sometimes I'd have to take myself away from the group and meditate with my own thoughts. I'd let the anxiety pass, see the emotion for what it was, try to let it go and visualise it and then ask myself "am I being rational or irrational?" I needed to be kind enough to let myself feel sad, or just be in pain. It was OK.

'Athletes were naturally goal orientated. They set sights on something, spent the rest of the time trying to achieve it, and if they didn't it was like the biggest upset ever, whereas, in actual fact, that was not the case.

'Dobbo often spoke about striving for excellence and that was really all we could do. You may not reach or attain every goal but the fact of the matter is you were striving to be better today than you were yesterday and then you would try to do the same tomorrow. In the job we were in and the type of people we were, failure wasn't an option.

'I'd been very fortunate that every squad I'd been in had been an open, willing and loving group. I was extremely fortunate. At Stevenage, we got promoted via the play-offs and you had to be in a real brotherhood to be able to do that, because these things didn't happen by chance. Graham Westley the manager there was a terrific guy but was he able to see what we needed emotionally? Probably not.

'I went to Wimbledon and that was the second coming of Darius because I'd been out for a year, came back, we got promoted after I'd been released from Burton and that gave me the euphoria I needed because I'd been so low. Then I came here. The gaffer and this club – I can't talk too highly of it.'

Darius started to choke up. 'I could cry, because I'm so overwhelmed by emotion. It's been such a rollercoaster but this club has given me *so* much, the support that I really needed.'

* * *

On the day he signed his contract extension, Darius Charles sent out an extended tweet. 'The last time I was this nervous was b4 I signed my first pro contract as an 18-year-old boy. This moment felt exactly the same (not because the money's the same!) This year has been the hardest I've ever endured, stripped of everything I thought I knew, my identity, my self-esteem, my sense of self-worth – depression, upset, hurt, tears, pain for many months. But one night I decided to take my destiny into my own hands. No words can ever describe how fulfilling this moment is. And as much as I worked harder than this for everything else in my life, I can't take the credit alone. I want to take this moment to tell everyone, team-mate, family and friend this wouldn't be possible without YOU, your love, kindness, care, empathy, support, praises and unwavering belief living in me is the only reason I stand here today living in my purpose.

'You were my shoulder to lean on, cry on, ears to hear my woes, you reminded me of the divine power that flows through me. And who Darius the man really is & what he stands for. I say all that to say this: No weapon formed against me shall prosper and when God is for you, who can be against you? I'M SO GRATEFUL FOR THIS MOMENT.'

This was a message brave and breathtaking in equal measure but was a mere surface-scratcher. 'In the last year, I lost myself. I didn't know who I was anymore because I'd attached who I was to the thing I did. The real blessing in having football taken away was that those closest to me, friends, family, team-mates, showed me who I really was. The things I thought I did because I was a footballer weren't because I was a footballer, but because I am the man I am.

'I truly believed the world was a mirror image of your thoughts and actions and if that was the case, I was extremely loving, kind, caring and empathetic because that was what everyone showed me. No one had anything but kind words to say. I didn't do it for plaudits, it was a case of, "I know I'm not the only one struggling in this profession. I can't be."

'I aspired to be a life coach, a mentor for pros young and old and people in general. The best way for me was to bare all, show my vulnerability in the hope that it allowed more people to show theirs and in doing that, which was extremely courageous, become the norm so people would stop simply trying to fit in and do what everyone else was doing.

'I had come away from myself and that was why I struggled with depression, panic attacks and anxiety. I went to therapy and that was the best thing ever. I'd tell anyone to go to it because it made me aware of why I was who I was.'

Having a young son had helped Charles in many enriching ways. Malakai – named for the Old Testament prophet – was nine years old and as bright as a button. He loved his football. Dad saw his son at least four times a week. 'I have a great relationship with his mum, we were childhood sweethearts, got together very young – young and dumb – and have a beautiful son.

'I was raised by women, my dad had his difficulties and I grew up not wanting to be like him. My son was also part of a broken home, and though it seemed in essence it was the same thing as happened for me it really wasn't. I was actively involved, we were co-parents. Malakai was doing incredibly well, such an intelligent lovely gentle soul, he played for Fulham under-10s. He really was a blessing.'

Charles talked life and football as reality. Fairy tales were for the rich and famous, he played at the breadline level, where every penny was eked and a moral compass was far more important than the pound in his pocket. The encroaching finality of Charles's career – he knew more than most it was near the end of his playing days – lent his words a challenging clarity.

'Footballers feelings were up and down every day. You could go from being in the team, to a substitute, to being injured, to not performing well, to getting a blast from the manager, to having some of your wages docked, to a pay rise.

'It was not a nine to five and this was no disrespect to those working those hours but this was not a job where you could coast. You had to be all engines running every day even if you didn't feel like it, if it was pouring outside, it was windy, it was nasty, or if you had an issue at home. I didn't want to say no one cared, but no one *really* cared because you had a job to do, people's livelihoods were at stake, a chain was only as strong as its weakest link, and if I turned up and I was weak that affected everyone else in this building.

'The need was to play. I wasn't paid to sit and watch. A plumber didn't watch another plumber do his job, did he? Imagine how I felt because if someone was in the side ahead of me they believed they were better than me. What did that do to a sense of self-worth?

'They may not have been better than you, they may have offered something different to you. But it didn't make me feel any better sitting on the bench week in, week out watching somebody else playing in my position.

'Could you step outside of that and say, "Well, it's not about *me*, it's about the gaffer and his ideas and what he wanted?" I was the one affected, it could affect how much money I got because there were bonuses to be had even at Wycombe. That was something I really, really toiled over. Why was I not playing? I went to train and did it as hard as I could every day and I did it really well but I couldn't get into the team. What did that do for my mentality and self-esteem?'

That is why visits to his therapist had been such an exceptionally transformative part of Charles's life. 'I could have a conversation with a team-mate about this and it would be, "Yeah, whatever." It was better to have someone from outside of the environment who could say, "OK I understand you feel this way but have you thought about it that way?" or "that it's really nothing to do with you and you need to focus on yourself and to train to the best of your ability because when you do get that opportunity, whether it was here or somewhere else, you could take that opportunity and fly high because it was not about this moment but about the process."

'When you could continue to strive for that excellence, then excellence is what you would attain, each and every day. But it was very hard to see that, to recognise it, when you weren't in the starting XI, when you were sat in the stands, when the boys didn't play well and weren't getting results for a period of time and you were still not in the team, what did that mean? What do I have to do? I was stuck.

'That's why footballers needed constant mental attention. In the gym we trained our muscles every day but where was the mental gym? You weren't given the tools and in such an intense environment you needed to be given tools, the coping mechanisms.

'My therapy was provided by the PFA and that was great, but I wouldn't have known there were 12 free sessions available through the association if a team-mate hadn't told me. It was almost like there were things there but they expected footballers to go out and search for them. We were adults and we were men, of course we were, but we were mollycoddled, hand-fed everything.

'We were told where to be, what time and what we were doing. Our only responsibility was to bring ourselves. Turn up – turn up and do what you were told. I wasn't trying to negate any responsibility, but they had trained us to be soldiers. You were trained to do this, like this, for this amount of time, in this place. For them to then say you needed to go and seek something if you needed it, I didn't know how that was done.

'I'd been a professional for 16 years, from a kid in primary school who was told what to do, to a teenager in high school told what to do and I'd gone straight from that into football to be told what to do. My whole life was that, so when or where did I get the skills to deal with the rest of my life?

'Everyone's perception is that you're larger than life but imagine when you go from football to being, say, a plumber. There's a real pressure because now I'm not a footballer and I've got to do a job that is normal. What would people think of me then?

'There was a real fear around football. For the first seven years of my career fear was my only motivation. That was insane. Then I made a decision. I'm really talented, I'm hard working, so why fear, why not love? Why didn't I do this because I loved it? As a kid, I loved it, I could do it for hours on end and so now I played out of love not fear but I was one of not many. A lot of people played in fear of being beaten or being replaced. The only certainty in football was the uncertainty.'

* * *

The hotspot story in the week's football press concerned Alexis Sanchez, the Manchester United forward, and the amount of money he was being paid – £300,000 a week if the tabloids had it right – to spend time warming his arse in his Bentley or on the substitutes' bench.

Wycombe paid their top-level players around 1/250th of that. 'Players require financial literacy,' said Darius Charles, not one of the top Wycombe earners.

'You needed the mental wellbeing to cope with the amount you had, it didn't matter if it was Darius on what I was on at Wycombe or Sanchez on his half a million a week. If you didn't have the tools to work you soon fell short, but we only really wanted to have the conversation when someone broke down, and for me that wasn't on.

'We trained our bodies every day and if the brain was our most powerful muscle then we needed to treat it better. Footballers are sheep – if you told them they were going to do a session with a psychologist every Tuesday, they'd do it. If the gaffer called me up on Saturday night and told me I was coming into training on Sunday morning, I was coming in to train. We were 24/7, 365 days, that's how it was.

'We could all do an hour with a psychologist but it wasn't something that was subsidised, football, the PFA, had all the money in the world, but with all the cases that we'd seen, there was nothing pro-active really. I went to a session once where

MIND partnered with the league but I didn't know what it meant. We had symbols on the back of our shirts but what did these mean for me who had really been struggling? Who did I go to? Who came to me to make sure I was okay? We did these things because it was the new hot topic and we wanted to be seen to be doing something about it.

'This was never an arena where you could coast. This would always be "push yourself to the maximum until you break". That's what this environment was, and it wasn't for everyone. We were gladiators in the modern sense. People could say they'd give their right arm to be a professional footballer but I'd like them to do one pre-season and see if they still fancied it.

'I'd love to see them come out when it was raining, freezing cold, go to bed early on a Friday and then on Saturday, when all their mates were having barbecues, going out just chilling, we were running around for their entertainment. We loved it, don't get me wrong, but these people should have really thought about what we don't do so we could become footballers.

'It must have been lovely to know when you were able to spend some time with your family and take 'x' amount of days off whenever. I had to live a particular way because I couldn't be seen out smoking, drinking or acting a fool. There were real ramifications to all my actions socially.

'You [the non-footballer] could do whatever you wanted within reason, return to work on Monday and keep your head down, but I couldn't do that. I couldn't mess up. For what I got paid, I sacrificed my privacy because my whole life was on show. If a footballer cheated on his wife, which I didn't condone, everyone knew about it. Not only did he have to deal with it but it was played out in the press, publicly. If Joe Bloggs cheated on his wife, they could deal with it, keep it in-house.

'Did you want to be a footballer? OK, but there was a lot that came with it. A lot of people struggled. Nothing worth having came easy. I worked bloody hard to be in this position that could be taken from me at any moment.'

* * *

The time had flown, it was 10.15am and the team were ready to prepare for a wider discourse on the MK Dons and how they might set up at the weekend. Charles was suddenly surrounded by a group of bustling men in blue who seemed to have shaken off the cup loss to Reading very quickly.

Josh Hart fired up the video of MK's most recent performance. Ainsworth emphasised the habit of the two wider of their three central-defenders to spring forward and Dons' manager Paul Tisdale's preferred set up for attacking corners – one man in the six-yard box, four or five mingling on the edge and one always free, floating. The front two were particularly strong. They would warrant careful marshalling.

The manager nominated his team: Allsop, Grimmer, Stewart, Phillips, Jacobson; Gape, Pattison, Bloomfield; Smyth, Samuel, Onyedinma. It would be Giles Phillips's first League One start; Samuel replaced Akinfenwa as the main striker with special notice for Smyth and Fred to keep close tabs on the marauding centre-backs. They could create havoc. Darius Charles would have to wait for his first-team opportunity. He'd be on the bench for the first time, which was progress.

As Ainsworth projected, MK Dons' two wider central defenders were deployed as auxiliary forwards, their first equaliser came from such a foray down the left and when referee Kettle penalised Joe Jacobson for something and nothing in the area it was 2-2, and the momentum (that vital commodity) was with the Dons.

Wycombe decided on a stronger physical presence. Akinfenwa came on, as did David Wheeler, who had been at MK on loan for the second half of the previous season, reuniting with his old Exeter boss Tisdale, with whom he had enjoyed a spell of 13 goals in 20 appearances that helped them to the League Two play-offs in 2017.

As Wheeler warmed up on the touchline, every opposing substitute hugged or high-fived him. It had to happen. A sumptuous ball from Nick Freeman in the final minute found Wheeler, who controlled it out of the air, stepped inside a defender and fired home. 'I had the lousiest preparation ever. I missed everything in training and then scored a goal like that.'

Wycombe would spend the weekend third in League One, their highest-ever position. Trevor Stroud bounded along the corridor. 'History you know chaps, history. It's wonderful but it's only another step forward in my eyes. The minute you stop and think you've achieved something is the minute you start to fail.'

Three days later, a draw at Fleetwood Town felt like a failure. The second half was played in lashing wind and rain. Akinfenwa rose from the bench to score with a header that looked like being the difference until a scrappy equaliser in the final few moments drew accusatory looks.

Richard Dobson especially loathed conceding goals, where concentration lapses proved his side's downfall. A cross from the left ought to have been dealt with, the ball spun from Ryan Allsop's grasp and landed at the feet of striker Paddy Madden eight yards out. There was limited consolation for Dobson when Fleetwood's manager Joey Barton told him he thought Wycombe had played rather well.

* * *

Southend United arrived in Buckinghamshire with the unwanted distinction of zero points, a record matched only by Bury who hadn't played yet. The football media were increasingly consumed by the story of a club for whom the last rites were being rehearsed.

BBC Radio 5 Live's *Wake Up to Money* programme devoted a half-hour segment to how the club had been driven to the graveside by unscrupulous ownership and depressing misman-agement. You could sense the fans' rage through the radio.

Compassion for Bury was sincere yet tempered by the realisation that bad business was bad business and the sport was infiltrated by fools. Bury had been granted more extensions than formed Britain's departure from the European Union.

On the face of it, the EFL didn't want to cold-heartedly put a member out to grass, but at the same time they said they had a competition to protect and Bury owner Steve Dale, with his Falstaffian beard and outbursts of petulant self-justification, was simply blowing hot air at the problem.

This state of affairs was both near and far from Southend manager Kevin Bond's mind as he slipped into a high-backed chair at the Holiday Inn, a regular stopover for the opposition before the downhill journey to Adams Park. In Southend's case the gradient was too, all-markedly, real.

My association with Kevin stretched to his 1980s playing days at Norwich and Manchester City under his charismatic dad John. Kevin was burdened by the handicap of his father, believing he was the best player on the books and constantly repeating his assertion in public. Mancunians resented that, especially as Bond Jnr was something of a stroller with an easy, laconic style as distinct from the man-and-ball mould of Dave Watson and Tommy Booth, previous City centre-halves.

Southend wanted Harry Redknapp to replace Chris Powell at the tail end of the 2018/19 season but Harry said he was conflicted by his association with BetVictor, the gambling company, and instead recommended Bond, his long-time assistant. Bond succeeded in keeping the club in League One, a mission accomplished thanks to a goal a minute from time against Sunderland on the last day of the season.

The new boss changed playing personnel, was assured by Southend's chairman Ron Martin that each new arrival was better than the player he replaced and that Martin was a fan of the 'pass-it-from-the-back' style the manager was attempting to inculcate in his squad. But unless nice passing delivered goals and thus points, a chairman's opinion would soon shift or supporters shifted it for him.

There was a fatalistic air about Bond only four games into the season. He didn't engage in social media but had a decent clue as to the vitriol that headed his way. He was even finding conversations with his wife at home in Southampton both disjointed and distracted. 'We sat at the dinner table a couple of times last week and didn't say a word. For all the use I am to her, I might as well spend a few more nights in the hotel in Southend.'

Only that he might find supporters grouped outside tossing pebbles at his bedroom window. The fickle nature of football support was long accepted as part of any deal but made it no easier to accept. Bond was suffering inside and only a result or two would make that ache subside. 'I can't be too heavy on the players. I want them to try to play with freedom but at the same time there's a fear there.

'We've lost four games in the season and won a cup game. That record might be lost if it happened in the middle of a season, but it's at the start and it's magnifying the problems. For us now, a goal changes the game and kills us. At the moment we're not going to score our way out of trouble, every club and every manager goes through periods when it's like that.

'We conceded first and then a minute into the second half at Lincoln last week. That was it. The Cowley brothers [management duo Danny and Nicky] told me when they went to Lincoln they were thankful to be in the National League with relatively little spotlight. They said it took them three transfer windows to change the club's culture. You need time but you also need to win and the wins give you time. That's what I need.'

Management was taking its toll, as calm as Bond appeared on the surface. He recalled something profound Sir Alex Ferguson said when his assistant at Manchester United, Brian Kidd, left to take over as the manager of Blackburn Rovers in 1998.

'He said, "I think the constant burden of having to make difficult decisions will weigh heavy on him." Fergie was right. The stresses and strains are unreal and football for so many people is disproportionately important.'

Ainsworth addressed his players as to what they should expect from a team on its uppers. 'Southend go pop, pop, pop, pop pop, boom. They want to play it out, fucking ridiculous. If you're Manchester City it's okay. But they are going to come here tomorrow and play hard, so respect them, but you're electric at the moment boys. Put yourself in their shoes, you've been there many times in the past few seasons. This is not going to be an easy game.'

Darius Charles was making his first full home appearance of the season. When he walked out on to the pitch and the formation took shape, he really wanted to cry. For 70 minutes Wycombe's entire defence appeared as if perceived through misty eyes.

Those with a disproportionate fascination in Southend's results were flying at a level of sensation they hadn't felt for many a day. 'We're winning away, we're winning away, how shit must you be, we're winning away,' their fans mocked those at the opposite end. But the players, though 3-1 to the good, weren't crowing at all. They looked petrified.

Scott Kashket intercepted a mis-hit shot by Nick Freeman and side-footed Wycombe to within a single goal before Jack Grimmer's scuff across the area landed at the feet of Adebayo Akinfenwa, who directed the ball into the path of Anthony Stewart. His side-footed finish drew the sides level. Three minutes into stoppage time, Freeman neatly found Kashket for a step inside and clinical left-footed finish.

Wycombe's bench exploded; Bond drove his hands deep into his pockets and kicked the turf in front of him. From a seat in the row behind, Adam El-Abd rose to slap me across the back.

Ten days later, El-Abd stunned everyone by leaving Wycombe, citing his reason as the need to broaden his horizons, and he joined Stevenage, languishing at the foot of League Two. Four days after that earth mover, Kevin Bond resigned as the manager of Southend United.

When Wycombe
went Top of the Table

THE loss of a football match to Wycombe Wanderers was inducing a managerial cataclysm. Ten days from a head-spinning collapse and after Rochdale had run his men in even greater circles, Kevin Bond departed Southend without a word to his staff. Mind you, he'd barely been there long enough to memorise their first names.

The next visitors to Adams Park were Lincoln City and within 48 hours of departing with tails between legs, manager Danny Cowley, with his brother and assistant Nicky, had been installed at Huddersfield Town of the Championship and their fields of relative plenty.

There was a comic-book element about the brothers' long haul from 2007 at a club called Concord Rangers from Canvey Island with their average crowd of 50 in the Essex Senior League to their present standing.

It was gratifying to see dynamic British coaches rewarded for good works as the club's double promotion, reaching an FA Cup quarter-final from non-league and winning an EFL Trophy from such relative geographical isolation, warranted. The boys were unquestionable dab hands at self-promotion.

The chat in Wycombe's coaching room when news broke of the Cowleys' *au revoir* from Sincil Bank mixed 'what the bloody hell?' at the wages they were about to earn with a proportionate sense of cynicism that their own efforts had again gone unrecognised.

Why not Gareth and Dobbo for Huddersfield, and not because Lincoln had been out-manoeuvred tactically and emotionally by a side that, with their 3-1 victory in the first week of September, moved to the top of League One? Even the press fixated on EFL matters was loath to give due credit. The *Football League Paper* splashed with 'Sky Blues soar to the summit'. Right colour. Wrong club.

Ainsworth wouldn't have been human if he hadn't wondered how premium jobs passed him by and papers printed stories that – premediated or not – discredited the job he was doing. He found solace in a quote from Kurt Cobain, the late Nirvana frontman, 'I'd rather be hated for who I am than loved for who I'm not.'

'Do people want me to change, to cut my hair, to alter my style, then might I get one of these jobs? Well, I won't.' He kept the front page image on his iPhone to emphasise his annoyance that Coventry had made the headlines when second in the table. 'If the season ended today, we'd be champions. No more to be said.'

The training ground canteen chatter was more boisterous than usual on Monday morning. Joe Jacobson learned the EFL's dubious goals panel determined he *had* scored a hat-trick against Lincoln, two direct from corner kicks, an achievement that would keep him in dinner-party conversation for life. His left foot was a national treasure.

When the roll call was taken, a couple of faces from Jacobson's generation were absent. Adam El-Abd's decision to move to Stevenage evoked significant ripples, not least as his new side were crushed 4-2 by Cheltenham Town in his first match and Dino Maamria, the manager who signed him, was immediately sacked and replaced in the interim by Mark Sampson, the controversial former England Women manager. El-Abd was already wondering if he hadn't made the most terrible mistake.

Matt Bloomfield had been given extra time to recuperate from the incident that overshadowed Jacobson's historic hat-trick as the major debating point of the victory over Lincoln that was self-evidently not the parting the Cowleys had anticipated.

Danny and Nicky were full-on rant and rave at Adams Park. Their standing with officials was deep into negative territory and evidence for that reputation was more than circumstantial. They took it in turns to belittle their goalkeeper Josh Vickers for nervousness at dead-ball situations. Screaming 'you're fucking costing us' over and over again was hardly likely to improve Vickers's ball-handling.

The brothers busied themselves, cursing the fourth official at each decision against them, though in that they were hardly unique. Trailing 2-0 at half-time, Danny marched across the pitch to finger-point referee Chris Sarginson, a largely one-way conversation that ended when the door of the officials' room was closed in his face.

Cowley hoped his show of open dissent might persuade the referee to think twice about penalising Lincoln in the second half and the plan worked to the extent Sarginson made – or *didn't* make – a decision that profoundly affected the match.

Bloomfield characteristically threw head and body at a corner and was caught when two Lincoln players collided and one struck him full on the temple. He collapsed in the six-yard area, lying prone next to Lincoln's Bruno Andrade (Gareth Ainsworth's first signing as Wycombe's manager in 2012).

The instruction was that play must be stopped if a player received a head injury. This incident didn't require an adjudication. Bloomfield and Andrade were out for the count. Sarginson put the whistle to his lips twice, didn't blow and signalled a goal when Lincoln substitute John Akinde nudged the ball home at the far post.

The Cowleys appeared indifferent to the players' plight, and demanded of the fourth official – 'Is it a goal?' They urged their players back to their own half. Ainsworth was denied entry to the pitch until the medics had made their assessment. In the stand, Blooms's mother Jackie was distraught seeing her son lying motionless.

The home players clustered around the referee demanding to know why he hadn't stopped the match. The stuffing had been knocked out of him. The hiatus lasted a dozen minutes.

Medical chief Cian O'Doherty was checking that Bloomfield was breathing properly and there were no potential fractures or signs of distress. He was concerned that the captain, lying on his back, was in a highly agitated state, at one and the same time struggling to make sense and wanting to leap to his feet.

O'Doherty settled his player but was not settled himself, demanding an explanation for a failure in communication between the four officials at such a critical moment. The touchline official was clearly distracted by the Cowleys' in-your-face antics but the linesman, with a direct line of sight across the penalty area, had offered no support.

When he was about to burst into the referee's room, O'Doherty found himself at the back of a decent-sized queue forming behind an equally indignant Richard Dobson.

* * *

When the melee around the skipper cleared and he was lifted onto a stretcher, Ainsworth disappeared down the tunnel to check on his man and console his mother.

The Wycombe players took time to clear their heads before Jacobson scored from a second direct corner kick, a stunning Allsop save denied Harry Anderson from four yards and the home side spurned multiple chances to extend their lead.

The substitutes had played a full part and Ainsworth called upon a novel threesome. Akinfenwa we knew, but Rolando Aarons and Nnamdi Ofoborh had joined on loan from the

Premier League, to the gratification of the coaching staff and utter amazement of supporters.

Wycombe trailed Ofoborh after an alert from chief scout Bob Rickwood prompted Dobson to watch him for Bournemouth under-23s, a match he recalled as much for the team's tendency to play out from the back under pressure of numbers as he did for the first sight of a muscular teenager in the middle of the park who possessed a decent touch whatever the furore around him.

Dobbo detailed Ofoborh's three performances for Nigeria in the 2019 under-20 World Cup tournament in Poland and was sold on him. The kid may not have had the lot but he had more than enough.

Bournemouth prevaricated – first yes, then no, then maybe – before manager Eddie Howe decided that first-team opportunities with Wycombe would be beneficial to the lad and allowed him to go. Nnamdi arrived at the training ground to sign with ten minutes to spare.

Aarons was definitely in the 'are you serious?' category of signings. Paul Smyth had inadvertently kicked a post during training – 'one of those stupid things' – and Fred Onyedinma wrenched a groin muscle. From the pre-season overload of forward players, Wycombe's numbers had seriously dwindled. On his usual Thursday visit to the training ground, Rickwood was challenged by Ainsworth to spend the morning coming up with half a dozen forwards who might a) be available and b) fit Wycombe's mould.

Aarons topped the scouting pile but there was a snag. Wycombe didn't have a ready contact at Newcastle for a report on his personality and was alerted that the player had once been involved in a bar brawl in the city.

Aarons told *The Guardian*, 'I've heard clubs have said no to signing me because they heard this and that. I had to go on loan to try and get games and do what I needed to do. It's been tough since my first loan [to Sheffield Wednesday] but I've learnt a lot. It's weird because I don't think I've done anything to deserve the reputation or words people say about me but the only way I can correct it is by playing well and scoring goals.'

Ainsworth judged people on his sense of them rather than any past indiscretions. He discovered Aarons and Onyedinma had the same agent and talked through a deal, the greatest complexity of which was that the forward was on Premier League money way beyond Wycombe's pay grade.

After a few hours of give and take, Wycombe agreed to pick up a fraction of the 24-year-old's wages which didn't extend Rob Couhig's cheque book as might have been imagined. Rickwood's grapevine had borne fruit again. Aarons was a Wycombe player for at least six months.

He was lightly built, sinewy and spry and had an instant rapport with the fans with his flashy touches and trickery. It might take time for his new team-mates to establish exactly what he was about because so much of his play was off the cuff. Sadly, at the end of a short cameo against Lincoln, he strained a muscle. Such were the game's fine balances.

It remained an historic week for all in quartered blue. Ainsworth's tactic of letting Lincoln have possession in their own half, hard pressing once they sought to cross the halfway line, throttling their routes to goal, the lethal left foot of Jacobson and the introduction of two lightning-rod players had combined to send the Chairboys to the top of the league.

The fans were in a stupor. This was all very new and quite wonderful.

* * *

On Sunday there was a break-in at the training ground. The burglars were amateurs. They stole Andy Fairman's mobile phone, a litre bottle of Jack Daniels from Gareth Ainsworth's bottom drawer and opened and closed a lot of cabinets but missed £15 in cash in full view on secretary Kelly Francis's desk.

Everyone was asked to check their boots and make sure the thieves were not wannabe players rather than dim-witted chancers. It seemed that one mobile and some decent alcohol had been enough to keep them happy. 'It was a bloody good bottle too,' Ainsworth said. 'It was a present from a fan. I was saving it for when I get the sack.'

He might have wanted to take a swig right now. His boys were on top. The pats on the back and cheery waves as he stopped for his regular Starbucks skinny cappuccino in Marlow High Street were sincere and gratifying. He was as proud as punch.

For Wycombe's support base, though, this Monday morning brought a significant element of alarm.

The departure of the Cowleys meant Lincoln needed a management team and, from an initial spot in the middle of the bookmakers' field, Ainsworth (and thus Dobson) had become the clear favourites to replace them. It was time to speak of that which should not be spoken.

Wycombe's fans pleaded that a move to Lincoln was sideways at best and the place itself was bloody remote. Then again it was financially more stable and thus highly attractive especially as the Couhigs were still not certain of taking control. The Imps would offer the manager and his associates substantially more than they earned at Adams Park.

Rob Couhig wanted to assuage the worriers. The potential owner insisted he would 'create a sustainable economic model that would allow the club to compete at even higher levels and justify your confidence in us. I am humbled and grateful that the manager has expressed a clear desire to remain at the club.'

He obviously knew what the fans didn't.

* * *

Being top of the league for a week was a little unreal and Wycombe were well acquainted with rises and falls. True to their *Grand Old Duke of York* past, no sooner were they up than they were down after a first league defeat of the season to Gillingham at the Priestfield Stadium, a ground that looked like a poorly assembled Meccano kit.

Nothing about the Wycombe performance was pleasing, a colourless, fruitless display that afflicted every team once in a while and, though hard to digest, injected a sense of reality into the system.

Steve Evans, a Scot with a tendency to controversy and colourful language, was Gillingham's manager. He had done the rounds from Corby and Boston United (where he was given a suspended jail sentence in 2006 when found guilty of conspiring to cheat HMRC out of £250,000) to Crawley, Peterborough and Leeds United and had a reputation for boot camp football. There was not a single smiling face in the 2019/20 Gillingham squad picture.

Gareth Ainsworth may have admired Evans but Richard Dobson wasn't entirely drawn to him. It was an accepted post-match norm that a home manager's office would be thrown open to the opposition boss and his assistants for the exchange of pleasantries even if the groups couldn't stand each other.

Dobbo usually played along with such nuances, though Evans and his boisterous assistant Paul Raynor and the Accrington pair of John Coleman and Jimmy Bell, who would visit Adams Park three days later, tested the most patient chap.

'I used to go in but, after most of the stuff I heard, I said to myself, "Why would I waste 15 minutes of my life on this?" Traditionally we wished each other well and talked through the issues in the game but more and more people would just bitch about the referee and why this or that decision hadn't gone for them. I just didn't want to be in there.'

Behind his desk on Monday, with 24 hours to prepare for Accrington's visit and an injury toll mounting, Dobson was pondering how it was that Gillingham – average if truth be told – had been first to beat his team.

Equally frustrated, Dominic Gape came into the coaches' room to ask for his personal clips to see what he could have done better. The pair chewed the fat for 15 minutes and agreed, 'We lost all our creativity in one afternoon.'

'When we used the diamond before, it was about frustrating the opposition's diamond, but after our start Gillingham chose to use a diamond to frustrate us and we didn't deal with it,' Dobbo said after a 2-0 defeat. 'Who knows this might have been a good moment to lose and see what our reaction was.'

* * *

Two home games in five days against Accrington Stanley and Portsmouth would demand a rotation across positions that was something of a novelty where Wycombe were concerned.

The team would have to respond without the ceaseless pressing of Alex Samuel, who had suffered a cracked rib and punctured lung in a first-half collision at Gillingham. Only his decent nature prevented Samuel saying what he really thought of the perpetrator of the barging challenge on him that went unpunished. Darius Charles, who had played five consecutive games, required rest, and Joe Jacobson, an ever present, couldn't be flogged to a standstill whatever his fitness levels.

Ainsworth selected Giles Phillips and Jamie Mascoll in defence, David Wheeler and Fred Onyedinma as a front two, with Nick Freeman and Scott Kashket as the wider influencers. The trouble was that for 45 minutes against Accrington there was no influence, though in Jordan Clark and Sam Finley the Lancashire side possessed livewire forwards who required a watchful eye.

Their basic attacking tactic was for Ross Sykes, a towering centre-back, to thump the ball high and diagonally to the edge of the Wycombe box where his forwards contested doggedly for first and second balls. Accrington took the lead through a Dion Charles header. Wycombe equalised when Kashket stumbled in the penalty area – a mite too dramatically for Accrington's liking – and Freeman was steadfast in Jacobson's absence to drive home the spot kick. It ended 1-1.

There was one Accrington tactic the home side could do nothing about – a quite brilliant high-press on the fourth official, a poor sod called Stuart Butler. John Doolan, the first-team coach, stationed himself a couple of feet from the area reserved for the referee's third set of assistant eyes and ears. Each time an Accrington player was touched, Doolan made his faux outrage loud and clear, often joined by Bell, so poses and profanities were delivered in stereo.

A posse of Accrington players would surround and scream at referee Brett Huxtable whenever a decision displeased them. 'They were street-wise,' Jack Grimmer said. 'We needed a little bit of that. If one of our players went down, he bounced straight back up.'

Dobson had 'the longest shower of my life' to delay his appearance in Ainsworth's office before protocol was breached. John Coleman spent 15 minutes in the referee's room before informing Ainsworth and his staff that he thought Wycombe would struggle against Portsmouth the following weekend as Huxtable wouldn't be on the team sheet. Dobbo wished he was back under the shower.

* * *

The prevailing sense was that the week of 14 September would be defining for Wycombe's future, short and long term. The matches against Gillingham and Accrington produced a solitary goal from the penalty spot, but the club were third in the league and the initial block of nine matches – the stations by which management judged the team's progress – were as good as they could have hoped for. This was play-off form by Dobson's measurable standard and if Wycombe made the play-offs, well, imagine it.

The financial reckoning (i.e. the legacy members' vote) expected to arrive early in 2020 had become increasingly imperative. The team's strong on-pitch performances, the arrival of Premier League players, the empathic nature and benevolence of the Couhigs and the general infusion of well-being around the club determined that it was time to make the decision on ownership sooner rather than later.

A fans' forum two days before Portsmouth came to Adams Park was a litmus test and the manager chose to join Trevor Stroud and Rob Couhig on stage. Ainsworth had avoided the first gathering but believed his staff and players should now express an opinion. This was not a gun to the head for a 'yes' vote, but it was as near as dammit.

Stroud stressed that the club would be free of debt, their heritage protected and the trust would still wholly own Adams Park. He told the gathering the deal in its entirety would be available for inspection once lawyers agreed the small print. Every legacy member entitled to vote could see the integral elements before they placed an 'X' in their preferred box.

Rob Couhig said he had fallen in love at first sight twice, when he saw his wife Missy and when he arrived in Wycombe. 'We're having the time of our lives. Now we believe we need to speed the engagement process. The club is in a unique space and we must take advantage. One of the many lessons I learned in business was that these opportunities don't come around again. We might not come back.'

The qualification for a vote extended to those who had been season-ticket holders for four years. The gravest concern for 'yes' supporters was an apathetic response, especially as every non-vote counted as a 'no'. The requirement for a 75 per cent pass rate was a frighteningly tight margin. The trust said it was a defence mechanism inserted to protect themselves against rapacious owners and had not realised it might screw everything up if they found someone they actually liked.

The manager was unequivocal. 'A few months ago we were talking about a budget that might be competitive at the bottom end of League Two. Let's do this now. I think we can achieve something. Rob was true to his word, he gave me a little bit more [cash to spend] and proved he was committed to the club. My expectation for the season was smashed by us getting to the top of the league.'

Ainsworth's emotional tie was as profound as those who had either supported the club over many years or were entirely new to such an attachment. Inside the room was a mix of those who'd seen it all and mixed support and sentiment with scepticism. Were spiced burgers going to sway their vote? Then there were the young supporters who aspired to follow a successful team, maybe in the Championship one day.

The Wycombe fans' forum Gasroom 2 was a popular venue for discourse, though much of the debate was carried out in the fog of anonymity. It could be witty but it could be pernicious too.

That said, regular correspondent perfidious_albion struck a chord with many fellow Chairboys. 'There are obvious cultural differences between we English lower league fans (I use each word deliberately) and our new American "sport as family entertainment" business-focussed friends. As has been pointed out, currently we are on a high and all is peachy as they might put it, which is fine. When Adams Park is full of can-do positivity they get that.

'However, Clan Couhig has yet to experience, or possibly even comprehend, our capacity for old world negative, sceptical cynicism. We won't always be third, there will be dark days. How they react to the implicit criticism will be the true test of their resolve. Small-time loan-shark heavies and shouty ice-cream vendors we coped with yet I for one would not want to be on the wrong side of Rob and the blood family.

'To succeed in the US, cold-eyed ruthlessness is the cost of entering the game. And I suspect post sale it will be "The Couhig Way" or the highway. Along with many others I see no practical alternative but we must go in with our eyes open and accepting of what we sign up for.'

Ainsworth's departing words that evening cut through the debate. 'I'm not going to scrape and scrap much more and you wouldn't believe what it has taken from the staff to get us to this position. We're on the verge of something spectacular and the people up here back me.' The rousing ovation suggested Ainsworth had a multitude of apostles.

Questioned about the club's constitution going forward, Rob Couhig said without fudge that he, his wife Missy, nephew Pete and consultant Mark Palmer would be four members of a six-person board to include two voted on by the trust, the favourites for which were Trevor Stroud and his redoubtable deputy David Cook.

Pete Couhig had officially applied for the post of the club's chief financial officer, marking out his financial expertise and linking it to a record of entrepreneurism in the entertainment business. His love of music – the same rock 'n' roll genre favoured by Ainsworth – would strike a positive chord.

He'd been involved in successful music venues in Louisiana, namely Tipitina's in New Orleans and SoGo Live in Baton Rouge. For good measure, he was 'one of the Founders/ Managers/Producers of Panic 2000, LLC; which filmed, edited and released commercially the Widespread Panic documentary.'

It did feel as if, for a few weeks at least and with Ainsworth cheering on the Couhigs, widespread panic in Wycombe had been averted.

* * *

Accrington sold 12 tickets for their fixture at Adams Park. The match was played with one stand entirely devoid of human life – a saving on stewarding fees, yes, but producing a morbidly one-sided atmosphere.

Five days later there was not a space to be had at the same end when Portsmouth rolled into town. To say that this famous old south-coast club's recent past had been chequered was a profound understatement. Tossed and blown by decades of financial indiscretion, the 2008 FA Cup winners and recent members of the Premier League had survived relegation to the National League in 2014 thanks to five wins from their five games under former player Andy Awford.

Relegation could have been the end of the story. It was a precarious sensation Pompey had become well used to. Two years earlier the club slipped into administration – not for the first time – owing over £50m to a string of creditors, including unpaid players and staff, and were staring over the precipice.

With the locals digging as deep as they could, a Pompey supporters' trust was formed that worked marvels and managed to secure a takeover that expunged the debts and placed the football club on a sound if slightly surreal footing.

In August 2017 the trust formalised the sale of the club to the Tornante Company (translating from hairpin bend in Italian) owned by the former chief executive officer of the Disney Corporation, Michael Eisner. The price was an estimated £5.6m. The deal had indeed spun Portsmouth's fortunes around.

But with such backing came the need for the club of Portsmouth's size and support to soar, and soar quickly. A loss in the 2018/19 play-offs to Sunderland meant Portsmouth would require a strong start to the new campaign to keep their support base tolerant.

When Pompey arrived at Adams Park they had played six games – Bury's EFL expulsion and the staging of a music festival in the city meant enduring two postponements – with only six points in the merit column. Kenny Jackett, who became manager as the Tornante negotiations neared completion, was under the cosh.

Such a scenario became further evident when Portsmouth's chief executive Mark Catlin was handed the team sheet in the boardroom. 'What the hell's going on?' he snorted. It was evident he didn't think much of the manager's choice.

The match was sparse in inspiration and quality. It was only when it became ten a side that any space opened up. Matt Bloomfield had taken another blow on the head and was replaced by Nnamdi Ofoborh. Twenty minutes into his stint, Nnamdi was shown a straight red for a challenge that a Sunday League player would have celebrated by blowing across his knuckles.

The referee consulted a linesman and showed a second yellow to Pompey's Ellis Harrison, who had decided to manhandle Adebayo Akinfenwa, which was spectacularly stupid given it could hardly be attempted without drawing attention to oneself.

Ainsworth kept two men up. Scott Kashket ran his legs to a standstill though he got on his manager's nerves by drifting more than once beyond Pompey's back line. 'Scotty, I'm going to bring on someone who doesn't keep fucking running offside,' he screamed. Dobbo had to politely remind him that he'd already made the three permitted substitutions.

Kashket's roaming mattered little when in the 82nd minute Tom Naylor stuck up his arm to palm away a corner. Sadly for Portsmouth, Naylor was a centre-half. Nick Freeman had scored from the spot at the same end against Accrington but this was different. Akinfenwa tucked the ball under his arm, concerned that if Freeman missed it could shatter his confidence for a long time. Bayo's aim was true.

Wycombe's 1-0 success was further wild encouragement but served only to enhance Portsmouth's woe. There was nothing in Jackett's touchline persona that matched Evans, Cowley or Coleman for permanent scowling rage. He was at his most animated when changing hands to shield his eyes from the sun. Maybe Portsmouth's fans took his lack of wild waving as an indication he didn't care.

A most gruesome sight was two boys who couldn't have been more than ten in club shirts leaning across a barrier screaming dog's abuse at the disappearing Jackett while each was clasping the hand of a beer-bellied moron I assumed was their father. It was disgusting. Ainsworth said, 'If I have as successful a career in management as Kenny Jackett, I'll be delighted.'

Ten minutes after the match Ainsworth and Stroud were standing at the head of the tunnel in mutual admiration at the result. Nnamdi Ofoborh approached like a sheepish schoolboy who'd been caught flicking ink at the back of the class. 'Sorry boss, sorry,' he said.

'You're here to learn,' Ainsworth told him. 'You were awesome. I wanted you to be committed and you were. It wasn't a dirty foul, just a little late. I don't think we can appeal it though. It's a three-match ban.'

Nnamdi nodded, tried to smile, shuffled from foot to foot, shook our hands and walked slowly back down the tunnel.

Balderdash

THE Wycombe coach didn't pass Gigg Lane on its way to the Village Hotel in Bury, the overnight stop before the appointment at Rochdale. I had wanted to re-visit the ground – now more of a shrine – the following morning but stair-rods were falling upon stair-rods and I feared catching my death.

The climax to Bury's status as a Football League club remained a despicable blot on the governance of the EFL and how it had allowed the club to rot without displaying any palpable sense of appreciation or interventionist drive.

The EFL's financial figures were released early in 2020 and published with a typically piercing commentary by Kieran Maguire (@PriceofFootball) who wrote that the League had 'only' £82m in its account as of 30 June 30 2019, 'which explains why they were unable to help Bury FC.' The league reported that 'no material events' had happened between the end of the financial year and the publication of its annual report. The death of a football club is not a 'material' event?

If Bury could go, so could a few others. Wycombe were still too poor to relax for a minute. Rochdale remained on the map even if to stay alive they allowed their main sponsor to rename the ground in their honour. In 2016 it was goodbye Spotland, hello The Crown Oil Arena, which might have looked good in

Riyadh or Abu Dhabi but felt weirdly inappropriate in the hills around Manchester.

It was a soak-to-the-skin day, though warmth was never far away in this neck of the woods. Each press pass had the message 'Free Pie' attached which, disappointingly in one respect, was not the club's protest against the incarceration of a local mafioso.

Instead northern hospitality remained abundant and Phil Catchpole of BBC Three Counties Radio was dismayed when we pointed at his badge after he'd forked out three quid for Rochdale's finest combination of beef and potatoes covered in a hearteningly flaky crust.

As with many clubs in the region, all roads to the ground tilted at a crazy angle, had to be negotiated in the dark whatever the time of day or year and were dotted with stone terraced homes that would stand resolute against tempest, flood or invasion force.

From my days as a boy football reporter based in Manchester – where Gigg Lane was often a Friday evening workplace – I loved these hills, these arenas and the inner strength they emitted. As a man of Blackburn, so did Gareth Ainsworth.

He was back to his roots. Sitting across from him as the team coach wound through rain-lashed streets and up past the local cemetery – he thought it macabre when I took a picture of the shop-front of Rochdale Memorial Services – I sensed a relaxed calm.

We chatted about our kids and as his were aged between ten and 16, he was anxious as any parent would be about where they were and how quickly they were maturing.

Then the vehicle lurched left into the car park and he was jagged into full match mode, 'come on ... rock n'roll,' he implored his team as they marched single file into the spartan away dressing room.

Twenty-four hours earlier, I climbed aboard the team coach for the first time expecting quizzical glances and grumbles as this was the players' space where they could be themselves without fear of intrusion, exposure or disturbance. There was nothing but good cheer and hearty handshakes.

'You're one of the team bro,' said Adebayo Akinfenwa.

* * *

As the last of the luggage was lifted aboard, Nnamdi Ofoborh ploughed a lonely furrow between the training-ground mannequins, trying not to look across at the coach. This was the professional's deepest anguish. Your team-mates departed as a group headed in one direction, you left, with the radio for company, going another.

Ever since the teenager's arrival from Bournemouth, Richard Dobson had said that his determination was to get Nnamdi to smile. There would be better days to go for that one.

When Ofoborh realised his sending off against Portsmouth – the first in his life – was not a dreadful illusion, he placed his fists to his eyes and his shoulders heaved. The only conclusion anyone could draw was that the lad was inconsolable. His manager promoted a counter theory. 'He was laughing because someone told him he was missing Rochdale away and he thought, "Thank fuck for that."'

Ofoborh was not the only player with Rochdale scrubbed from his itinerary. Nick Freeman and Joe Jacobson were on adjacent exercise bikes putting a brave face on niggles, Paul Smyth's foot still wasn't right and Matt Bloomfield – disqualified because of football's concussion protocol – clucked around like a mother hen making sure no one had forgotten anything.

Bloomfield recalled the dressing room scene a few days earlier when he came around from a latest knock to the head to find Nnamdi sitting across the room, as numb as the captain. 'At the end of the match, Dobbo asked if I might have a word with Nnamdi and I said I'd already been sitting with him for 45 minutes. He was distraught, the lad, but this was what we'd always done here, taking care of each other.' 'Blooms' hated being away from the lads but at least he'd have a weekend at home with his girls.

It was clear that this was the least cliquey group and a richly diverse one. There were the bookworms – Bob Rickwood, the chief scout-cum-temporary-kit manager was devouring the pages of *Living on the Volcano*, the excellent essay by Michael Calvin on the art of management, while Giles Phillips was alone at the back engrossed in George Orwell's *1984*, a rather deeper offering.

Phillips developed a love of reading once his parents had drummed into him the beauty of the written word. His favourite was John Steinbeck's *Of Mice and Men* and he revered *The Alchemist* by Paulo Cuelho, described by Waterstones as, 'a beautiful parable about learning to listen to your heart, read the omens strewn along life's path and, above all, follow your dreams.'

There was the card school using casino chips for money (well, this was impecunious Wycombe), those deep in their musical world, taking images of team-mates in embarrassing forms of repose or joining the debates that became more animated the longer the journey extended. The voices of Akinfenwa and Sido Jombati were distinct, which was apparently commonplace. It was difficult to pick out every word but the most vociferous exchange was definitely about a chap called Pogba.

Through pouring rain and across the roadwork-strewn motorway system we rumbled on. Each time brake lights flashed ahead – this was the M6 on a Friday afternoon so it became numbingly regular – Scott Boylin, the driver, received a mouthful of friendly abuse. He was well used to it.

Once we had stopped for a coffee and relief at Norton Canes services, it was time for those in the front seats to engage in a little frivolity. The serious stuff of football was around a few more corners yet.

* * *

Two parlour games were long-standing Wycombe favourites – In One Word and Balderdash. Dave Wates assumed a writer would possess innate word association qualities and dropped regular partner Josh Hart without debate. He was soon regretting such bravado.

We divided into three teams for In One Word. One player from each team had five words/names/items on a card they had to get his/her partner to say within 60 seconds. The bidding started from a maximum 25 words and teams haggled over how many they thought it would take for his/her partner to answer all five correctly. The foreplay was often as intense as the actual performance.

Any time you depicted a word and your partner's reaction was an open-mouthed, glazed expression, it ate up precious seconds and spelt almost certain humiliation. No hand signals, rolling of eyes or gesticulations of any kind were permitted. On the return journey, I teamed with Josh, had to describe 'Lion Tamer' and when he shouted 'Penguin', I really thought the manager of Wycombe was going to have a coronary.

Nevertheless, Ainsworth and Dobson were long-practised artists at the game and as intuitively on-message at word association as they were when it came to team selections and culture building. It was quite something to behold how instinctively they read each other's mind. They breezed it.

We moved on to Balderdash. The format was that one player in turn read out a question from the categories film plots, people, words, acronyms and the law. The entire group wrote what they thought was an appropriate answer and the papers were handed in. The questioner read them out, along with the correct answer that only he or she knew. Points were gathered by answering correctly (which rarely happened) or, alternatively, how many of the group believed your answer was the right one.

A lot depended on an ability to mask emotion when reading out the responses so the group were unable to distinguish between the correct answer and the utter Balderdash, of which there was plenty.

One question was, 'What is a H-A-B-O-O-B?' The compendium of replies included, 'a blanket wrapped around a baby while being breast fed' (I was proud of that), 'a wooden tool used by tribesmen to entice termites from their mounds', 'an Indian wind instrument' and 'an intense Saharan dust storm'. It was the dust storm.

David Wheeler had tired of the Pogba polemic and joined with us, at the same time being treated for a dead leg. It looked like a very uncomfortable process having to re-adjust his leg position beneath a table every few seconds as suction pads attached to his thigh muscles induced stimulation. He kicked me under table twice and had the good manners to apologise.

As befitted a bit of a brainbox, he pondered every question with total focus but Dave Wates, sports scientist supreme, was crowned king of Balderdash to prolonged applause (all his own) as we reached the Bury New Road.

It was an established tradition that away-trip newcomers endured an initiation ceremony. At Wycombe the players were ritually serenaded after the evening meal. The three stooges this trip were the two recently recruited physical therapists, Aly Vogelzang and Sara Waterton, and me.

Sara asked to go first as she had become a bundle of nerves about freezing on stage – in this case standing on a chair. To be honest, I couldn't remember the title of her song and the players pretty much drowned her out with boisterous accompaniment. I went next.

Adebayo Akinfenwa was a self-appointed MC and asked for personal particulars before drifting into more delicate areas: to 'write a bestseller or Wycombe promoted?' My whispered 'bestseller' was not a popular response. 'A night out with friends or a night out with your wife?' I pleaded the Fifth.

My chosen song? On assignment to New York in the mid-80s, I was in a group of writers who acquired seats for Frank

Sinatra's one-man show at Carnegie Hall – Ol' Blue Eyes, a pianist, a glass of scotch and a spellbound audience of 2,800. I presumed 'My Way' would do the trick for 25 people in a basement room at The Village in Bury. Bayo handed me a spoon. That was my microphone.

The boys applauded dutifully but were much more animated at Aly's rendition of 'Ain't No Mountain High Enough' – a hugely appropriate choice given Wycombe's standing. Aly's surname translated from its Dutch origins to 'Birdsong'.

* * *

Eileen had worked as a waitress at The Village for 19 years. 'I came for six weeks one Christmas to help my niece and never left,' she said, fussing around the Wycombe players as the midday team talk beckoned. A few of the company gently cleared their throats. Dexy's Midnight Runners came into my head.

Eileen rolled out the last table-top and closed the door from the outside (she could have been a Rochdale spy). Gareth Ainsworth had a tactical novelty to explain, as his side would play 3-5-2 with Jack Grimmer a touch further withdrawn as the right-sided player of the midfield five than Fred Onyedinma on the left.

The middle three were Dominic Gape, Alex Pattison and, making his season's debut to a burst of applause, Curtis Thompson. I had never seen the lad play. David Wheeler, his dead leg restored to life, would be Akinfenwa's partner up front.

'I want every nerve tingling with excitement,' the manager said. 'The only person you need to worry about taking shit if this doesn't work is me. It's on my shoulders. They're broad. We need to have belief in this, there's no justification for not believing in it. We're away from home, they're expected to have most of the ball, so let's be solid. Bayo, we've got an extra-large armband to cover your bicep.'

The depletion of so much experience – no Bloomfield, Jacobson, Freeman, Samuel or Smyth – might have sparked a sense of impending calamity as Rochdale had been inspired the previous Wednesday night to a performance against Manchester United in the Carabao Cup that delivered back-page praise. The League One side lost on penalties at Old Trafford but gave United a mighty scare.

Rochdale's starlet was 16-year-old, tousle-haired Luke Matheson, who scored a beautiful goal and had the press eating out of his hand before he headed to school to sit a psychology exam. He said he wouldn't be turning on his iPhone that night because all his friends were United fans and he needed a decent night's rest.

When the team sheets landed in the press box, it was no surprise the exhausted kid was on the substitute's bench. Rochdale's manager Brian Barry-Murphy preferred a three-man forward line whose combined age was 105.

The players, young and old, would need a long stud. Rain had sheeted across Greater Manchester for 20 hours, relenting in the nick of time for referee Darren Handley from nearby Bolton to declare the pitch playable. 'He's old school,' Ainsworth said.

Indeed, when Handley emerged for the warm-up, he stopped to greet each member of the Rochdale groundstaff so heartily you presumed they were regulars at the same local. His linesmen left him to it and did the exercises on their own.

The match was three minutes old at most before Ainsworth was bellowing a new set of instructions through the pouring rain. Rochdale liked to tippy-tappy across their own area but then slashed the ball towards the front men with little pretence to precision. Grimmer tucked around, Onyedinma pressed on and 3-5-2 shifted into 4-3-3. Gape's red boots and Thompson's limes were powerfully prominent after Pattison hurt his back in a crunching fall.

Soon enough the away side was two-up. Beyond the stands the landscape kept disappearing and reappearing as cloud levels fluctuated between low and ground level. Ainsworth's fear was that a couple more downpours could render the pitch unplayable.

Then the sun peeped through and concern turned to elation when Grimmer burst from deep, substitutes Josh Parker and Scott Kashket combined, Parker struck a post and Fred pocketed the rebound. A first away win of the season had been an uncomplicated stroll.

Ainsworth and Dobson made their way to the side of the ground where 344 supporters were in a euphoric state. The manager didn't want to select one player for special mention, though the dynamic return of Thompson, the irrepressibility of Gape and the resolution of Phillips swirled in his head.

It was put to him that to win a match with less than 30 per cent possession distorted statistical norms. I preferred the local who grabbed me by the lapel in the annexe to the directors' room, obviously thinking I was on the board, 'You deserved that today. Much the better side. We had plenty of the ball but did fuck all with it.'

During the first half, an announcement went out for Scott the driver to return to his coach. Someone suggested it had been spotted floating down the high street. Instead some bloody idiot had hurled a brick at it, smashing the front door and windscreen.

A replacement coach duly arrived with a driver willing to make the 400-mile round trip to Buckinghamshire. Scott would be able to put his feet up for once.

The team were invited into Rochdale's boardroom for post-match comfort as secretary Kelly Francis was rushed off her high heels sorting the paperwork. What struck me was a singular lack of gloating. Satisfying though a first victory away from home was, this was not a time for exuberance. The players were reflective, almost subdued. The job had been done, three points accumulated, now to get home safely.

When we pulled into the training ground just before 11pm in the midst of another soaking downpour, Ainsworth gently reminded his players they should each take one piece of luggage from the coach as well as their own.

Adebayo Akinfenwa lifted a massive metal kit container without help. I had neither seen before, nor expected to again, a player hoisting one of those with such ease and then returning for another without a murmur of complaint.

* * *

It was flagged on the Chairboys Central twitter account that the team (and subs) who restored Wycombe to second place in the league had cost precisely: free, free, free, free, loan, free, free, free, free, free, swap, free, free and free. Alex Pattison tweeted, 'This Team Is A Madness.'

The absurdity was cranking new levels. Matt Cecil, the head of media, sent out a tweet mirroring the mood, 'Official: Better than @manutd'. When Cecil suggested to his manager in the pitch-side interview that Wycombe had achieved something Manchester United couldn't by putting three past Rochdale, Ainsworth said, 'Don't you start,' mixing humour and mild exasperation.

The reaction was astonishing. Cecil's tweet had thousands of hits and retweets within a day and induced a Mancunian meltdown. 'Wow, muddied by fucking Wycombe'; 'Man Utd ffs trolled by a group of park rangers', and last, but by no means least, the resurrection of Crystal Palace manager Roy Hodgson's spectacular rant on BBC Sport when he took offence at a line of questioning.

Hodgson, 'Let's not take the piss here.' Reporter, 'I certainly wasn't.' Hodgson, 'Well I think you are.'

* * *

Wycombe had become immune to having the piss taken out of their football, their results, their standing as a team and now had the opportunity for a decision that might inspire a role reversal. The Couhigs were soon to reach a point of no return. Solvency – and thus salvation – was within the club's grasp.

The results of the team were lightening spirits and spreading a positivity that might encourage more of the 889 eligible to vote to tick the 'Yes' box. At the back of the minds of those fearing a negative outcome nagged the lawyer's mantra of 'reasonable doubt'. Who was this guy and what did he really want out of becoming Wycombe's top dog? Rob Couhig remained an enigma.

Joe Stevens was the original Wycombe terrace drummer boy who had long been an implacable 'No' in the matter of private ownership. Stevens – who now lived in Los Angeles – was born 100 yards from the old Loakes Park ground, 'Just too late to catch a game on my first day, having arrived at 6pm on Saturday evening.'

He was ten when he first saw Wycombe in the flesh. 'It was my Christmas present on a grey Boxing Day, we beat Slough 1-0 away with a Steve Guppy goal. It was damp, freezing and brilliant. At 14 my parents deemed me old enough to get the bus to Adams Park unaccompanied. I went to around half the home games in 1995/96 and bought my first season ticket in 1996/97 for 46 quid. By December 1997 [28 December was Southend away, a 2-1 win, and Keith Scott scored both) I was travelling away too and loving it.

'The memories from those days are pretty much sacred, good times and bad. From being one of the 46 who witnessed our first-ever golden goal [Jermaine McSporran, Shrewsbury away, in the Auto Windscreens Shield] to turning our backs after 15 minutes against Blackpool when Lawrie Sanchez had managed us to our lowest ebb, it was like being in a rollercoaster – trapped in, just like everybody else, going where it took us.

'An overnight bus ride to Dublin, only to find the pre-season tour was cancelled as our full-back had contracted meningitis and quarantined the squad, was just part of the fun of being with Wycombe. The rest of the crowd were there so we went to watch Shamrock Rovers v Boca Juniors – rolling with the punches, flying the flags and confusing the heck out of the locals.'

The task at Wycombe now was to win over their own *confuseniks*. The plans would be laid out for all who were allowed to see them on Tuesday, 15 October, four days before the visit of mighty Sunderland, the biggest fish in the League One sea. The legacy members needed to be persuaded that the Couhigs had the most honourable of intentions.

Stevens wasn't the only supporter concerned about the chequered history of those with a fortune to play with who set sights on a football club, got their fangs into it and bled it dry. He had been a regular at meetings of the Football Supporters' Federation through the years, listening in horror to the tales of butchery across the country.

'All those encounters made me very aware that securing the long-term future of a club, the simple existence of the team for us to congregate behind and support, was the most important thing for any fan. On-field results and promotions could never be chased at the expense of safeguarding a future and the best people to guarantee that safeguard were the fans themselves.

'Wycombe had a rough year in 2004. We were awful on the pitch, and off it the board proposed a vote to allow a minority stake in the club to be privately sold off. To the masses this was fine as we would retain the majority and therefore control of the rudder to steer the ship. To me it was opening a door to the unscrupulous and self-interested.

'We had no benevolent backer waiting in the wings, so who would want to plough in money to a club that had landed back in the fourth tier and was somehow broke three years after reaching an FA Cup semi-final?

'It screamed hostile takeover. I argued my case, debating with everyone I could. It wasn't enough. We lost the vote by a squeak, and Steve Hayes [a local entrepreneur who also owned Wasps rugby union club] came in.

'Football was different then as wages were lower and clubs in the bottom leagues still hoped to receive a decent transfer fee for a top prospect. Wycombe had an academy that produced first-team players. We had full ownership of our own ground.

A "no" vote then was a no-brainer for me and had it happened we would have been fine.

'Those with Hayes needed to bear a portion of the blame for allowing him to ladle in money, but what choice did they really have? The club was budgeting at a loss and a director with a minority stake was willing to dole out funds. By 2009 we were screwed. We were a vote away from being Bury.

'The 2009 vote [in which Hayes took full ownership of the club while writing off £3m of the club's debt in exchange for shares] was a referendum solely on an individual who had executed a hostile takeover. He had shown no association with fans or the club, as shown by his later statement when he attacked a lot of us with whom he'd not been willing to work anyway.

'I was stoked to see the trust take over once Hayes cut his losses and ran [in June 2012]. We could not go back to 2004 or 2009 and view the current situation through those eyes. The trust didn't inherit the club as it was in 2004, they acquired the bits that were left on the terms Hayes gave them.

'The trust struggled to keep it going, laden with debt and on a shoestring budget. Gareth Ainsworth's role in the club's survival cannot be under-estimated. His achievements on virtually no funding have been remarkable. It was no surprise that the minute he had the funds to assemble something like a squad we started to fly.

'From the outset Rob [Couhig] asked that his actions were used to judge intent and has made every effort to reassure the disaffected. The current model was unsustainable. I know Rob hated the "plucky little Wycombe" school of thought but it's what we were last season for sure – a tiny, clever fish that survived in a big pond of trouble.

'The trouble was, in the natural world, sooner or later you were going to get chomped.'

Going Dutch

THE gate-crashing arrival of The Athletic into the British sports writing genre in the early autumn of 2019 was as spectacular as the New Year's Eve pyrotechnics on Sydney Harbour Bridge.

Many of the finest football scribes in Britain were hot-footing it to the land of online subscriptions where the writing was stripped of editorial ideologies, promoting long reads and meaningful insight. As long as enough people were prepared to pay for it, this was the future.

One of the younger recruits was David Ornstein, who had honed his skills at the BBC, developing a reputation for trusted and insightful reporting. On Saturday, 28 September we were reacquainted at Rochdale of all weird places. He was in the boardroom before and after the match being matey with the Wycombe group. It struck me as a little odd. Why here? Why now?

It made sense a few days later when Ornstein's debut article for The Athletic resounded through Wycombe and its fan-base like a sleep-awakening thunderclap. 'Exclusive: Bergkamp, Larsson and Kuyt's bid to buy Wycombe.' That spun a few heads.

Ornstein articulated the Wycombe investment picture as it pertained to American Rob Couhig and then outlined the philosophy behind a European offer with the former Barcelona, Everton and Southampton manager Ronald Koeman on board as an advisor. It had at its heart, 'catapulting Wycombe to stardom.'

Ornstein wrote, 'As players, they collectively accumulated 48 major domestic honours, including 21 league titles across the Premier League, Scottish Premiership, La Liga and Eredivisie. Koeman also won the European Cup with Barcelona and the European Championship with the Netherlands. If anybody is precluded from taking part [Henrik Larsson had been strongly linked to the vacant Southend United job] the project will proceed regardless and the door left ajar for them to return.

'They retain a long-held ambition of becoming the first set of leading former players to purchase an EFL club and personally work there on a day-to-day basis. They committed funds and can access further private equity if necessary.

'However – and Rob Couhig shares this vision for Wycombe – their priority is sustainability. They intend to wipe out all debts, cover running costs and use their expertise, experience and contacts to help Wycombe grow organically towards self-sufficiency and success. No costly signings or exorbitant salaries. Furthermore, with Larsson, [Dennis] Bergkamp and [Dirk] Kuyt spearheading the operation, they believe commercial revenues can leap to a level that would be virtually impossible by other means.

'The initial idea was to gain maximum power via a minority shareholding, but the realisation that maximum power tends only to truly come through a majority shareholding shifted the objective.'

Recent reports from Holland mentioned former Liverpool striker Kuyt's interest in becoming an investor in a club named Wanderers. The assumption – given its proximity to Liverpool and current perilous state – was that the club in question was Bolton. Rather, at a meeting in Bergkamp's home in June and with Wycombe being the sole 'Wanderers' in the group's mind, there was a unanimous conclusion that the target was ripe.

'We're not coming over pretending to know everything,' a source close to the group said. 'We know a lot and we're going to bring that together with the people working at the club to make it a joint venture. It's a family club and we have to treat family as family.

'Trevor Stroud and Gareth Ainsworth had been invited to meet with the ex-players in the Netherlands, but, despite indicating they would attend, a date could not be fixed and alarm bells began to sound.

'A deal in principle was close, yet the group were made aware – more than once and with increasing urgency – that Wycombe faced cash-flow difficulties that needed resolving. With Stroud showing concern that the process was starting to drag, the consortium sought to ease his worries and meanwhile ploughed on with fine-tuning their structure and approach.

'At that point they had not handed over the unsecured funds as an agreement had not been struck and due diligence not completed. Then, on 21 June, Stroud dropped a bombshell.

'He phoned to state that Wycombe would be pursuing a separate path. No take-it-or-leave-it ultimatum. No prior warning of competition and no chance to match the rival offer. The board was consulted but stood firm. Time was up.

'Despite sympathising with the consortium's "incredulity", Stroud underlined that the chosen route was felt to be in Wycombe's best interest long term. Case closed. Stroud told me he is sure they have made the right decision and was unable to discuss the former players' bid. "All of the discussions we had before we went down the route with Rob are covered by NDAs [non-disclosure agreements]," Stroud said. "I've been asked a few times, people have picked up rumours, but all I can say is, yes, we talked to a number of parties. That's the position I have to hold."'

Stroud later indicated that trying to get anywhere with the Dutch group was like 'walking through treacle'. Better to stick with the jam from across the Atlantic.

* * *

It was on these shifting sands that Wycombe entered the season's Leasing.com Trophy, once the Freight Rover, Sherpa Van, Auto Windscreens and, most recently, the Checkatrade Trophy. This was the EFL's competition for League One and Two, 16 sides from academies in the Premier League and Championship, with a Wembley final and prize pool of £3m. In its palsied financial state, it was well worth Wycombe giving the competition every consideration.

The first of three opponents in the group stage of the competition (clubs were initially split into groups of four on a regional basis) were Stevenage, bottom of League Two, without a win all season and desperate for a fillip of any description in whatever match. What made the evening especially eerie was the sight of Adam El-Abd stepping from the visitors' bus.

He was so side-tracked he walked into the wrong dressing room. He played the second half as a substitute and left the ground in a state of bewilderment matching precisely that in which he had departed a month earlier. Amid the many peculiarities of the first six weeks of the season, the disappearance of El-Abd from Adams Park was top of the 'I-didn't-see-that-coming' moments.

OK, he was 35 and not as quick as he once was, but no one imagined El-Abd would up-sticks so soon into the campaign. He had been keener than most to shine a light on the club and himself. Now he was estranged in more ways than one.

'How freely can I talk?' he asked as we drew chairs closer. I said that was entirely up to him. He had hidden that fact that he'd begun the season in a troubled state with upheavals in his domestic life matched by distinct concerns about his position at Wycombe.

'The gaffer and I agreed at the start of the 2018/19 season that I was to get a new deal at Christmas, my contract ran for two years and I said my terms weren't on a par with some others. Gareth said they were.

'He said to come back to him at Christmas if we were in the top ten. We were eighth around Boxing Day. I'd been playing well. I knew the club were struggling financially so I left it until the end of the season. I explained that I was coming now [at the end of the season], but he said, "There's no new contract." He said he'd speak to the new owners and get back to me.

'Then he said I had to prove myself to the new owners. I said, "What if I say I don't want any more money just an extra year?" He said, "No." I said, "OK, what if I played 25 games with no extra money but there's a clause in my contract that said if I played 25 games, I get a new deal?" The answer was, "'Sorry, no."

'For me it was a sign that the club were putting me to one side. I may have been wrong but to not even entertain a conversation was like, in my head, I was done. And I loved it there. How many games did I play last year, how many more would I have played this year? If the club wouldn't even entertain an appearance-related contract, I could see the writing was on the wall. I was being eased out, so I'd try to get a new contract elsewhere.'

El-Abd's simmer came to a boil at AFC Wimbledon, where he was on the bench after a three-week absence with a calf strain. When Anthony Stewart required on pitch treatment, Ainsworth asked Giles Phillips to warm up and El-Abd remained rooted to his seat.

'I realised then I was fourth-choice centre-back. Nothing against Giles, but he was a 21-year-old on loan. It sent me the messages I needed. I knew then I should have left in the summer. I told the manager I felt he'd let me down. He said he was still working on it but I said, "No, I've seen enough."

'I needed to say that before we fell out properly, I had to leave. I didn't want to fall out. Gareth said, "Well, if you feel that way," and I said, "Yes, I do." Thinking about it now, I might have been calmer, it was heat of the moment but it was how I felt. He [Ainsworth] didn't say, "No I don't want you to leave, you're with me." On Monday it felt as if I was being pushed through the door, but that was OK, no problem.

'Maybe I was too big a character. I won't go into any more but a few things happened and I didn't know if people were sending me messages. I felt I'd been let down and I couldn't see beyond that. No one said, "Come on Adam if you were in his [the manager's] shoes what would you do?" But, having been promised a deal at Christmas and not got it, well it was what it was. I couldn't reverse it now unfortunately.'

If Wycombe had become a frying pan, Stevenage were most definitely a fire. Within a couple of days the club had sacked the manager who signed him, Dino Maamria, and Mark Sampson was promoted to a caretaker role. El-Abd did get to prepare for Maamria's last match, a 4-2 loss at Cheltenham Town.

'After the first day I thought, "oh God what have I done?" It was more like a running club than a football club. I covered close to 10k on the first day of training, running box to box, completely aimless stuff. It was no wonder we lost on Saturday, no one could move.'

El-Abd was staggered at the numbers in the squad, from a tolerable 24 at Wycombe to an unwieldy 36 at Stevenage. If getting into the Wycombe first team had become such a concern, how would he manage in Hertfordshire? Not only that, Sampson had made it plain – "How can I make this easy for you?" the manager told El-Abd at their first meeting – that he wasn't going to be considered as a starting player. In fact, he would not be considered at all. Sampson offered him a scouting role.

'I had to sit on the bench for the first game and then he [Sampson] brought in a 17-year-old from the academy who had never played in front of me. He played every combination of centre-backs he could possibly find without me. I went to see him the Monday before the Wycombe game and said, "What's the reason behind this? Who sanctioned signing me?"

'Surely the chairman would have wanted to make sure I was part of the next manager's plans because he knew he was going to get rid of the old manager. So don't sign me. Let the guy have his last game, sack him and then get in those you want to get in.

'I said, "Look if I don't play another game of football again, I'd be upset but I'm not going to go home and cry into my pillow. I'm 35 years old, I've played a lot of games and I think you've used me. You sent me home last week, you've got a load of young lads in the team who could use experience in the dressing room and even if you're not playing me, I know I could add something. I want to play and I'm pretty pissed off that you're shunning me."

'He thanked me for coming to see him and said we'd see what happened moving forward. He called me an hour later and said, "I've had a change of heart, do you want to play 45 minutes against Wycombe?" I said, "Yes, of course." So I played, and his assistant said after the match he [Sampson] had it in mind to start me the following weekend. He didn't.'

* * *

If the intransigence of his new manager at Stevenage was difficult to comprehend, things were hardly sweeter on the home front. El-Abd was in the throes of what he admitted was a less-than-amicable divorce.

In January he separated from his wife, three months after all had seemed right with the world. El-Abd said his finances were in order, he felt he was in a position to be comfortable once his career ended, he had rental income on one of his two homes in Brighton and his career at Wycombe was as steady as it could ever be for a player in the lower leagues.

'I genuinely didn't see it [the divorce] coming. On my wife's birthday in October we had a big row. We'd been eight years wed and together for 13. Two kids. I invested a lot in our future that stretched us and I said that for six months we needed to tighten our belts. Then for her birthday her sister bought her flights to New York. I said, "Look we need to tighten, so no, don't go."

'That sparked the argument. It didn't help that her sister was married to Brighton's Lewis Dunk, a Premier League footballer living on £70,000 a week. My wife saw her sister going to Dubai seemingly every week and living the life. I don't know if she saw stars but it wasn't something we could afford. To be honest, now that I'm out the other side, I'm hoping it ends up being a good thing, but my life has been altered like you wouldn't believe.

'This time last year, me and my wife and two kids (football-loving Xavier, 11, and Sophia, seven) had our finances in order, we were going to be set after my football career but by no means wealthy. Then I felt as if I'd been chopped in half, my wife was in the main house and had all of my equity. It was really tough for the kids and for the first six months, they struggled.'

El-Abd saw them three times a week, on Wednesday, Saturday and Sunday evenings. The rest of the time he was training, playing (not playing actually) and staying in a hotel in Stevenage. The one occasion he had taken his children away from the Sussex home was in 2016 when he signed for Shrewsbury and thought the ballast of a two-year contract would not upset their education. Micky Mellon signed El-Abd and was sacked within three months. The minute the player met Mellon's successor, Paul Hurst, he sensed something wasn't right.

El-Abd scored the first goal of the Hurst era, a thunderbolt against Southend, and 'felt as if I was on fire'. Then he was dropped. By the end of that season, Hurst had got rid of 22 of the initial 24 players in his squad, though El-Abd was spared from being among the initial cull of 11 in the January transfer window. 'I had to move the kids back to Brighton after a year. Thinking back, I shouldn't have moved them up in the first place, but I thought it was too far for them to remain at home and I'd never see them. In football, you were never settled.'

He wanted his next move to be commutable from Brighton, so Carlisle – even with the breathtaking Lake District scenery on its doorstep – was rejected. Wycombe made a positive gesture. 'It was the perfect club for me, and I loved my whole time there.

It's a really good club, with good people who are a massive part of its success.

'I arrived the season the club were promoted. We took our time to get going and then got the balance right between attacking and defending. The obvious moment was Dom Gape's clinching goal at Chesterfield. We knew in the dressing room at half-time that results were going for us. It was 1-1, we'd missed a few chances and the nerves were building. I'll never forget the amazement on Dom's face when he scored and we felt "we're going to do this". We defended for our lives and when the whistle went the feeling was incredible.'

Wycombe's style of play under Ainsworth was the subject of debate and conjecture. El-Abd, as its defensive embodiment, saw how it unfolded ahead of him and would often wince. 'We were never afraid to risk. We had a player like Bayo who could bring the ball down on his chest, set someone up and there was the chance of a shot. No one else had Bayo.

'It could be a double-edged sword. If you played that ball, didn't have a shot and didn't score, the opposition would have the ball, and if they were good with it, you could be outnumbered for a good passage of play and if that snowballed you were in trouble. We were always either attacking or defending, the game never settled down.

'There was no active rest, giving the ball to the full-back, passing it square, giving it to the goalkeeper. The opposition was chasing but you were chasing as well. There was no time to take the sting out of the ball but that's the way Gareth played. There was no right or wrong way, it worked and it still works, but one thing was for sure you had to be incredibly fit because the game never slowed.

'Jesus, you got value for money and goalmouth action if you were a spectator. It was like basketball – they attacked then we attacked.'

* * *

One image remained stark from El-Abd's cameo for Stevenage at Adams Park, a sharp yank on the shirt of Adebayo Akinfenwa as the two men challenged for aerial possession inside the penalty area. Bayo tweeted that if his old captain had wanted a souvenir that badly, he could have asked for it.

El-Abd had come on at half-time with Stevenage a goal to the good – there were so many Wycombe defensive faults with the goal it would have taken a chapter to describe them all – and that was how the match ended. The 30 doughty fans who travelled from Hertfordshire were in raptures, especially the 25 who had had their tickets paid for by the players.

The Wycombe management were at a loss to explain so much of the performance. It fielded a shuffled side with number-two goalkeeper Cameron Yates, Sido Jombati, Jacob Gardiner-Smith and Josh Parker having their first starts of the season and Joe Jacobson returning as a left-sided central-defender. But that couldn't properly explain a performance so lacking in direction and individual confidence.

Ainsworth picked over the pieces and his points needed to be made, and strongly. He would ask the squad to look at their own contribution and, more widely, why so many had been so poor. It was not often the manager suggested he didn't believe his side had been brave enough.

The coaching staff did at least find levity in a discussion of the antics of the referee and his team, especially the fourth official. I'd wondered what could have prompted Richard Dobson, usually the most controlled of men, to brush him away at one stage late in the match.

It transpired that having asked how much time would be added for Stevenage's persistent time wasting, Dobson was told, 'At the moment, seven minutes.' When Andrew Williams, the fourth official, held up the board it said six. 'What the hell is this? I suppose the referee's told you he's got to be away early,' to which Williams replied, 'Something like that.' There was much smacking of foreheads in the technical area.

'Is this the first time you've done this job?' the fourth official was asked. 'No!' came his offended reply, and even the Wycombe staff felt a bit sorry for the guy as he slumped back into the 'reserve official' perspex shelter, cheeks reddened and eyes beginning to glisten.

But Williams's response to Dobson over the added time breakdown had nothing on that from referee Josh Smith to Dominic Gape, a second-half substitute. The first time Gape protested one of Smith's many fanciful decisions, the referee stopped him in his tracks. 'The match kicked off at 7.45, where have you been?'

* * *

On the day of the Stevenage debacle, Sunderland, Barnsley and Reading had all chosen to jettison their managers. Jack Ross, Daniel Stendel and Jose Gomes became ex-employees in the space of a few bloodless hours.

Millwall still had a vacancy after the departure of Neil Harris. The timing sucked. Gareth Ainsworth was either the bookmakers' favourite or in the top three on the lists for all four clubs. Consternation gripped Adams Park like the evening chill.

Pete Couhig had probably been angrier in his life, and I wouldn't have wanted to see it. Much of the steam generated in the aftermath of a pretty rotten night against Stevenage was coming from his ears. He preferred I explained The Athletic's Bergkamp story to El-Abd rather than talk it through himself and risk imploding. 'But it won't have any effect on the outcome of the vote will it?' El-Abd said. 'It might just fucking ruin it,' Pete replied.

The crux of Pete's anger was not the veracity of the story but its timing. Was it a trap set for the American offering to fail which might cost the club a viable future, the manager a significant percentage of his squad and allow the Bergkamp consortium to have a free run? We'd likely never know.

Within a few days of publication came the first hint of a possible destabilisation. Sunderland contacted Trevor Stroud and asked for permission to speak to Ainsworth. The chairman granted it. This occurred the very moment I proposed to sit down with him to reflect on the opening two months of the season. He asked if I wouldn't mind postponing. 'It's all going off,' he said.

In these instances, turning to fans' forums was a masochistic necessity. Sunderland's didn't disappoint. It looked as if Ainsworth would be in for an uncomfortable ride if the job was offered and accepted. One contributor said, 'His team are fucking wankers.' Another noted that, 'He [Ainsworth] looks like a cross between Mick from *The Walking Dead* [Andrew Lincoln], the hotel manager in *Room in Rome* [Enrico Lovero] and a homeless guy just out of court.'

A search for pragmatic logic amid the swirling, fevered support of a football club tended to go unrewarded. But there was the occasional ray of objectivity. 'Ainsworth's a manager on the up, there's a reason half the clubs in our league and the one above are after him. What do people realistically expect?' cried one voice in the Sunderland wilderness.

What ran through the comments was the sense of entitlement as if Sunderland were still in the Premier League and shouldn't be soiling their shorts against tadpoles like Wycombe. As news of an approach to Ainsworth broke, Sunderland were four places and four points behind the Chairboys with a game in hand. And guess who was next to visit Adams Park?

These were turbulent times in the city whether or not you were a football fan. The front page of the *Sunderland Echo,* on the day it led with the Ainsworth story on the back, expressed deepening concern that the business model for Nissan, the town's major employer and the UK's single biggest car-making site, would be jeopardised in the event of tariffs likely to be imposed on automotive exports should the UK leave the EU at the end of the month without a deal.

The *Financial Times* reported that the factory's night shift was to end, though the decision would have no immediate effect on the Nissan workforce of 6,500. Tension and fear were rising, not least because the Japanese company were the North East's largest private-sector employer and their plant in Sunderland was crucial to thousands of supply-chain jobs in the area.

Any workforce upheaval could have seismic consequences for the local economy and people would inevitably turn elsewhere for solace, especially to a new football manager delivering success for their club and, as a consequence, lifting local morale by its bootstraps. All of this weighed heavily on Ainsworth's conscience.

It was ironic, too, that the talk concentrated on 'big' Sunderland so soon after Ainsworth reported on his players' growing sense that, 'We're not little Wycombe any more.' Judged alongside Sunderland, though, the reality of Wycombe's inferior standing was reflected in the doom and gloom spreading through Wanderers' supporter base as they felt the net closing in.

There was a shared awareness of, 'it's bound to happen sometime'. After all, Ainsworth's stock was rising and his ambition to manage at a higher grade could only be postponed indefinitely. When he said he'd rather the ambition was fulfilled at Wycombe he wasn't bullshitting to keep the loyalists onside. It was his heart talking.

Taking everything into consideration, promotion was more likely with Sunderland, even if the Wearside club were not a rock of financial stability. The sacking of Ross was lamented in local quarters, a decent coach seized by a desire to make the Sunderland project work but not afforded the time to see the task through. In that, he was not an uncommon victim. The word 'toxic' was used by many to describe the situation at the Stadium of Light.

The desperation to secure promotion back to the Championship after the loss to Charlton in the 2018/19 play-off final was a pervasive force. It had begun to feel as if it had to happen this season or a prolonged chill would set in. And Sunderland still had a £10m wage bill from the £40m the latest owners had inherited when they moved in two years earlier. Ainsworth had never dealt with such financial excess before.

For him to take the job – if offered – would require enormous family upheaval, but the compensation of a surge in wages and an inner conviction that he was well prepared for such a task had to be aces in his pursuer's hand. The following day, Millwall of the Championship announced they were interested in talking to him. How would the cards fall now?

All of this was a disconcerting inconvenience as the final legal t's were being crossed and i's dotted on the deal that might deliver 75 per cent of Wycombe Wanderers into the hands of Rob Couhig, as long as a similar percentage of the enfranchised legacy members ticked the appropriate box for him to lead the club forward.

Though due diligence matters required resolving, a four-page letter was emailed to the members on the evening of Monday, 14 October in advance of a meeting at Adams Park where the finer points would be debated and the first ballots cast.

There were two weeks in which to vote so Tuesday, 29 October was stay and play or cut and run. Couhig didn't attend the 15 October gathering but sent a video message from his office in New Orleans that struck a positive though non-triumphal chord.

Trevor Stroud was contacting those members who didn't possess an email address (such people existed in the 21st century) by old-fashioned letter or phone call to make certain they were aware that any abstention or failure to vote would count as a 'no'.

The chairman said it would be a crime if apathetic dereliction held sway because he knew that if it did then Gareth Ainsworth would not be seen at Adams Park for the dust from his brown boots.

The Jump Start

HAPPY pills were flying off the counters across Buckinghamshire as one by one the plum managerial vacancies were offered to anyone but Gareth Ainsworth. Sunderland preferred Phil Parkinson's record of periodic success in the lower leagues by a unanimous board vote and general antipathy from the terraces.

Ainsworth flew north to meet Sunderland's hierarchy and sensed during the meeting they were going through the motions. He was recognised at Newcastle airport, which led to frenzied chatter on local forums, but on the day of Parkinson's appointment those insisting they had seen Wycombe's manager downing a celebratory one in the Colliery Tavern across from the Stadium of Light were mischief-making.

The trusted counsel from those with connections in the north-east told Ainsworth that Sunderland's decision to look elsewhere and not give him a choice to make was a blessing. Moving so far would have meant an immense upheaval and disruption to the family time that was increasingly precious to him. And the club was in a right mess.

In the ensuing days, Millwall of the Championship appointed Gary Rowett, once of Birmingham City, Derby County and Stoke City, the latter two for a season apiece. Rowett had never been allowed to build a club in his image and this might be his time.

Reading, whose posh new training facility was five minutes from Ainsworth's home, promoted their football director Mark Bowen, who insisted he'd had nothing whatsoever to do with the sacking of Jose Gomes. Forgive the eye-rolling.

Delicious timing meant Parkinson's first game in charge of the Black Cats was at Adams Park. Seventy-seven days from the opening day of the season, Parkinson was once more winding down time in the away dug out, mired in pensive thought. We shook hands and with all sincerity I again wished him well. He'd had one training session and a few snatches of video analysis on which to base his team selection, which sounded vaguely familiar.

For Ainsworth this had turned into an occasion where desire for success was stinging. He wouldn't touch social media with a bargepole and couldn't remember the last time he'd read a paper, but he wasn't deaf to the negative noise generated by his prospective engagement on Wearside. He just wanted this win.

Matt Cecil, the head of media relations, knew more than most of the manager's inner feelings and decided to add a pinch of spice by putting Ainsworth's picture on the cover of the match-day programme. The temperature on the Adams Park grill, already heading towards 'toasty,' had become decidedly warmer.

Luke O'Nien bounded off the Sunderland coach and through the foyer like a puppy-dog left at home all day suddenly spotting its owner. O'Nien remained a hugely popular figure at the club where, for 101 appearances in three seasons, he was an enthusiastic, driven element in Wycombe's engine room. Who would ever forget his contribution to the promotion cause and the camera-stealing show after it was secured at Chesterfield?

His frisky nature hadn't changed one jot, and those who knew him from his Bucks days weren't surprised when he took irrepressibility to the limits. He tugged at the special protective headband worn by Matt Bloomfield after his two recent concussions. Dominic Gape told him to put a sock in his griping every time a decision went against his side.

O'Nien would often get under the skin at the Wycombe training ground where he would push boundaries to win a practice match. Not enough of his current team-mates looked as badly in need of this win as he did.

Darius Charles scored the only goal with a right-foot volley, which was one for the Antiques Road Show. Charles went to the away end and cupped his ears. Adebayo Akinfenwa leapt onto his back. This would normally have been an unsustainable burden for a human with an arthritic hip, but Charles could have borne the world on his shoulders at that moment.

At the start of a week entailing trips to Blackpool and Rotherham, a 1-0 victory over Sunderland was hearty sustenance. Charles did the rounds of local well-wishers, collecting awards and resounding cheers. Everyone loved Darius, and the more so when he told them, 'Their fans came here and were smug. They had this Sunderland presence. I wanted to let them know this is our house. You play by our rules. We're second in the table – you are wherever you are. Respect us.'

This was a recurring theme with Wycombe. The opposition consistently looked down their nose at a team forever banging on about their impoverished state, playing ugly, scuffing football, taking hours over free kicks and throw-ins and managed by a rock-and-roll fan in jeans who leapt around the coaching area as if he was at Glastonbury.

Wycombe's football wasn't the most cultured. The boys never said it was. The team was unlikely to play the opposition off the park in neat one-touch triangular movements. Michelangelo didn't sculpt their marking at corners, Dobbo did. If you paid a £1,500-a-week pretty much top whack, you shouldn't expect Grindhouse Rolling Thunder Super Caffeinated Roast but contented yourself with a single shot of espresso.

Why couldn't opposition supporters get their heads around this? Actually, the less stupid ones did. The same with players, though they appeared few and far between. Jack Grimmer overheard one Sunderland player say to another, 'This fucking lot will tire soon,' so he jogged closer and said, 'No we won't.' They didn't.

At the end of a thoroughly uplifting afternoon for the home side, Rocky Allsop rather audaciously tapped Chris Maguire on the cheek as the teams walked off and said, 'Never mind son.' It looked as if the whole thing might go off. No one liked losing to Wycombe. Sunderland *really* hated it.

* * *

What would be an acceptable return from Sunderland at home, followed by Blackpool and Rotherham United away in the space of seven days? Wycombe wouldn't turn their nose up at three points from nine, five would be terrific, seven marvellous and a full house out of this world.

A third overnight stay in a month – secretary Kelly Francis's calculator was doing overtime – brought further initiations and insight into Richard Dobson's role at the club. The FA Cup first-round draw was taking place at 7.15pm – an hour after the team arrived at the seaside – so the latest version of *The Voice* had to be rushed.

Jack Grimmer was first on to the chair, his pale complexion turning redder at Akinfenwa's unsubtle probing. 'Black or white?' Jack was asked, which had nothing to do with how he took his coffee. He responded 'black' to rowdy applause.

Jamie Mascoll sang, as did 'Rizz' Aarons and Nnamdi Ofoborh, the teenager swaying back and forth to the lyrics of 'So Sick' (not a song with which I was familiar). Nnamdi's graceful gyrations were lost as half the room was spellbound by the screen in the opposite corner display balls with numbers on them. The manager breezed into the room as number 47 was drawn to visit Tranmere Rovers. He breezed straight out again.

At lunch the next day the players returned to the function room with twin extended tables and a third for the staff. Dobbo was running an eye over the seating arrangements to see who was getting closer to whom. I sat with him.

'We're a diverse group and I'm intrigued by how comfortable certain players are in whose company,' he said and pointed out David Wheeler, a thoughtful man he had marked down as a future general. Wheeler had turned 29 a few days earlier, had signed a three-year contract and Dobbo had noted his sensitivity.

The coach pulled into Bloomfield Road as the seaside winds buffeted the corner flags and the screech from the local seagulls intensified. It was a collar turned up, two-pie evening in the press box, one before the match and another at half-time, for warmth rather than nutritional goodness.

Ainsworth told his men Simon Grayson's team wasn't comfortable kicking it long so urged them to compete in a deep press that lured the Tangerines into doing exactly that. Once again the Wycombe boss wasn't concerned if the opposition had a majority of the ball.

Wycombe went ahead after eight minutes with a goal of route-one simplicity. Rocky Allsop's free kick soared into the stiffening breeze, Akinfenwa applied downward thrust and Scott Kashket had shrewdly read his partner's intent and the angles to lift the loose ball past a stranded goalkeeper.

Blackpool's fans began venting displeasure at Grayson's keep-ball tactics and demanded the team be more direct. If Wycombe could survive until the hour the frustration would intensify. A soft free-kick four minutes into the second half was the side's undoing, central defender Ben Heneghan escaping his marker to loop a header over Allsop.

The Wycombe lads thought he was trying to head it back across goal and got lucky. That said, a 1-1 draw was pretty acceptable against a side Ainsworth believed would be among the promotion challengers. We'd probably be home by 1.30am.

The players started to clamber onto the coach and Scott the driver turned his key in the ignition to fire the engine and generate warmth. Nothing happened. Not a spark. The kit piled up on the pavement but it wasn't worth loading anything unless the coach would start. 'Anyone got any jump leads?' went out the desperate cry.

The Blackpool stewards were initially sympathetic but had begun to shrug their shoulders, wanting us out of the way, especially as the Wycombe supporters' coach had loitered and fans were disembarking to see what the fuss was about. This was getting fretful and tiresome. Kelly Francis was on to her Blackpool counterpart, who said the groundsman was still on site and should have the tools to help.

A white transit appeared but there was not the space to manoeuvre it close enough for jump leads to reach the battery on the near side of the coach facing the ground. To add to the evolving farce, Scott had misplaced his reading glasses and couldn't distinguish between the positive and negative elements.

The players ate their fish-and-chip suppers by the light from mobile phones, oblivious to the back-and-forth of the van as it inched towards Bloomfield Road's brick-walled exterior that threatened to strip the paintwork. 'What about retracting your wing mirrors?' I said, exasperated, to the driver.

A couple of worse-for-wear Blackpool box-holders stumbled around in the dark, colliding with the metal kit holders, thinking they were helping whereas all they did was keep getting in the way. Then Ainsworth appeared, gripped the jump leads with one hand and demanded the van driver have another go at getting as close as he could. The leads magically reached.

'Thank God for that,' said Kelly, who feared having to locate, book and pay for 20 hotel rooms as the shutters were coming down. 'I hope you fucking go up,' one of the well-oiled supporters said, thrusting a bottle of zinfandel into my hands. 'Have that on me.'

The players leapt off the coach to help load the kit and assorted medical and musical paraphernalia. At just past 11pm we reversed from a dimly car park and headed south.

Rolando Aarons's four-year-old son Lorenzo had come in the hope of watching him play and was clinging to his dad on the pavement. Rolando was last to climb on board, by which time the food had gone. I gave him my cod and chips.

* * *

It was a well-thumbed ritual that players with small cameos or those who didn't make it off the substitutes' bench would warm down after the game. Dave Wates ushered four players out for quick-fire sprints to loosen stiffened muscles and sinews. Matt Bloomfield had come on in the last minute and was back on the pitch but away from the others. Half an hour later, he was still there.

The lights were going out and his team-mates had long since showered and changed, yet Wycombe's captain chugged across the pitch on the diagonal, recovering from corner flag to corner flag along the goal-line before another flat-out sprint. He paused, only to replace stray divots. Distracted, I lost count of the crossings but there had to have been six at least. He finally re-emerged in the corridor. 'Loved the workout Blooms,' I said. 'Got to pay the mortgage Neil, got to pay the mortgage.'

Matt Bloomfield was approaching 36, though you wouldn't have known it. He was lean and sharp, big blue bush-baby eyes, open face, neat cropped hair, the embodiment of self-preservation. I doubted he'd sniffed alcohol since the day Wycombe won at Torquay in 2014.

His career had had its bleak moments: a cruciate ligament injury at 24 that kept him out for a year, the clash of heads in 2009 when plates were inserted into each cheekbone and an elastic band was required to keep his jaw in place and then a horrid groin injury – *osteitis pubis* – that meant 12 months from the summer of 2012 to 2013 was spent spectating and fretting.

At that time he was hoping to start a family, but making ends meet was a real burden. Blooms wasn't on 'a proper playing contract', rather an agreement that kept him in the game with the hope of making up the financial balance elsewhere. 'I needed to provide for me and my wife and pay the mortgage because football alone wasn't paying enough. A mate of mine had a lettings agency so I helped him with viewings which gave me extra cash.'

Bloomfield acted as his own agent, and not because he was the untrusting type. 'I never considered I earned enough money to warrant giving someone else any of it. It was easier to do it myself. I'd only ever signed two-year contracts max at any one point.

'As soon as I signed a contract, I regarded it as a countdown to earn the next one. For me, it wasn't "two years, let's go and enjoy myself" but I had signed for 18 months. I'd like to sign a new contract six months before the two years was up so in that period I had to excel. A couple of times it went to the summer and I spent my holidays on the phone negotiating a new deal, fighting over 25 or 50 quid.

'I knew what other people earned, what I needed to get by and pay my way and what I felt comfortable with coming to work, so I decided to do it all myself. One problem with that was that I didn't have someone going in and getting the bonuses for me. My contract had to be the simplest one pager in the EFL. I never really haggled.'

Bloomfield was five years on from his testimonial when Jose Mourinho brought Chelsea back to Adams Park, a repeat of the 2007 League Cup semi-final when a side including Mikel, Makalele, Cole, Ballack and Essien (with Frank Lampard on the substitutes' bench) was held 1-1 by the League Two boys thanks to a late equaliser by Jermaine Easter. In total, Blooms had made over 500 appearances for the club and wanted quite a few more.

'There were times when I was left out or my contract came to an end and I considered my future – every player had those moments. There was never a hankering to leave, on the contrary there was always a reason to stay. The first couple of years I didn't have an affiliation or love for where I was. That grew.

I never wanted to push the issue and no one wanted to push me. There was obviously something I offered over the years to different managers.

'The last seven years with the gaffer have been amazing. Had we dropped out of the league five years ago we may have gone part-time and the club gone into administration. It would have been dire. My future would have been out of my hands. Look at us now. It was so energising to be on this journey with the gaffer and Dobbo.

'Torquay in 2014 was the most euphoric moment of my football career. Celebrating near failure was not a good thing but it was much more, it was my testimonial year and I knew what was happening behind the scenes. To all intents and purposes we were down and out. We had to win, which I knew we'd do and it was whether the two other teams couldn't get a point.'

Bristol Rovers had won at Adams Park the previous weekend, their fans mocked the demoralised home support and invaded the pitch before the end in the belief they had survived and Wycombe were sunk. Rovers manager Darrell Clarke walked into Ainsworth's office to offer his condolences. 'We're really sorry for you,' he said. That stuck in the Wanderers' craw.

Seven days hence, Wycombe were at Torquay while Rovers entertained Mansfield, who had nothing to play for but were getting increasingly annoyed at the haughty attitude of the home side. Mansfield journeyed down on the morning of the match, stopped at a fish and chip shop for lunch, realised they'd left their kit at Field Mill, had to beg to play in Rovers' third change strip and, as if taking the mickey, led 1-0 with a quarter of the match left.

Time seemed to stand still; Wycombe were 3-0 up at Torquay, they had done their part. Gareth Ainsworth remembered not watching much of the final 20 minutes as he was continually gesticulating towards his allies in the main stand to ask how much time there was left at the Memorial Stadium. There was much furious tapping of watch faces, but the second hands wouldn't move any faster.

Finally news came that Rovers, who had laid siege to the Mansfield goal and struck the woodwork three times, couldn't break it down. So much for the previous week's patronisation. Rovers, instead, went out of the Football League for the first time in 94 years. Wycombe survived and their future – that would have hung by a thread – was at least temporarily reprieved.

Ainsworth had told his children that week that he believed in fairy tales. One Wycombe fan went to Devon clothed as Jesus Christ, carrying a cross across his shoulders with the word 'Believe' attached. Someone took the banner down and handed it to the manager, who brandished it on the pitch.

Bloomfield remembered the coach journey home as the giddiest five hours of his life. The team stopped at an off licence and emptied it of anything brown in a can. There was a celebration back at Adams Park, though that was a blur.

The following season Wycombe reached the League Two play-off final at Wembley, a gloriously insane occasion in which they led Southend United 1-0 deep into extra time's injury time before a crappy equaliser meant the dread of a penalty shoot-out. Bloomfield was the first Wanderer to miss from the spot in a 7-6 loss. Just recalling it hurt: 'I was distraught for a long time.'

By then Blooms had passed 30, which is considered a professional footballer's point of minimal return. 'Everybody told me it was a slippery slope, I'd put on weight and find myself out of the game. I decided I was going to show that I didn't want to finish yet. I looked at my nutrition, my exercise, mental health, psychological mind-set and did everything to stay in the game as long as I could because I loved the job.

'That was why I did the 125-mile trip from Felixstowe [where his wife Madeleine and two pre-school daughters lived] a couple of times a week, to train, it was why I got out of bed wanting to prove people wrong. Well maybe saying "people" was a lazy thought process but the general sense was that you got to 35 and retired.

'I had far too much energy and desire to let that happen soon. I wanted to be part of a squad going somewhere and moving forward. Each year under the gaffer the squad improved and the club improved. I had a real desire to be a part of that so every season I had to find ways to stay ahead of the competition.'

Bloomfield had been at Wycombe longer than any present player, any member of the football staff, and the beat of his football heart chimed perfectly with what the club had strived to be, and never more so than under Ainsworth and Dobson.

'The manager recruited players and characters who wanted to go out and play for him. He was fortunate that he was such a good man and man-manager he could make people believe in the process and with what we were trying to do here, even if the money wasn't what they could undoubtedly get elsewhere.

'On the whole there was a reason why footballers moved – to make money. If that had been my priority I'd have moved around more, but the grass wasn't always greener on the other side. I liked to work for good people trying to do things the right way. I believed people wanted to be treated correctly, they wanted to be spoken to correctly. If it meant missing out on a couple of hundred quid a week, well that was the situation here.

'The culture at Wycombe was very inclusive. It was a manly environment, we wanted to win and go out and do the best we possibly could, but equally, if you came in, you were who you wanted to be. We still had the banter and all that stuff but I never wanted to think people felt uncomfortable when they walked through the door.

'As the club captain my responsibility was to introduce myself, make everyone feel wanted and explain how it worked. I'd been here forever so I knew the score. If I'd ever gone somewhere else I'd like to think someone would have done that for me.'

* * *

When the coach pulled into Wycombe's training ground from Blackpool it was 2.45am. Matt Bloomfield had a further couple of hours behind the wheel to get home to Suffolk where he'd spend what was left of the day being the best dad he could to his daughters, Mollie, five, and Rosie, three. Mads, his wife, was well used to being woken up at absurd hours.

Most of the rest of the group would be in bed by four, after brief snatches of sleep en route. Dave 'Big Bird' Wates had somehow managed to squeeze his 6ft 4in frame under the table between him and Cian O'Doherty, who was sound asleep, as befitted the father of a newborn son.

Josh Hart was flat on the floor by the front steps, wrapped in a Wycombe gilet. Richard Dobson tried to get comfortable by curling up on his favoured front seat but it was impossible.

The manager hadn't slept, and his mind continued to whirr with the possibilities for his team. He hadn't had much rest in his own bed when his phone buzzed and Trevor Stroud's number lit up.

This was not another club asking to speak to him but the news he'd longed for since mid-July. Wycombe had a new majority shareholder, the 75 per cent legacy members' threshold had been met, Rob Couhig was his boss and the club's future had been protected. That worked better than any shot of espresso.

'Amazing what is happening here,' he said after Couhig and the chairman had spoken to him and those wanting to deliver best wishes stacked up. To be fair to Stroud he had always seemed upbeat and it clearly helped that his manager consistently declined interest from elsewhere. 'I'm me and what you get is me,' Ainsworth told the local press. 'We've put Wycombe on the map and raised the profile. We're tagged with a style, but as far as I'm concerned that's about trying to win every game, by hook or by crook.

'We have a big man who plays most of the time so we're labelled as being direct. We need the moments he gives us.

People don't see what Bayo does off the field. I can't quantify the importance of that. This is the longest he's stayed anywhere, remember that.'

When it was time for an interview for the community station Wycombe Sound, he was chuffed that Keith Higgins, the resident Wanderers man, curtailed a song by The Doors – his favourite band – to go live to the training ground. 'Wow, Keith, fading out Jim Morrison for me, that's a special moment.'

* * *

Rotherham's railway station was flooded, anything with a basement was flooded, the New York Stadium's car park was under water and the pitch looked so lovely it lulled Bob Rickwood – once more taking on the kit man duties – into a false sense of balance. The chief scout was collecting the last of the balls after the pre-match routine when he lost his footing, landed on his wrist and smashed it.

He was not the only one suffering. Adebayo Akinfenwa was struggling with a high temperature and decided to travel on his own by train on Friday evening rather than risk infecting his team-mates on the coach. He had been told he wasn't in the starting XI and still made the trip north. This was a team thing.

Rickwood was on his way to Rotherham General Hospital when Anthony Stewart clipped a delightful 30-yard pass with the outside of his right foot that invited Scott Kashket to run at a defender, cut inside and, on what was supposedly a weaker right foot, curl a shot home from the edge of the area. Four minutes had gone.

What followed was 86 minutes that did management hearts good. A robust, athletic, physically superior South Yorkshire side could not get a definitive look at Rocky Allsop's goal.

When Rickwood was having his arm jolted back into position (the doctors re-set the bones, found they were five millimetres out and he would endure the process all over again when he got home), Wycombe's players were sprawled across the floor of the dressing room, utterly spent from the endeavour which secured a 1-0 win.

It had been a performance of steadfast endurance, unremitting belief and inverted trapezium. Wait a second, what? Nothing fazed Phil Catchpole with microphone in hand, but when Ainsworth said he had deployed an inverted trapezium in midfield, there was an understandable sense of 'come again?'

They were clearly big into their convex quadrilaterals at the Wycombe training ground and the geometry used against Rotherham was dictated by David Wheeler, often retreating from his forward role, Rolando Aarons roaming, Curtis Thompson dropping, while Matt Bloomfield and Dominic Gape remained solid (you know, Wycombe's usual one-dimensional shit).

Throughout the match, the Wycombe bench was verbally assailed by one fan seated with his young son in splendid isolation ten rows back. The man never let up, constantly screaming 'fuck off' to Ainsworth and Dobson as they shouted instructions at the same time as he ripped what he assumed was Wycombe's more basic approach.

For the umpteenth time he yelled 'offside' when Wycombe launched an attack that prompted Dobbo to spin on his heel, 'You can't be offside direct from a goal kick.' The response came back in broad Yorkshire, 'Well you live and learn.' Dobbo almost spilled his tactics folder.

Every win, and especially those with a clean sheet away from home, was manna for the troupe. The euphoria was seeping into the players' bloodstreams. This put the coaching staff in an unprecedented predicament, wanting to douse excesses of optimism while not dulling the team's natural exuberance.

The coaches were elated for a different, yet just as poignant, reason. The resignation of the manager of Morecambe did not usually cause tremors as far away as the Home Counties, but when Jim Bentley left the League Two side for AFC Fylde of the National League, it meant Ainsworth became the longest-serving manager across the entire English professional game.

We knew it was a special occasion because two packets of Maryland cookies adorned the desk that morning, an assortment of dark as well as light chocolate. Not for that reason alone, Ainsworth cartwheeled across the room, though his response – 'Fuck me I think I've done both my groins' – suggested his playing days might soon be a happy memory. The manager of Woodley United, the Berkshire semi-pro outfit in the Hellenic League he still turned out for at 46, would have wanted a word about excessive celebration at his age.

Ainsworth had considered calling Bentley the previous day but resisted lest he might be seen too celebratory. He was full of admiration for the job Morecambe's boss had done on a budget probably tighter than his own. He'd make the call later in the day. There was, though, real pride in his achievement. Dobbo said, 'I suppose that makes me the longest serving assistant manager.'

* * *

The first match after the validation of the Couhig takeover was celebrated by Rob and Pete lapping Adams Park in a monsoon. Louisiana was renowned for its crazy weather and here was Buckinghamshire getting in on the act. Rob carried an umbrella under his arm and any moment I was sure he'd give us his Gene Kelly. Soaked to the skin they may have been but inside the Couhigs were singing in the rain.

When the figures were announced, they came as a reassuring shock. Of the legacy members eligible to vote, 95 per cent cast their ballot and just short of 97 per cent of that number said 'Yes' to foreign ownership. Only 21 voted against. Pete declared he'd round the dudes up.

The trust had served its period of office with diligence and sincerity but the time had arrived for a reality check. Rob talked of his family's 'daunting sense of obligation'.

He was reintroduced to the squad two days before the home match against Shrewsbury Town. 'I've tried many lawsuits and the will to win predominated. I prevailed a lot of times as you have, and that is what makes you so special. Think about the remarkable transformation you've already created in this community. My family is already on the ground here, but now is the time to hit it even harder. The real work starts now.'

Shrewsbury threatened to throw a spanner in the works being the more eager, creating more chances in open play and moving the ball smartly. Scoring was the difference and that's what Wycombe did – Joe Jacobson's free kick nodded on by Darius Charles and spring-heeled Rolando Aarons slid in his first goal in the colours. That brought the inevitable 'how we did lose to, blah, blah; I couldn't watch that every week blah, blah, how are they in the top two, blah, blah,' diet of the opposition's self-flagellation after a loss to Wycombe.

'We are pushing expectations higher,' Ainsworth said. 'It is difficult to talk now about just surviving. The midfield boys ran their socks off, especially laterally because I played three up and wanted to be the aggressor. We have seriously good players to come back so those in the team know they need to be on it all the time.'

The vapour was rising from naked bodies in the dressing room where Akinfenwa assumed centre stage. His oratory may not have matched Henry V's *cri de coeur* at Agincourt (this was following a win rather than preparing for battle) but Bayo's words stirred the hearts of Wycombe's happy few.

He referred to war in the manner of the side that was winning a string of battles. He evoked fervour. His team-mates sang heartily. 'Never seen anything like this, never been in anything like this. The game is changing man, the game is changing.'

I understood the management's desire to keep a lid on this elation. But it was hard, very hard, when someone as sensible as Jack Grimmer admitted that every night he went to bed he couldn't get out of his head the thought that he could soon be part of a Championship club. Whatever spells Ainsworth and Dobson cast on the players, they couldn't stop them dreaming.

I walked back out to the side of the pitch. It was still teeming down, the lights in the sponsors' boxes were all illuminated, much drink was being taken behind steamed windows and a lone sodden partridge was doing a lap of honour of the centre circle.

Wycombe were three points clear at the top of the pear tree.

Up (and Down) for the Cup

WYCOMBE Wanderers' participation in the Carabao Cup lasted one night; the Leasing.com Trophy was done and dusted in two. Beaten at home by both Stevenage, who were propping up League Two at the time, and Fulham under-21s, the only realistic chance of a Wembley date Gareth Ainsworth considered for his club at the start of the season went up in smoke like a lot of other loose kindling on 5 November.

The manager had been moved to dismay twice in the first four months of the season when his players allowed the least of trophies to slip from their grasp. After all, these losses came at a cost and Wycombe weren't well off enough to cock a snook at potential income streams.

They pocketed the £20,000 Leasing.com participation fee but only another £10,000 for the defeat of MK Dons when already out of the competition. That might buy a year's supply of worm infestation treatment for the training ground.

The manner of the losses was not something Ainsworth could let pass without airing his concerns. His reaction may be critical to careers. The enriched state of the club's finances thanks to the Couhig vote coincided with the approaching January transfer window and the consequent growth in wiggle room for Ainsworth to bring new faces in and send any failing ones out.

What made life deeply frustrating for those on the first-team fringes was Wycombe's lack of a reserve/B side delivering regular competition and challenge. There were few opportunities to show off – a ten-minute burst here or there from the substitutes' bench to make an impression. A couple of poor examples of ball control and that could be it. It was impossible to build any momentum.

Playing in front of a couple of hundred relatively disinterested folk on a shocker of a Tuesday night was hardly fun. But, as Ainsworth rightly said, these were professionals, or aspired to be. 'Ninety-eight per cent effort doesn't cut it,' he said. 'I need 100 per cent all the time. That performance just wasn't us.'

Though he didn't imply it directly, you knew from the intensity of his delivery – 'Shit defending that boys, shit defending,' he said as the video was played – that loyalty to those not reaching the levels he demanded was being stretched. Time for the season's first round of defining decisions was moving up fast. Edginess crept in.

The loss of the second chance for cup glory was swiftly followed by the arrival of the third and most prestigious of all. The FA Cup may have diminished over the years but still had the power to unlock the heart of the football romantic, even if Tranmere were not exactly prominent in erotic hotspots. The first-round draw sent the Wanderers to Prenton Park, a week before they'd return for a league fixture broadcast live on Sky Sports, their first such exposure of the season.

The ground was in an unprepossessing spot. On the approach you could look across the centre of Liverpool to the famous Metropolitan Cathedral, the Liver Building and the Radio City tower, signposts of prestige and pulling power.

The panorama from the press box at the top of the main stand at Tranmere was row upon row of terraced homes, as tight-knit as the people who lived there. The wind hurried through the rafters and empty seats and it felt as if you were trapped in some hollow appendage of the Mersey tunnel.

As the two teams would meet again so soon, Ainsworth adopted a tactical approach he hoped would startle Micky Mellon, his opposite number, and get him thinking twice how Wycombe might look Sunday hence. He left Adebayo Akinfenwa on the bench and restored Alex Samuel for the first time since his lung puncture at Gillingham.

David Wheeler and Rolando Aarons were to play off Samuel. Sido Jombati came in for his season's league debut at right-back for the injured Jack Grimmer. 'Intelligence, patience, desire,' were the manager's keynote words.

Tranmere's team sheet was handed to Richard Dobson who counted ten players. It was an administrative error but if uncorrected and the player missed off the list – in this case Kieron Morris – started the match, Wycombe had every right to stop play and bring it to the referee's attention. The consequences might be severe. Imagine if they did nothing and Morris scored. Imagination became reality inside three minutes.

The omission had been corrected by then. Dobson showed the sheet to Ainsworth and the pair debated for a few seconds before deciding honesty was the best policy. Mellon was duly thankful and marched off to give a member of his backroom team the sharp end of his tongue.

What made Morris's goal more sickening was that he was much coveted by Wycombe's management. There was a chance he could have joined in the summer but the time spent weighing his options meant sights were set elsewhere. Not only did Morris put Tranmere in front, the so-and-so went and equalised after Wycombe – through Joe Jacobson's sweet free- kick and a prodded finish from Samuel – got their noses in front. A 2-2 draw and a replay meant the teams would now meet three times in 12 days.

The second instalment was the single League One fixture on the Sunday of a 2020 European Championship qualifying weekend where internationals took priority and lower league clubs scrambled to rearrange fixtures. Tranmere butchered another team sheet – this one had Jack Grummer in the first team and Alex Damson among the substitutes. His name was Pattison.

Not to be outdone, Sky TV invented a player. He may have been the most recognisable face and physique in the Football League but Adebayo Akinfenwa – restored to the line-up – was 'Akinfenway' throughout the first half. Why didn't someone scream into the commentator's headphones? Bayo was a regular Sky pundit, making the mispronunciation of his name doubly absurd. The man with the mike didn't know his Grimmer from his Grummer and, to add insult to injury, Joe Jacobson became Yakobson.

Compensation for these malfunctions was found in a share of Sky's largesse – always a handy dollop of sustenance for a League One side – and a resolute 2-0 victory thanks to goals just before half-time from Akinfenway and Yakobson.

Not everyone – the commentator clearly included – was thrilled that this was *Sky*'s selection. On Twitter, @GMElement1 said, 'Tranmere v Wycombe on Sky. Fuck me, they've really set us up for a Sunday afternoon nap there ain't they? 90 (+10) minutes of "injuries", goal kicks, throw-ins that take five minutes and Gareth Ainsworth. I'm going back to bed.'

As GME slept, Wycombe produced a master class in being Wycombe, a team performance without a weakness. 'The shift they put in today was phenomenal. Curtis [Thompson] was cramping near the end, you should have seen the size of his fucking calf, and we had to push him back on but that's the way it is. I can't be without these boys.'

Two days before the trip, Matt Bloomfield and Akinfenwa had approached the manager asking for a few minutes with the squad without management in the room. Trusting his generals, Ainsworth acquiesced. What happened in the privacy of 15 minutes as a squad was a stirring example of the Wycombe squad's enduring belief in each other.

Blooms and Bayo wanted to double down on the attitude that had got the team to their prominence in the league. It was confirmation of the message drilled into them the day they signed. Jack Grimmer walked out feeling ten feet tall. 'We could have had this meeting after we'd lost a couple of matches – that would have made sense, but the fact the generals wanted to drive home the message when we could go clear at the top was so this club.

'We knew what had got us to the top, we needed to keep those standards if we wanted to stay there. Everyone was allowed to have a say. We all came out of the room buzzing.'

That buzz intensified when the team gathered to watch the video of the game on the eve of the third in the Tranmere trilogy. The highlight reel was infused with positivity, not least when David Wheeler was pictured on the edge of Tranmere's six-yard box as one attack broke down, then flashed across the screen at what you could have sworn was a piece of deliberately speeded up film, to arrive on the edge of his own six-yard box within ten seconds. 'Usain Wheeler,' Ainsworth said. 'This is us. This is so fucking us.'

His team-mates applauded as 'Wheels' hid his embarrassment behind a prolonged swig of water. The reaction to JJ's penalty was then shown, with Dominic Gape burrowing *under* his colleagues' huddle rather than leaping on top of it. The laughter was contagious.

'We're a force boys, we're a force,' the manager said. 'Now take all that good stuff, that intensity, that serious talent, and go turn it into another win. I'm sure they [Tranmere] will start tomorrow with the team they finished with on Sunday, they'll come at us but that gives us big counter-attacking opportunities.'

* * *

In Micky Mellon's office after another Wycombe league success on the road, Tranmere's manager suggested out loud that Adebayo Akinfenwa would be left out of the cup replay because of the physical burden so many matches in quick-fire succession would have on the big man. Ainsworth nodded without saying anything. He was beginning to formulate a cunning plan.

He would give Bayo the first 45 minutes on Wednesday night then bring him off. The hope was that Mellon would set up his team and brief them not to imagine being roughhoused around at the back. Such psychological edges could be vital.

Ainsworth's more pressing concern was niggles to Bloomfield, Jacobson and the need to rest Darius Charles. That was a huge chunk of experience shorn in one fell swoop and having to bring in Giles Phillips and Jamie Mascoll – novices still – ran a risk the manager would rather not have taken. The situation nagged at him.

Paul Smyth's return after three months of inactivity was cause for relief. The Northern Irishman offered trickery in tight spaces on the left to balance the cunning of Scott Kashket around the target of Akinfenwa. Wycombe's task was apparently made easier when Kane Wilson went over the ball to Jack Grimmer and was sent off in the 41st minute. From a corner on the stroke of half-time, the ball was kept alive in Tranmere's area and Anthony Stewart lashed it home.

The decision to bring Bayo off looked sound, though the team would lack a piercing on-field voice – an army without a general. But Tranmere weren't exactly cock-a-hoop either, depleted in numbers, away from home, ten minutes to reorganise, massage life into dispirited minds and heavy legs and draw inspiration from some quarter. Step forward the captain and goalkeeper Scott Davies.

We'd seen it before, a night when a keeper morphed into a giant in green, his errors made to look like world-class interventions and the world-class interventions seem routine. Behind Tranmere's blockade of two ranks of four, Davis was as impenetrable as the door to a vault, dealing with deflected shots and finely struck ones with steely assurance. He even made time-wasting look like an art form.

Wycombe had too much time, too many options, wanted to be too certain in their passing and, off to the side,

Akinfenwa cut an increasingly agitated figure on the bench. He could sense what was coming. From a stray midfield pass and simple ball over the top, Morgan Ferrier's decisive finish revived the ten men. Into extra time, players came off, players went on, but Davies was resolute. The best save of all came from a free kick from substitute Josh Parker that was headed into the top left-hand corner. Davies set off early and got a glove on it.

The more times Wycombe threw bodies and balls into the box, the less they looked likely to score; the few times Tranmere broke, their pace had the potential for devastating consequence.

Of course it had to be Kieron Morris – the one-time Wycombe target whose name had been left off the team sheet 12 days earlier – who settled the tie in the 115th minute, low and slow into the bottom corner. The Chairboys' FA Cup journey was over.

* * * *

Pete Couhig watched the tie unfold from one of the sponsors' boxes in the Frank Adams Stand and emerged through the lights, vapour rising as he marched across the pitch. 'Two hundred fucking grand, man.' That may have been a conservative estimate.

The second-round draw had pitted the winner of this replay at home to Chichester City of the Isthmian League South East Division, the lowest ranked side in the competition. Chichester usually mixed it with teams like Sittingbourne, Herne Bay and East Grinstead. Wycombe could, and probably would, have made vegan mincemeat of it.

The match was also scheduled for live coverage on BT Sport, so there was additional revenue blown away (mind you, BT called the club Wycombe Warriors in a press release so their interest in the tie was only half-hearted). But what of the possible gift of a Premier League club away in the third round? 'I can't watch that draw, man, imagine Tranmere getting Liverpool,' the demoralised Couhig said. They drew Watford and would eventually lose in the fourth round to Manchester United.

For once, the sound coming from the home dressing room was of silence. Next door, much to their opponent's anger, Tranmere's boys were blasting out the Wycombe anthem, 'Seven Nation Army.' It was like a boxer sent sprawling on his back in the ring, being toe-capped in the groin for good measure. It *really* hurt. Ainsworth would remind his team of the disrespect later in the season when the Rovers returned.

In the meantime, there was no scope to mope. Wycombe had Doncaster Rovers at home on Saturday and then Ipswich Town, their main challengers, at Portman Road within 72 hours. But not often could a bunch of players sitting on top of the league have looked so in need of pulling themselves together.

The Peaks of Performance

GARETH Ainsworth graduated on 3 December 2019 with distinction in professional studies in football management, a diploma run by the University of Liverpool in conjunction with the League Managers' Association. The ceremony was held at Liverpool's Philharmonic Hall where Bjorn Again, the Abba reincarnation, was scheduled the following evening. Could you hear the drums Rolando?

Ainsworth cut quite the academic in his mortar board and cloak, proudly displaying his certificate. His younger brother Liam sent a text asking why Hermione and Ron hadn't stuck around for the official picture. There was a definite hint of magic about a delightful family occasion that honoured how hard and with his whole heart and soul he worked at his profession.

Matt Gill, Ipswich Town's first-team coach, had also done the hard learning yards to take his talents as far as they could go. He was recognised at the same occasion, an indication that the club's tradition for progressive football burned bright.

I frequented Ipswich many times in the 1970s and 80s, when Bobby Robson and John Lyall were the managerial men of distinction and the whole enterprise was controlled by the mildly aristocratic Cobbold brothers of the East Anglian brewery dynasty. Mr John and Mr Patrick ran a tight ship in that they were quite often tight.

Bobby Robson was 'Robson' to them, and in the crowded boardroom after a match either Mr John or Mr Patrick would be heard to say, 'Robson, get [so and so] a drink old chap'. Imagine a Premier League manager today being told by his chairman to make sure a journalist's whisky glass was topped up. Imagine a journalist in the board room.

That was just the way it was. Ipswich's enterprising brand of football was not all that attracted the finest from Fleet Street to ignore Arsenal, Tottenham (even West Ham) on a regular basis. A number of these stout fellows would wake in railway sidings the morning after a match at Portman Road unaware how they got there or where it was they lived.

Time, dynasties, writers and drinking habits had moved to a different place – as had the club. Ipswich were in League One, a comparatively impoverished status, unsure how to deal with relegation from the Championship the previous season and – much like Sunderland and Portsmouth – rather resenting the fact they were mucking in with Accrington, MK Dons and Wycombe.

Sunderland and Portsmouth would have been delirious to be second in the league rather than festering in mid-table with Christmas fast approaching. Ipswich were in second spot but also in a right funk. Five points ahead were Wycombe and that was almost as degrading as having to watch Norwich City – their bitter East Anglian foe – trying to fend for themselves in the Premier League.

Paul Lambert, Ipswich's manager, had previously been in charge at Wycombe (and Norwich) which had to be why he was so agitated as the Chairboys' visit dawned. This was not a match he could countenance losing. A draw would be just about bearable.

At half-time on 26 November neither side had scored and Ipswich had a goal ruled out that sparked incandescence in their dug out and the stands. This was too much – some idiot linesman flagging for offside. Fucking hell, still 0-0 against this lot. Benedict Musola, the Wycombe chaplain, recalled noticing a distinct difference between the two benches, Ipswich all agitation as opposed to Wycombe's calm.

As the players gathered to return to the field, David Wheeler spotted Matt Gill and held out his hand in a friendly gesture. They had played together at Exeter City. Gill's reaction was to walk over and plant his studded boot onto Wheeler's foot. He was soon heard from the Wycombe bench to shout 'do him' to his players whenever the ball headed in Wheeler's direction.

Mr Patrick and Mr John would have shown him the front door and told him not to return.

* * *

We were a couple of weeks into the Christmas General Election campaign. Professional footballers tended not to divulge political preference, sensing it best that the dimmer lights on the terraces or social media did not have a reason other than wearing the wrong colours to profane them.

David Wheeler was not an activist in any sense but a man with a social conscience who pondered the state of the nation and its political classes with considerable disquiet. His parents hadn't been politically active. 'My dad had socialist liberal values and often shouted at the TV when *Question Time* was on but that was about it.'

Wheeler was content and confident in political discourse. We were so engrossed on a coach journey home (from Tranmere I think it was) debating anti-Semitism in the Labour Party, we didn't realise we were talking loudly next to the table where Scott Kashket and Joe Jacobson were in their regular card school. They took our conversation in good part.

There were occasions when verbal passions flared. Wheeler was soon to enter his 30s and become a father for the first time, giving him pause for much reflection. The global eco-systems were shifting at an alarming rate and those of his generation and the next would be the ones whom it might affect with the most hideous consequences.

'The number-one issue in this election shouldn't be Brexit but the climate. The fact that it isn't is really concerning. We have the facts in front of us but the problem, initially, is convincing people that it is a problem. A lot of powerful forces said it didn't exist because they gained financially from it, which was totally disingenuous.

'The current electoral system hasn't been fit for purpose for decades, which is another barrier because if people feel they can't vote their way into change on the climate the two main parties aren't going to feel the pressure to take action. If you had electoral reform and a subsequent boost in Green Party votes and representation, Labour and even the Tories might think shit we need to have decent policies and actually deliver on this stuff otherwise we could be in trouble.

'The classic problem of the left has been the inability to have a consistent message. Extinction Rebellion [an environmental movement that used non-violent civil disobedience as a means of pressing their climate agenda], had an incredibly powerful run of action. They pissed people off but it was a consistent message of blocking roads and disrupting airports before a few idiots decided to climb on top of a train.

'How was that consistent with the message? They needed to encourage people to use the train yet decided that disruption was the be all and end all to get attention when they needed the public's support. Once the message was trivialised, it was also diminished.

'I worried a lot about the climate. People like Piers Morgan on TV encapsulated the problem of trying to get an articulate message across. A well-meaning vegan would be invited on to his show with a serious point about the meat industry being a huge polluter of the environment – which it is – and he would batter them unceremoniously the entire time, shouting things like, "You're wearing a leather wrist-watch, you're a hypocrite."

'Instead of a rational debate, viewers just enjoyed watching Piers monster his guests. That wasn't going to help educate those people who had genuine concerns.

'I read a tweet which said that if a million of us improved just a little rather than a 100 people being perfect, the world would be a better place. There would be a lot more scope for change if you got everyone to do a tiny bit better rather than listen to puritans.

'In the last few years I've gone from someone who ate meat three times a day to not eating meat or fish. I haven't quite gone vegan, everyone has their human flaws and even though I'm passionate about the cause, I love cheese. It's that simple. A majority of people have felt that way about meat, and you have to give them a chance. I've got to the brick wall of cheese and I can't get past it.'

* * *

'Get Brexit Done' had become as commonplace in the lexicon of late 2019, as had 'are Wycombe still six points clear in League One?' Actually it could have been eight.

Two minutes from the end of the match at Portman Road, an Ipswich player did indeed 'do' David Wheeler, though replays suggested contact was made in the 'D' rather than inside the area. Nonetheless a penalty was awarded and a momentary hush descended.

Joe Jacobson, who had rolled his last couple of penalties low into the corners, decided to aim higher, that aim was true but Ipswich goalkeeper Tomas Holy raised a giant left palm and deflected the ball back into play. The save inspired a headless chicken end to the game that finished without a goal.

Lambert slagged off referee Alan Young and his assistants while ignoring the fact that his side had not laid a defining glove on 'inferior' opposition. Oh he was going to complain to this person, that organisation and probably the Supreme Court for good measure. Yes, Young had booked 11 players including Rocky Allsop for time-wasting for the first time in his career, but the Ipswich press boys largely rolled their eyes.

For Wheeler the result and its manner were further endorsement of the decision he had taken in July to join the club to which he seemed destined. 'I'd come close to signing for Wycombe a few times. When I was leaving [Brunel] university and trying to get into pro-football it looked as if I'd have a trial and ended up going to Dagenham and Redbridge and then Exeter, who I signed for. When I was leaving Exeter I heard Wycombe were interested again but nothing came of it.'

The defining moment was a chance meeting with Matt Bloomfield at the wedding of Wheeler's agent Joe Burnell when the pair were seated on the same table and conversation inevitably turned to their respective careers. Wheeler heard exactly what he hoped to hear.

'The point I was at, and because of the things I valued, Blooms sold Wycombe because of the changing-room environment and the characters inside there. It was a such a big consideration.

'I knew how much I valued my day-to-day experience and wellbeing as opposed to the pure ambition of playing at the highest level I'd had as a young player. I'd seen the other side of how things could be if you weren't playing, the dressing room wasn't how you'd want it to be and how your mood could drop and whole life change if things weren't going the way you wanted. Blooms said it simply wasn't that way at Wycombe and a lot of praise for that had to go to the gaffer and Dobbo. I only heard good things about them from everyone I asked.

'I didn't know if the club was in a position to offer me anything. I did my due diligence and they were in a situation where they were tipped to be relegated and that was still the case when I signed. I had played against most of the lads over the years, I was quietly confident in them and backed my own ability. I thought "let's give it a good go".

'My expectation was quickly surpassed. There was a lot more professionalism than I expected, players staying long hours to look after themselves. Standards were high at other places but the additional stuff was nowhere near the Wycombe level. Looking after your body and doing all the right things in that sense was different.'

Wheeler had moved to QPR in 2017 and in the manner of his fellow Rangers Paul Smyth and Giles Phillips an economy of opportunity and months of unfulfillment beckoned. Rather than a short-term loan to Wycombe as in the cases of Smyth and Phillips, Wheeler negotiated a three-year deal to move a few miles up the M40.

He accepted the club possessed different and dynamic forward options so permanence in the team was not a given. Even with Bloomfield's assurances, he worried if he would fit in. How would he get on with his fellow forward Adebayo Akinfenwa, the celebrity-hugging antithesis to his camera-shy nature?

Richard Dobson recalled Wheeler's sheepish arrival. 'David had his guard up for quite a while, not sure about anyone or anything here. One day he came into the coaches' room to break the ice. We were in mid-conversation when Gapey and Alex Samuel burst in and started chatting about any old thing. That was when he realised this was a different place.'

The look and bearing of Wheeler and Akinfenwa was singularly the sharpest contrast of any two men in a team. 'Bayo and I came from very different worlds. I grew up in a very middle-class southern town [Brighton] and I'm sure he had a much tougher time, but the nice thing was all these lads from varied backgrounds had a mutual respect. That wasn't common.

'We were both forward players and it was the same with Alex, Smythy, Fred, Scotty, if one of those was playing there would be less chance for me and the stats, bonuses, racked up against you. A significant reason for our results, irrespective of who was on the pitch, was that everyone wanted everyone to do well and the team to win.

'I'd been at clubs where the lads on the bench or in the stand were actively willing their side to lose because then there was more chance of them being involved.

'Bayo stood for everything in the Wycombe ethos. He may have been a public figure, the most famous league footballer in the country, but I hadn't expected him to be so grounded, humble and down to earth. He would actively dissuade any flamboyance or extravagant behaviour and had a rule where if a player came in wearing an outfit he deemed worth more than a certain amount that player was fined.'

The psychology of football fascinated Wheeler in much the same way it infused so much of Dobson's thinking about the game and its consequences. 'Wheels' was taking his Masters in sports psychology and the club permitted him time away for his classes.

There was an increasing need for care among the football community where personal issues could be spoken of freely and without fear of raising self-doubt lest you were regarded as emotionally lame or lacking in machismo. Once more, it was clear that the Wycombe dressing room was an open, tolerant, inclusive place, which drew the best from people rather than sending them into darker corners.

* * *

The election campaign rumbled on. Scott Kashket had no inkling that team-mate Jacob Gardiner Smith was the son of a Labour MP who was becoming a mainstay in TV debates, often seated alongside leader Jeremy Corbyn.

One morning, before training, Scotty was agitating over a press conference he'd seen the previous night, especially the behaviour of the Labour politician who dismissed a reporter's question on anti-Semitism because the subject matter in hand was NHS funding. Kashket let rip in the changing room. Jacob began to fume.

I Googled a picture of Barry Gardiner and showed it to Scott across the canteen table. I swear I had never seen a human so completely and utterly lost for words. As he tried to speak, nothing came forth but a stream of indecipherable dribble. His team-mates were in hysterics.

When, on the night of the count, the initial exit poll showed the Tories heading for a whopping majority, David Wheeler's exclamation point of a tweet – 'FUUUUCCCK!' – didn't really require its exclamation point. He was uncomprehending and demoralised in equal measure.

'I'd done a lot of reading on the EU but I hadn't needed to because I saw who was lining up on the side of "leave" and that was enough for me, by and large. Those like Boris Johnson, Nigel Farage and Iain Duncan Smith couldn't have been further from my way of thinking, what I valued and what society should have been striving towards.

'I didn't want to be one of those "I hate all these guys and what they stand for", so I taught myself a lot about the subject. There was a lot of misinformation spread and I suppose the public shouldn't have been blamed for believing what officials were telling them, because who else were they going to believe? I sensed people lost the reasoning behind why they voted the way they did in it [the 2016 EU referendum] in the first place. It became like supporting a football team when that wasn't what it should have been about.

'I know people who would vote the same way regardless of what had happened and that's bonkers. For instance, Dominic Grieve and Jacob Rees-Mogg were both Conservatives, Tony Blair and Jeremy Corbyn both Labour, but the choice had become far too binary like the referendum in the first place. It was "leave" or "remain" when there was so much grey in between. I don't think people voted for Brexit, they voted for Brexits – multiple different versions of it.

'In this day and age, electoral reform should be inevitable. The majority of developed countries used proportional representation as their electoral system and it encouraged co-operation, coalition, cohesion and compromise.

'If you had compromise, more people were represented rather than fewer.'

* * *

As Wycombe entered a 17-day competitive hibernation on top of League One (and knew whatever happened they would still be there on their return) the choice of Nick Hollis as speaker for their second development day of the season might have been considered a surprise.

Hollis was a remarkable individual who had climbed the highest peaks of six continents he verbally crossed off as one would the contents of a shopping list at Sainsbury's. Then came the need to tackle the one that required him to pause and reflect on deeply – to reach the top of the world, the ultimate, Everest.

I was reminded of a back-page story by a long-time travelling companion Harry Harris of the *Daily Mirror,* who once wrote that Joe Kinnear, then Wimbledon's manager, was 'speaking to me exclusively from his hotel room *overlooking* Mount Everest'. Imagine the view.

The story of Hollis's Himalayan heroics stilled the Wycombe common room to reverent silence. The gasps came when we were shown images of blackened feet, the effects of frostbite too scary for words. That and when he talked almost matter-of-factly about stepping over frozen dead bodies both on the way up and as he and his sherpa Pemba (who had climbed Everest six times) retraced their steps to base camp.

The most staggering element of his story, though, was when he stood atop the peak, expecting to witness the greatest view of all and was stricken with snow blindness, the effect of ice particles lacerating his eyes on the final arduous assault. So, when he got to the summit all he saw was a blur.

Hollis was talking to a group of men who had scaled their peak and yet were less than halfway through the operation. It made for an intriguing calibration of time and circumstance. So far, too, none of the players had suffered from any form of sight loss. Indeed the boys' focus remained incredibly clear.

The essence of the Hollis talk was one that struck a defining chord, that one man didn't climb a mountain alone, it required a dedicated team, a team that worked together for the common cause where the celebration of a single achievement was regarded as a win for all.

He espoused the need for leadership – 'not the barking orders type, that is so last year' – and for a collaboration of leaders. He asked Bayo if he was a leader and the big man said that he was 'but that it gets moved around, through the forwards, the midfield players and the defenders'. 'That's exactly what I mean,' Hollis said. It was the Wycombe generals typified.

Richard Dobson asked if he could interject. 'A few years ago we looked at the structured leadership at football clubs. There was a captain and a vice captain who were two similar types and we felt that wouldn't work for our dressing room. We believed that instead of two people trying to help 25 people, we'd split it between four and five to make it easier to get around to everyone.

'Each of these would have personality traits that would connect with different parts of the dressing room. We knew that we could also pass the armband around to any of four or five and they could be the captain at any one time. If we were in a ditch, there would not be one leader, but the four or five would take the lead.'

* * *

Nick Hollis was about to climb Everest and was shit scared. 'The fear was real, but most of the time when we feel scared as people there's actually nothing to be scared of at all, it's the irrational, impulsive, monkey mind taking over trying to run the show, and if we can find the reasons for that we can also intercept that fear. Do you talk about getting into a flow? I'm sure you do, and when that happens you're disengaging your primitive mind. If you come out of that flow your performance goes to crap.

'I knew I needed to interfere with that fear, I needed to man up and face it, but it was truly understanding the fear and then making rational decisions and that's what I did on Everest. The next stage was to commit. To take the plunge. And then to find the person I needed to stand shoulder to shoulder with me, who I could rely on totally.

'You guys know who those people are, those you could trust, in my case, with my life, and also those with whom you could have a good laugh along the way. And also you need to work with people you like, otherwise life isn't much fun.'

Hollis flashed a picture of the team behind the team, the extraordinary sherpas, those who spent their entire life on the mountain, earning a touch more than the £400 a year that was the average income in Nepal, whose numbers would fluctuate as those who died on ascent or descent were replaced by the next in line.

'When you watched them on the mountain, they were magic, absolute magic. What made them the best team I'd seen in my life? The first thing was they knew the team objective, there was no ambiguity. It was all crystal clear. The second was they knew their role, what part they played in the bigger picture.

'Let me throw it back to you. What's your big picture? It is that you guys win the league. That is your collective team goal. The sherpas know what part they had to play in that. They know what their function was in the team goal. These guys would literally die for their mates. That is how they operated. And what was it they valued above everything? Friendship.

'They are all Buddhists, they transcend ego. It was a really nice place to be, hanging around these guys. There was never anyone to blame, no one was better than anyone else, no one was more powerful than anyone else.'

Mind the Gape

*'Twas the week before Christmas and
all through the ground, was a chorus of
mocking, a rotten old sound.'*

(with apologies to Clement Clarke Moore)

ENOUGH steam to power a small town for a day was rising from the forlorn and departing figure of Adebayo Akinfenwa. A sending-off, the club's third in the league, screwed the planning and caused all manner of page rustling in Richard Dobson's tactics folder.

We were 25 minutes into the closest Wycombe had to a local derby, a lovely cross-county journey despite the dismal weather that encompassed the villages of Piddington, Forest Hill, Lewknor and Milton Common before we swept into Inspector Morse country.

The Wagnerian melancholy was appropriate as Akinfenwa marched off and half turned his back from his manager's attempt at a consoling pat. The scene was at demoralising odds with the season, though it was still faintly absurd that Wycombe topped League One at any stage of the club's ring cycle.

Even the regular Wycombe storytellers had begun to struggle with context and they had witnessed much in their time. A dedicated handful of media folk travelled in the team's slipstream – Matt Cecil and Conor Shaw, the unfailingly helpful, indefatigable communications duo, Phil Catchpole of the BBC, Keith Higgins from Wycombe Sound, snapper Andy Rowland and Dan 'The Cam' Brown poking his nose (and camera) in wherever he could.

Catchpole and Higgins were enjoying remarkable seasons of their own. Phil's *Ringing The Blues* podcast, a weekly diaspora of everything Wanderers topped off with a Mexican mate reading the League One results (Shrewsbury sounded so romantic in Spanish) was named in the country's finest by the Football Supporters' Association. Wycombe Sound was nominated for best local radio station against a raft of BBC opposition. Not only on the football field was the town punching well above its weight.

Listening to the chatter, they had never missed a meaningful match, recounting the Hail Marys and horror stories from the immediate past and days long gone with a savant's clarity. Cecil and Shaw were club employees so their favour was assured. Catchpole and Higgins were devoted to the cause but had to remain professionally neutral. That wasn't getting easier as ambitions soared.

Our tiny knot watched Akinfenwa depart with that gnawing sense that this was going to be a shitty day. The atmosphere was already unreal for we were tucked together high in a corner of the Kassam Stadium, the one ground in England from where the Hollywood Bowl was visible from the press box.

The Kassam had three stands with a gaping chasm behind one of the goals, beyond which were the varied delights of a family entertainment block. There was a car wash attached to the main stand. The ladies selling burgers were disconcertingly cheery, or perhaps they were laughing at you, rather than with you. After all they probably knew what was in the meat.

Manchester City had been at the ground three days earlier for a Carabao Cup quarter-final in which Oxford registered more shots on target against Pep Guardiola's Premier League champions than any previous club in the season. A return of one goal from those 18 strikes was not going to be sufficient and City ran out reasonably comfortable 3-1 winners.

Confidence was rightly flooding through Oxford veins; the Wycombe staff knew this would be a thorough examination and thus its talisman would need to be fully concentrated on what he was best at. That meant being robust and self-contained.

Akinfenwa was booked for an innocent early collision before he sprang (ambled with intent) to the defence of a prostrate Scott Kashket who had been taken out by a tackle that pre-empted a scrum, with players stepping over him as if he was at the bottom of a ruck.

Oxford's centre-half John Mousinho – who played 79 times for Wycombe a decade earlier – manhandled Akinfenwa, who was silly to retaliate. There was so little impetus in the push that had Bayo, with all his muscle, done the same to me I was confident that after an initial wobble I could have stayed on my feet.

Mousinho's sack-of-spuds routine was of such quality that Lee Swabey – another referee short in every respect – was suckered into thinking something really nasty must have happened when it hadn't. The red card represented a second bloody nose for Wycombe in no time after Rocky Allsop's record sequence of 602 minutes without conceding in the league was shattered when Oxford scored what was to be the game's only goal.

It came straight from the opening page of Gareth Ainsworth's 'don't let them do this to us' preparation: a 40-yard right-to-left, cross-field pass, swift interplay, insufficient pressure on the ball and lack of defensive reaction when it landed back at James Henry's right foot after Allsop's instinctive double block.

Everything – especially his players – had fallen into place for Karl Robinson, Oxford's Liverpudlian manager. A good side, with belief in itself, its standing, its methods and with a little bit of cunning, were ahead, and the one player who might rubbish it all was bad company in the dressing room. Dominic Gape was already there, having sensibly decided that a worrying twinge in his hamstring would worsen if he stayed on.

The ten men did well to bear the strain of meagre possession for 65 minutes with enough composure to suggest they could earn a point that would have been remarkable in the circumstances. In truth they didn't create one worthwhile opportunity.

Wycombe had never won the match immediately after a loss to Oxford – Chairboys Central's Tom Hancock was a whizz at such statistical treasures. Their record on 26 December was an absurdly awful return of five wins from 22 matches in the Football League, leaving them 80th across all four divisions.

The Boxing Day match, the first reunion of the season, was at Portsmouth, where the choppiness of the waters lapping the south's coastal defences was not an auspicious portent.

That Wycombe started the match seven points ahead and ended it six clear was evidence of the startling inability of any club in League One to play with self-belief. The sparking Bristol Rovers came a cropper on home soil, as did Peterborough. Sunderland were held at home by Bolton in what must have been an out-of-body experience for Phil Parkinson. Ipswich were outplayed by Gillingham at Portman Road, but hung on for a point and moved up a spot to second.

As for Wycombe, Jack Grimmer, struggling with a pelvic injury, was in Aberdeen doting on his new baby niece, Matt Bloomfield was given respite from the intensity of the festive programme, the suspended Akinfenwa was doing his best to raise morale from the bench and Gape preferred to stay home to rest his hamstring, occasionally glancing at his phone for score updates.

Portsmouth trained on Christmas Day; Gareth Ainsworth gave his men the full day with their families. Who was to say who made the right call, though Wycombe would send out a new front three of Rolando Aarons, Paul Smyth and Alex

Samuel, who might have profited from more time to work out each other's mind and movement.

Ainsworth was counting on speed and thrust to rattle the Portsmouth centre-halves, who were considered susceptible to swift inter-action. A pity Wycombe never got going. It rained all afternoon and neither side was on its mettle, though Marcus Harness, a £1m player (Wycombe could only marvel at such things) who came on as a substitute after six minutes offered clever close control and infusions of pace.

The visitors conceded twice in six minutes midway through the second half. Ainsworth raged that a free kick was allowed to bounce without challenge in the build-up to the second goal as much as he was at the consequent lack of defensive solidarity.

It was a weakness he emphasised in the period between that loss and the arrival of Coventry City three days later to complete the set of clubs Wycombe would face in the first half of a stand-on-your-head season.

The squad was summoned for a two-game loss debrief at 10am on Saturday, when Ainsworth and Josh Hart replayed over and over again the goals conceded against Oxford and Portsmouth – 'Only the second time I've had to do this which speaks volumes for what you have achieved this season,' the manager said.

'It's been rosy and super positive this season and that's me, super positive. But I don't think our set plays have been as good. Did we believe in our runs at Portsmouth? Were we properly dying for it [the ball] against Oxford?

'We have to keep believing in what we're doing. Let's get something from these next two games [Coventry, followed by Ipswich Town at Adams Park on New Year's Day]. Let's be proud. Let's be Wycombe. We can do something this season, we definitely can.'

His was not the universal take on matters. On Twitter @ PompeyPedro wrote, 'Wycombe Wanderers are absolute dogshit, I'd be embarrassed to be a fan. Once their plan A of being dickheads falls apart they're even worse. Wish it had been them instead of Bury.' Merry Christmas to you too.

* * *

Few footballers I'd met loathed inactivity more than Dominic Gape. Summer holidays were an unwanted intrusion into his life. He squeezed into his third-row chair in the common room but was mentally disconnected as he agonised over a hamstring injury.

Before the summons upstairs he had been contorted across a wicked looking piece of gym equipment as if freeze-framed in a back somersault. Cian O'Doherty didn't want him disturbed from remedial work and the physiotherapist's command was disregarded at one's peril. We'd chat later.

Wycombe were missing the indefatigable Jack Grimmer, suspended Adebayo Akinfenwa and rested Matt Bloomfield at Portsmouth and had all but forgotten what it was like to see Fred Onyedinma. Of all the missing persons, Gape was the one missed the most.

He viewed the analysis and wondered what might have been had he been in the crux of the battle. 'We got small defensive details wrong for the first goal which didn't often happen with us, and for the second the goalkeeper kicked it in the air, it bounced, we didn't compete, we headed it, they headed it, they got in down the side and crossed it. Where was the defence-splitting pass there? There wasn't one. That's what a lot of the games were decided on in this league. Small margins.'

It was no shame on his team-mates when the manager let slip that Gape's was the first name on his sheet whatever the tactical nuance. It had not been greatly different since a 22-year-old arrived on loan from Southampton in September 2016 and after one morning's training was introduced as a substitute at Luton Town.

'I was chucked in at the deep end. I signed on Thursday, trained on Friday and then came on for 30 minutes. I smashed someone early. I had it in the back of my head that I needed to prove I could cope with that side of things because, coming from such a good upbringing at Southampton, my technical ability wasn't in question. My agent told me Wycombe liked me, I was a good footballer and the common theme was could I hack it physically?'

The sight of a Luton player writhing at his feet from his first touch suggested he had put that argument to bed.

Gape, the youngest of four siblings from Dorset, joined Southampton at seven and, though he lived beyond the permitted mileage range, was given dispensation to stay as the Saints was the one club that wanted him. His dad Chris was a self-employed builder who managed his schedule to drive his son to and from St Mary's. If his workload prevented it, mum Jenny took over the responsibility.

'When I was 14, Southampton asked me to come in full time, but my parents wanted me to stay at school and do my best so I wasn't there permanently until I signed a scholarship at 16. I thank them now because I know a lot of lads at Southampton went in at the age of 12 and when they got the sad news about not being retained, it was "where am I, what am I going to be?"

'It was a catch 22, your son could be in the Premier League and life was rosy or it could be devastating if he was released and had fallen behind in football and education.'

Gape captained different age-group levels at St Mary's and. like Wycombe, the club was solidly reliant on developing the person as much as the player. 'The place was full of really top-quality people. My age group had well-rounded individuals with the skill sets appropriate for the real world. We were special, going two years without losing a match in youth football, and from the squad over 50 per cent went on to do well in the game.

'Although I was a young captain everything was rotational. In four quarters of a match you'd play two or three positions and never the same one. I was centre-half, on the wing then

Fun at the squad photo-shoot for 2019/20.

Matt Bloomfield [back to camera] and Gareth Ainsworth [far right] are introduced to Missy and Rob Couhig and Mark Palmer by chairman Trevor Stroud [second left].

Wycombe's ethos explained to the new boys by Richard Dobson.

Pete Couhig, Mark Palmer, Rob Couhig and Trevor Stroud face the Wycombe supporters on the day a potential takeover was announced.

The squad was taught the Maori Haka by Bruce Simpson of Haka UK. Here they perfect the tongue-poke.

Bolton manager Phil Parkinson is alone with his thoughts before the first match of the season.

Paul Smyth celebrates with a back somersault after scoring Wycombe's first goal against Bolton.

That's my boy. Adebayo Akinfenwa lets Smyth know how much the goal means.

Wycombe's FA Amateur Cup Final side that lost to Bishop Auckland before 95,000 spectators at Wembley in 1957 is reunited at the Bull Inn, Bisham with other players from the era. Len Worley, Dennis Syrett, Michael Wicks and Jim Truett are in the group.

Skipper Matt Bloomfield leads the pre-match huddle before the team faces MK Dons.

Paying homage to the Wild Thing, a group of young Wycombe fans pose in front of the poster of Gareth Ainsworth.

Joe Jacobson is mobbed after a hat-trick – two direct from corners – sent Wycombe top of the table with a 3-1 defeat of Lincoln.

The directors' box rises to acclaim Adebayo Akinfenwa's penalty winner against Portsmouth.

Rocky Allsop flies through the air to deny Peterborough a late winner in the 3-3 draw at Adams Park.

Anthony Stewart, who played more minutes than anyone in the season, chests clear from Sunderland's Marc McNulty.

Darius Charles volleys home on his 'wrong' foot for the only goal of the game against Sunderland at Adams Park.

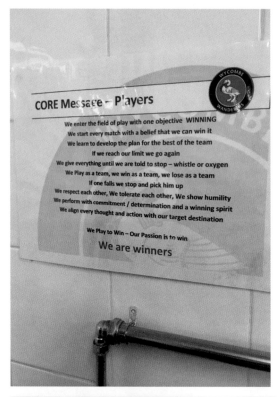

CORE Message – Players

We enter the field of play with one objective WINNING
We start every match with a belief that we can win it
We learn to develop the plan for the best of the team
If we reach our limit we go again
We give everything until we are told to stop – whistle or oxygen
We Play as a team, we win as a team, we lose as a team
If one falls we stop and pick him up
We respect each other, We tolerate each other, We show humility
We perform with commitment / determination and a winning spirit
We align every thought and action with our target destination

We Play to Win – Our Passion is to win
We are winners

Blackpool's groundsman squeezes his van close enough to the Wycombe coach to attach jump leads to the dead battery.

Wycombe's culture is imperative to the success of the club.

Football in a monsoon: Wycombe v Shrewsbury at Adams Park.

Pete Couhig acknowledges the acclaim of the home crowd as the takeover of the club was confirmed.

Phil Catchpole of BBC Three Counties radio interviews Gareth Ainsworth after victory over Shrewsbury.

High-flier Josh Parker celebrates a goal against MK Dons in the Leasing.Com Trophy.

The Times *applauds Rocky Allsop's response to homophobic abuse from the stands at Tranmere. Why the pink kit?*

Shaking hands at Ipswich where a Joe Jacobson penalty was saved in the last three minutes of a goalless draw.

Adebayo Akinfenwa can't believe referee Lee Swabey's decision to send him off at Oxford.

David 'Wheels' Wheeler celebrates a goal against Burton in customary style with Nnamdi Ofoborh and, background, Anthony Stewart.

David Wheeler's equaliser earns a point against Ipswich at Adams Park on New Year's Day.

Fireworks at Adams Park celebrate Wycombe entering 2020 on top of League One.

On-loan Rolando Aarons enjoys a joke as the squad poses for its second official team picture of the season.

Luke Matheson tackles Paul Smyth to give away the injury time penalty that earned Wycombe victory at home to Rochdale.

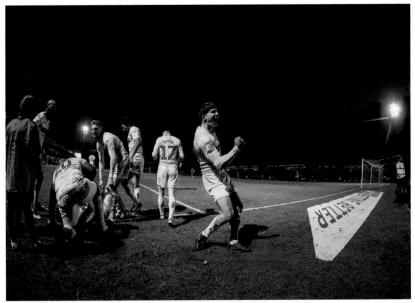

Here's what the goal means to the team, and Matt Bloomfield [right] especially.

'Judge' Rob Rinder, Sky Sports' Mark McEwan and Gareth Ainsworth endorsing Stonewall's Rainbow Laces campaign.

Thames Valley air ambulance lands at Adams Park when supporter Mark Bird was taken seriously ill before the match against Blackpool. He died later that evening.

Gareth Ainsworth shows off his 'Mark Bird – he's one of our own' shirt at MK Dons where a minute's applause sounded in his memory.

Jason McCarthy and Alex Samuel, the disciples.

The Vegan twins Darius Charles and Josh Parker greeted by fans outside Adams Park.

In full Beast mode, the remarkable Adebayo Akinfenwa.

Matt 'Mr Wycombe' Bloomfield in full flow, watched by Rolando Aarons.

Plotting a way through, 'Dobbo' Dobson and Gareth Ainsworth make their points on the touchline.

Akinfenwa's equaliser against Doncaster wasn't enough to prevent a 3-1 defeat, the last match before the virus hit.

David Stockdale in isolation at the training ground after complaining of a temperature and cough. Football shut down the next day.

The goal that never was – head of sports science Dave Wates scores against Hungerford in the Berks and Bucks Cup but the competition was annulled.

It's all balderdash. The winning card for the author and Dave Wates, completed with ten seconds to spare!

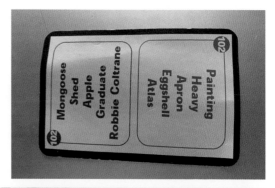

Missy and Rob Couhig mix with the fans in the Rebellion tent at Adams Park.

Adams Park erupts as Wycombe's supporters relish another remarkable victory.

centre-mid; it wasn't until I reached the under-16s that it was specified where you played.'

At age 21 Gape reached a crossroads at Southampton. He couldn't see a long-term future there, nor could they for him. 'I needed a loan move but at 21 with no experience I wasn't in a strong position. I was small for a central midfielder and I had to play in one of the most physical leagues out there.

'I believed I could cope because I enjoyed that side of the game. It got to deadline day and I was called by my agent. Southampton said they had accepted Wycombe's offer of a loan. It was a no-brainer.'

After a four-goal defeat at Luton, another four were conceded at Portsmouth on Gape's full debut. 'In the tunnel at Fratton it was relatively quiet, then I stepped out and the noise hit me. I said to myself, "This is it now, this is what it's all about." We lost but I had a good game and from those first two games I played every week until the end of my loan in January.

'Playing for the Saints' under-23s was an experience but there were 20 matches a season and they didn't mean a great deal. The emotions, the fans and the passion at Wycombe was like a drug for those six months. Having the feeling of being part of something real, I couldn't get enough of it.

'I came into a fantastic dressing room with a lot of good old pros and I hung on everything they said. For me the Wycombe loan was make or break as to whether I'd be a pro footballer. I was a sponge wanting to take in everything and thankfully the gaffer could see that, what type of person I was, how I'd play and I guess I was the kind of player he liked 100 per cent.'

* * *

Southampton recalled Dominic Gape at the end of his half-year loan but he wasn't prepared to drift. He told them so. Wycombe would have their man for a further two and a half years. Then the club drew Tottenham Hotspur in the fourth round of the FA Cup.

The coach pulled into White Hart Lane, Gape disembarked and was greeted with a bear-hug from Tottenham's manager Mauricio Pochettino, his former boss at Southampton. 'He said, "Dominic, how are you?" and embraced me. I'd only trained with the first team a bit but he was always great with the young lads and it was nice to know he thought that much of me.

'It was a crazy match – we led 3-2 with a couple of minutes to go, should have won and ended up losing 4-3. Poch asked me to come into his office where he was with his family and the coaches from Southampton, Jesus, Tony and Miguel. We sat around drinking tea and chatting like old friends. He didn't have to do it but it spoke volumes for the man he is.'

Gape had a dodgy spell after the Tottenham defeat, losing his touch for the first time in his life and having to deal with the weirdest sensation of his four-stroke engine hissing and spluttering. 'How could I go from playing really well to not doing well at all? Dobbo reassured me it happened with all young players. I didn't play much towards the end of that season and didn't deal well with it. I always struggled when I wasn't picked.

'One of the main reasons I started to study [a six-year, part-time Open University course in business management] was exactly because of my struggles if I felt I wasn't moving forward. I over-thought everything. Having an assignment to complete gave me the breathing space to think about something other than my form and our results.

'I'd been in a side that had over-achieved since I arrived. To do that meant getting the tiny details right, and mostly we did. The gaffer and Dobbo liked that – doing the small things a lot of people didn't want to do made us such a good team. If one of our team ran for 90 minutes, didn't touch the ball, but we won that was fine because everyone would do it.

'People looked at our results, saw who scored and made their minds up. We did score a lot from set pieces, a lot off the big man, people watched the highlights and branded us a long ball team but we didn't care. If we needed to play direct for 90 minutes and get a 1-0 win, 100 per cent we'd do that. If the game required us having to pick a lock and break a team down that way, we'd try to do that.

'Our philosophy was about how to win the game rather than worrying about this or that style.'

* * *

The defining campaign for Dominic Gape, the one over which he still broke out in goose-bumps, was the farewell to League Two in 2018 that ended with him fighting to hold back tears at Chesterfield's Proact Stadium. And not because his only goal of the season sparked scenes of mania.

This was the culmination of a cranky few months in which Wycombe shipped a lot of goals but time and again found a way to score more than the opposition. Adebayo Akinfenwa and Craig Mackail-Smith registered double figures, Paris Cowan-Hall, Luke O'Nien and Nathan Tyson chipped in regularly. A guy named Eberechi Eze, on loan from QPR, scored five times in 20 appearances then returned to Loftus Road and flowered into a talent that had Premier League scouts frothing at the mouth.

In January 2018 the Chairboys scored three goals or more in five of six games and on Saturday, 3 February Marcus Bean, a 33-year-old midfield player with a blind spot for goal, secured a 4-3 victory for ten men over Carlisle United at Adams Park, a blast from 25 yards that went into club folklore with the simple commentary line, "Bean with a shot!"

Gape said, 'We were behind in the 85th minute so many times and told each other, "We'll win this," and that spirit took us through. There were so many incredible moments, everyone talks about Chesterfield but few mention the week before.'

On Saturday, 21 April Wycombe were on the cusp of automatic promotion to League One – another pinch yourself moment in the club's almanac – when the leaders Accrington

Stanley arrived at Adams Park. Gape was picked to play at the base of a diamond but couldn't help prevent his side shipping two goals inside half an hour.

'I said to myself, "Keep trying to get on the ball," but for some reason I never had a pass on. We weren't comfortable with the formation and I ended up giving it away a few times trying to do the right thing. I was taken off after 37 minutes and felt I'd been punished for being too honest.

'If I'd hid and stood behind someone else maybe I wouldn't have been substituted, but I wouldn't have been trying to affect the game. I was embarrassed. I'd never been taken off before half-time at any level, but I was more upset that we lost 4-0, they were promoted and we still needed to win one of our last two to secure it.'

That evening Gape's phone rang off the hook. Richard Dobson asked the senior players to put their arms around the shoulder of a crestfallen team-mate. Matt Bloomfield called, as did Bayo Akinfenwa and Adam El-Abd. Gape had wanted to knock on Gareth Ainsworth's door and talk it through but the manager got to him first.

'The gaffer said he'd watched the game back and it wasn't my fault. He had to make a decision quickly. When you've been dragged off after 37 minutes you probably won't be playing the following week. I had one bad evening. Building up to Chesterfield, I had the bit between my teeth because I needed to put it right.'

* * *

In November 2017 Dominic Gape's fiancée Maggie had lost her mother Jane to terminal cancer. The date of Chesterfield v Wycombe – 28 April – was Jane's birthday. The night before the match Gape told Scott Kashket – the two shared rooms on away trips – he was going to score the next day. He hadn't scored all season. 'That's not me, saying that kind of stuff. It's more like Scotty who says he's going to score three every game.'

Maggie went to visit her mother's grave when the sun broke through at around 3pm on what had been interminably grey day. Later in the afternoon, her grandmother called to say her man had scored the winner at Chesterfield and Wycombe were going up. Maggie and her grandma went to dinner that evening and the harpist in the restaurant began to strum George and Ira Gershwin's 'Summertime'. The Ella Fitzgerald version had been sung at Jane's funeral.

> *'One of these mornings you're gonna rise up singing*
> *And you'll spread your wings and you'll take to the sky*
> *But till that morning, there ain't nothin' can harm you*
> *With daddy and mammy standin' by.'*

'It was a weird day in so many ways. I would love to have been with Maggie but she just wanted me to play. I didn't have a brilliant game, the ball bounced to me on the edge of the box near the end and I just hit it as hard as I could. I'm getting goose-bumps now. Look at my legs.

'There's a picture at the training ground of me grabbing my shirt after the goal. Even now, when I use the gym equipment, I get the same sensation every time I see it. The goal was the icing on a dream season, the things that happened, the results we had, the things we overcame.

'Bayo had been a massive part of our season; he dragged us through so many times and then he was injured and we didn't have him for the most important games. We were 1-0 down to an own goal at Chesterfield and, as we had done all year, we found a way to win. Results were crazy that day.'

Wycombe had become a League One club, seriously surpassing expectations and testing their financial resolve. Takeover talks shifted into gear, the players were in line for better returns on their contracts, everyone deserved more. The increasingly penniless trust were under serious pressure. Success had a price Wycombe couldn't afford.

And yet once more the club scraped a living and pulled rabbits from the hat. They were favoured for relegation and yet survived, despite a rocky period in the middle of the season when they couldn't buy a win; player numbers dwindled and those left had begun to feel as if they were trapped in a never-ending spiral.

The best £1,300 the club ever spent was that which chairman Trevor Stroud wrote off for the match at Southend over Easter. Ainsworth convinced Stroud that if his team were allowed to suck in some sea air it would end a run of four consecutive defeats. The purse strings were loosened, Ainsworth and Dobson took a ride on the pier-front rollercoaster on Friday evening and the following day's brace from Akinfenwa were perhaps the two most important goals of his many for the club.

Enough momentum was generated from that victory for Wycombe to win two of their final four matches and secure a second season in the third tier. More tough negotiations were required. Gape's contract was among a few expiring.

'I was 24 years old, played 150 games in three seasons, it was a case of, "I love it here, I love coming to work, I enjoy my job massively and had immense pride every time I played for Wycombe." It wasn't about not being happy, I was honest with the gaffer and the chairman all along, I didn't want to leave but if an opportunity came up to further my career and play at the next level I'd seriously consider it.

'In the summer there was so much talk and I didn't know what to believe. I was getting 100 calls a day asking where I was going and then it came to the end of the window and I didn't have an offer I felt was big enough to take me away from this place.

'I sat down and went through everything. I made the decision I wanted to stay. They were honest with the club's situation and I understood there was potential investment. If it hadn't been there and we were going to have a dogfight, I had no problem with that either.

'I could do a fight, especially under this manager with this staff. Then as the summer unfolded and the training improved I thought, "We've got a really good squad now and we're not thinking about where are we going to find a starting XI but about good players missing out completely."

'This season has been a dream. We've been doing everything our identity said we would do. We're not the highest earners, we don't have the biggest budget but we never say die and with those ingredients you can't go too far wrong. We could be sat here 15th and it would still be a good season for us.

'The year we went up we were seventh, fifth, fourth, third. When you come towards the end of the season a lot of things go out of the window. When you're in a relegation scrap you have to do everything you can to win games. You find out a lot about your team at this time of the year.

'There are so many teams who are unbelievable in August and September, with no points on the board, the pitches are immaculate, you're wearing your moulds, it's nice and warm, you're going to get the ball off the keeper and play total football, it's a dream.

'When you're in April, that's when the players who are mentally tough will still be doing the things that brought them success. It's easier said than done. You get teams that don't turn up, suddenly the results are strange, there's a battling bottom of the league team that is doing everything to win, against a team with incredible talent and the tough battling teams win. You're facing players in do-or-die mode who will do anything to win. Or there may be a team that needs to win and doesn't fully believe in its team-mates and that's when the cracks show.

'The closer we can get to the end of the season still in this position, the better we'll fare because there's 100 per cent trust in each other in this camp. We went through a terrible spell last year and it was still Wycombe the whole way. If we were going to fall out, bicker, play the blame game, we were going to be relegated because we were staring it in the face.

'We were conceding in the last minute, emotions were high, if we were going to crack, we'd have cracked then. We faced snowballing losses, looking down the league, people were gaining on us all the time and we still kept what we are and got the job done by being us.

'I speak to people about Wycombe, and when I tell them the dressing room is unbelievable I feel they don't understand it. I mean it 100 per cent.

'It's very rare for any human being to go into work every day and love what they do, especially on a Monday morning. But that's where I'm at and it's been like that for a while, it's not because we're winning. I can't think I've ever woken up and said, "I don't want to go in today."'

* * *

Over the Christmas period of 2019, Dominic Gape's love of the football life was being properly tested. There was only so much bending, stretching and spectating he could endure. He was redundant for both the Coventry and Ipswich matches, two fixtures to be celebrated more for how far Wycombe had come than the once mighty had fallen.

Wycombe had not lost at home, Coventry had not won away, so both sides were laying claim to the most absurd League One statistic. Watching the analytical expertise of Josh Hart in the manager's room on the eve of the Sky Blues' arrival, it was clear they would pose a distinct threat. Gareth Ainsworth's Siri went off in mid-conversation and, quick as a flash, he asked, 'Siri how do you beat Coventry?' That threw it.

There was another shuffling of counters on the tactics board. The manager needed to get a clear thought in his head about how best to utilise his resources, hoping that the advantage of Wycombe's relatively tight pitch and a potent crowd would lift the team from its festive torpor.

The last thing Ainsworth said to his players as they left the dressing room was not to do anything stupid early on, stay tight, narrow and concentrated. Darius Charles needed another rest and with him went so much organisational prowess. Sido Jombati continued to deputise for Jack Grimmer at right-back and Nnamdi Ofoborh was having to learn his trade at the sharpest of sharp ends.

The first quarter of an hour would be an eloquent summation of the hesitation suddenly prevalent in the ranks. Was the fact they led the table for so long becoming an impediment? It was four months inside the top two now and there was bound to be some wear and tear in the head.

Week in and week out, they were having to protect a lead that leapt between three and seven points, one point forward, two back. The manager said opposition teams were eyeing them differently in the tunnel.

Coventry had an astonishing 50 players in their squad, yet no home of their own. There was hardly enough white space on the back of the programme to fit all the names in, and double-spacing was used to make Wycombe's 28 stretch that bit further.

With such numerical excess, how Coventry had gone five months without a win away from their temporary home of St Andrews in Birmingham became an increasing mystery as the match progressed. Not in that time could they have been treated to the freedoms Wycombe presented.

Bayo Akinfenwa equalised after Sam McCallum's early strike from a gift when Ofoborh tried to play out from the back and Matt Bloomfield slipped, running on his pass. Then Wycombe gave away a calamitous penalty. Jombati had plenty of time to clear his lines, turned back towards his own goal, under-hit a back pass and tripped Matt Godden. He should have been sent off (an instinct confirmed by the referee's assessor at half-time).

By then Coventry led 3-1. Godden was on his way to a hat-trick, confirmed by the best goal I'd seen all season that comprised a quick ball forward from Liam Kelly, Jordan Shipley's flick with the outside of his foot and the striker's first-time finish.

David Wheeler, the most unflappable guy, was booked for a foul late on and told referee Kevin Johnson he was playing a guessing game. 'I was as angry with our performance as I was with myself and the referee and I knew that when I challenged the guy the ref was looking the other way. He said he'd seen it. I hated it when people didn't tell the truth.'

Ainsworth talked of 'fundamental errors that are foreign to us' and that he was 'big enough to take whatever stick is going to come. These lads will run through brick walls for me but we need to find our legs again. My job is to get results, I totally understand that.'

For his opposite number Mark Robins, the importance of such a victory could not be downplayed. His boys passed it to feet, whereas Wycombe passed to where they hoped feet might be. 'We had to prepare for this differently to any other match and we responded with our best football of the season.

'The job that Gareth has done here is really amazing, they're probably worse off [in a financial sense] than we are and yet he has a team that sprints, runs, covers and throws themselves in front of the ball. They do the ugly side of the game so well.'

* * *

Even Bodger, the Wycombe mascot, was getting ants in his pants. He was seated in the home dug out for a picture with the smaller match-day mascots when he was tugged on the sleeve and his place taken by Paul Lambert, once Wycombe's boss and now Ipswich's for the foreseeable future. It took a lot to wipe the painted smile from his face but I had a sense that behind the mask Bodger didn't like being budged.

Lambert was, by contrast, laughing all the way to the bank. The day before he returned to Adams Park he signed a five-year extension to his contract at Portman Road, not bad for a manager whose team had been stuffed five at Lincoln three days earlier.

This had turned into a massively important New Year's Day fixture for both sides. Wycombe had lost three on the spin and didn't want to ape the previous season's four-loss Christmas calamity. Ipswich hadn't won in the league since Bonfire Night. The clamour at the top of League One was becoming more extreme by the day.

Ainsworth demanded honesty from his players in that those who wanted to play but were carrying a knock came clean. 'Tell me, tell any of us if you're not right. We're stretched, we know why we're stretched but we can't afford to take unnecessary risks.' The loss of Curtis Thompson, who struggled for longer than he should with his hip against Coventry, was clearly a case in point.

'I want to try something against Ipswich, nothing mental, but in attack, very explosive, getting forward, go. I want to have one in the space, a little Jack Russell, which is a good analogy for this player, an Irish Jack Russell, who never stops yapping. Paul Smyth, I want you clipping heels, getting the ball back, and when we do we can run at people and that's what's going to happen.' With that in mind, Alex Samuel would lead the line rather than Adebayo Akinfenwa.

'This is a new decade, a new start, new people coming into the club and no matter what happens tomorrow we're going to still be top of the league. Come on.'

This mattered to all, but it mattered to Matt Bloomfield more than most. Ipswich had been Blooms's only other club and he coached in Suffolk as he worked towards his UEFA licences. He had played for Lambert at Wycombe through the toughest of times.

'I was 24 and my contract was running down – Paul was the manager – it looked as if we were going to get into the play-offs that year and who knew what the future held from there. I had interest from elsewhere but before I knew it – typical me – I was into a full-blooded tackle, my cruciate went at home to Darlington. The doctors thought I'd just done my medial ligaments, Paul was keen for me to be fit for the play-offs so I went in for the op and when I woke up they said, "Sorry it was the medial and cruciate and you'll be out for nine months."

'I went from a young, aspiring professional who was invincible to "this all could get taken away from me at any point". I decided to take a journalism degree, professional sports writing and broadcasting at Stafford University, because from that point forward if the game was ever taken away I wanted to earn something and provide for any future family I might be lucky enough to have. I found it therapeutic to write. My first port of call at the end of my career could be coaching but you could never be too prepared.'

I stood at the head of the tunnel as Bloomfield gathered his troops on Wednesday, 1 January 2020. There was a real look in his eye. On the pitch, he was thumping his fist into his hand before the warm-up began in earnest. He did it for about two minutes – I had not seen him this animated before a match.

Wycombe should have been ahead after five minutes. Samuel gnawed at a defender and crossed low where the Jack Russell was on his own at the far post, two yards out. Smyth had to keep his eye on the ball until it made contact with his boot and it was a certain goal. But he half turned as if beginning his celebration and swept it the wrong side of the post.

Composure in critical moments had begun to betray Wycombe and the rest of the first half was played on the edge of everyone's nerves. Free kicks were routinely delayed for so long you had forgotten what they had been given for and so it was a joy when Ipswich took a quick one in the 54th minute. Luke Garbutt's cross caught the entire defence unawares and James Norwood headed, unchallenged, into the net.

Akinfenwa was soon warming up and within two minutes of replacing Smyth he flicked the ball on, Samuel was poleaxed on the edge of the area and David Wheeler nipped in to flick the loose ball over Will Norris into the net. It secured a second draw between the sides in six weeks.

The teams had barely left the field before Rob Couhig bounded on with his extended family to press a button that would set off a New Year's firework display in the car park. He asked for the crowd to join him in a countdown from ten to one – 'which happens to be our position in the league'.

The manager undertook his familiar bound around the pitch, acknowledging support from all four corners, shook hands with the entire Ipswich team and was about to disappear down the tunnel when one of his own fans approached screaming, 'Fuck you Ainsworth.'

'We'd lost one game at home all season and that was the thanks I got. I looked the fella in the eye and I think if he could have got to me, he'd have hit me.'

The League One season may have been mad but this was taking madness to a new and menacing level.

A Singular Goalkeeper

RYAN Allsop put his hand up to play in goal when he was four, a year younger than his elder son Charlie – a blond, blue-eyed spitting image – was in 2020. On reflection would he do it again? He proffered a half smile. 'There are times when I would. Then there are the other times.'

Goalkeepers lived a life apart and Ryan 'Rocky' Allsop was no different than anyone else in this association of the slightly scrambled. It was not easy – or sensible – for anyone other than a goalkeeper to understand why someone would *want* to volunteer to play between the posts with its entirely ludicrous pressures and responsibilities.

Allsop said that in the 2018/19 season, when Wycombe survived in League One against distinct odds, he counted three mistakes in 41 appearances – against Luton at home, Sunderland at home and Scunthorpe away. He was genuinely shocked to learn before the new campaign that a caste of supporters suggested he was a weak link and the manager should look around for a replacement. 'I deleted Twitter a long time ago. Now I know why.'

In fairness the debate took hold as signings rolled in through the initial heady days of the anticipated Couhig takeover. Each squad position was addressed except the one many supporters felt the most important, which conveniently overlooked the fact that Cameron Yates, Allsop's 20-year-old understudy, had signed a new contract.

In the first four months of the campaign, Allsop made several head-turning saves, the pick coming in the frenzied sixth minute of added time against Peterborough when he spun on his axis in the six-yard box to pull off a terrific stop from Mo Eisa to secure a 3-3 draw. A late one-handed upward lunge to deny Sunderland's Aidan McGeady was another 'worldie'.

As he leapt through the autumn damp in a distinctive black jersey, comparisons began to be drawn between Rocky and the Russian Lev Yashin, who always wore that colour and was rated the finest in his era. By the new year the side were shipping goals and he was being picked apart – such were the vicissitudes of the goalkeeper's life.

Why 'Rocky' was the inevitable question? I presumed he was a Sylvester Stallone fan or his parents were devotees of the 60s US cartoon *Rocky and Bullwinkle*. It was quite a nickname to bear, not least if he should have a dodgy spell and 'the rock crumbles' clichés multiplied. The story of how Ryan became Rocky and never went back to being Ryan was instead quite inspirational.

When Ryan Allsop was delivered at the Queen Elizabeth Hospital in Birmingham on 17 June 1992 he was premature and placed on the critical list. Baby Ryan couldn't breathe without assistance and had suffered a collapsed lung. He required intensive care for days. 'I was on 100 per cent oxygen. I got through that though the doctors didn't think I would.

'Inside a couple of weeks I contracted meningitis and almost died from that too. One of the nurses decided to call me Rocky because I was such a fighter. When I went to school everyone called me Rocky. I can't remember anyone ever calling me Ryan.'

He recalled that his mum Dawn thought for quite a long time in his childhood that he might be deaf. 'My parents used to bang pots and pans behind me and I wouldn't react, I just carried on playing with my toys. I had to go for hearing tests but they never found anything wrong.'

Turning a deaf ear to complaints about their performance from any quarter was the prerequisite of any goalkeeper. Rocky would not be the last in his position to say that, when it came to the finer points of his art, most people didn't have a clue what they were talking about.

The ooohs and aahs, the 'fucking get on with it!', the 'you're shit, aaaahhhh!!!' nonsense from the imbeciles behind the goal, the general ribald cacophony in football grounds, was all noise. He had never really taken that much notice, though at one stage in the season he would react to it to profound effect.

From the time he was a little lad with Beacon Colts in Birmingham, Rocky simply wanted to do his best and – not in a malevolent way – resented those who picked holes in him mostly through ignorance.

Like many goalkeepers he lived a nomadic lifestyle, shunted around clubs and to the odd different country – in his case an Icelandic outpost – seeking the consistency and acceptance that might allow him to settle. He hoped to have found it at Wycombe but needed to keep on his yellow-booted toes.

* * *

Rocky Allsop was a Brummie, a bluenose, a Birmingham City fan and so, in Wycombe, he at least landed at the club with the perfect colour scheme. It was an irony not lost on him that he was on the books in some form or another of every West Midlands club, except the one he truly loved.

Trials came and went at Coventry City – too prohibitive cost-wise for his mum Dawn to keep driving him there and back – Aston Villa (where he stayed for six weeks) and then to Wolverhampton Wanderers, who also took him on a six-week trial and after his first training session wanted him to sign there and then.

The association didn't last too long and the next stop was Walsall. 'They messed me around a lot and I said to my parents, "I just want to go and play with my mates."'

He joined another local club, Rushall Athletic, but told his father Colin he thought he was better than their level. 'Dad called West Bromwich Albion and talked about me and I was invited to a community session. My parents paid for it but after the first go the guy in charge gave them the money back. They wanted me to have a trial.'

At 15 he was playing for Albion's under-16s when, a couple of months into the season, he was promoted to the under-18s side, an elevating experience in every way. 'The under-18s was a bit of a golden age, we had a great crop of youngsters. But we took a bit of a hammering at Nottingham Forest one day, lost 4-2 and I was pretty down.

'That night the academy manager Mark Harrison rang. I thought he was going to have a go, but he said, "Are you sitting down?" I said, "No, why?" He said I'd been called up by England for a Nordic tournament in Sweden. I just went very quiet.' Rocky made five England appearances and kept four clean sheets.

His domestic career was in a state of regular upheaval, which was never easy for any teenager, especially a goalkeeper. From Albion he went to Millwall, where he stayed for a few months until he was released at 19, just when he thought he'd be given an improved deal. 'They had David Ford as the first-team goalie, Steve Mildenhall in reserve and then signed Mike Taylor as well, so I was released.

'I spent three days at home when my agent called and said, "What do you think about Iceland?"'

* * *

'What do you mean Iceland?' Rocky Allsop asked in the same way he might have said, 'What do you mean Aldi?' His agent explained the finer details of the move and said he should try it for a couple of months and then return for trials in England with greater experience under his belt.

Three days from the call sounding him out about trying his hands abroad, Rocky flew to Iceland already knowing he was in the first team the next day for IF Hottur, a club he assumed was from the country's capital Reykjavik. He trained with the squad that evening, was driven to a hotel and told he'd be taken to an apartment after the match the next day.

'I had an unbelievable game and the team was buzzing for me. I said, "Is someone going to take me back to my hotel?" They said, "No, no, no, we're flying now." "Where to?" We flew across the entire country to the Austurland region. The coach said the population was 3,000, everyone knew each other and I'd be fine."'

Rocky shared an apartment with American trialist Kris Byrd. 'There were no TV channels in English so we sat there chatting the first night and there was a knock on the door. It was one of our team-mates, who said, "Get changed there's a house party." We didn't know anyone there, but we were involved straight away. As time went by, I absolutely loved it. I don't think I'd be playing football now if I hadn't gone there. I was getting games and was really match sharp.'

IF Hottur, based in Egilssataoir, played in the Icelandic second division. 'By the end of ten matches the top clubs in Iceland were asking me to play for them, but I decided to come back to England. Maybe I was a bit naïve. My agent thought I should have more trials back home, and if nothing came of them I could always go back.' He never did.

Allsop was a free agent after his release from Millwall. The two clubs most keen were Bournemouth and Leyton Orient. He went to Brisbane Road where he was one of five trailists, alongside goalkeepers from Manchester City, Everton, Stoke City, West Ham United and Sunderland.

'The other lads were in a hotel and I was put up at the ground. I was walking in for training one morning when the goalkeeping coach told me I wasn't to tell the others but they wanted to offer me terms. I signed for Orient.

'They had Jamie Jones and Lee Butcher, who was injured, and they signed me to be second choice and said they could only give me a six-month contract. I think the idea was to keep me on until Butcher came back and then get rid of me, but I ended up playing the first match of the season because Jones was injured.

'We won on penalties [in the League Cup] against Charlton, and then Russell Slade [the manager] pulled me aside and said they were bringing Jones back against Everton at Goodison Park in the next round. He [Jones] was a big Everton fan but we lost 5-0 and he hurt his shoulder so I played the next league game, did well and Slade kept me in.

'In January my contract was up. Bournemouth and Bristol City put deals on the table. Eddie Howe had just gone back to Bournemouth as manager in League One, they'd won nine in a row, were just outside the play-offs and I spoke to my agent who persuaded me to sign for them for two and a half years. I stayed five.

'Eddie was unbelievable, his knowledge and tactical understanding, his ability to get the best out of people and improve people was second to none. If you bought into him, did what he said and took everything you could from him, he'd get the very best from you, he was that good. His sessions reflected that. He improved me as a goalkeeper, both him and Neil Moss, the goalkeeping coach. They were brilliant.'

Loan spells became a staple of Allsop's Bournemouth career when after contracting glandular fever he couldn't break back into the side. He would be bounced from Coventry to Wycombe, Portsmouth, Blackpool and Lincoln. From Blackpool, he could at least take a flight to Bournemouth to see his wife Sophie, but there was no straightforward way to get back to the south coast from Lincoln.

'Logistically, it was worse because you couldn't fly and the train took five hours. Driving was four and a half. I was living in Lincoln and going back to Birmingham as often as I could [where both sets of parents lived so his wife could meet him halfway]. That was a very difficult year but it's what we had to do. I needed the work.'

That work would include playing at Wembley for Lincoln and keeping a clean sheet in its EFL Trophy victory over Shrewsbury Town in April 2018. Allsop suspected he would be released by Bournemouth that close season and was enthralled when Wycombe pounced to sign him on a permanent deal.

He would become the club's number-one choice. His first season would go pretty well, the three mistakes aside. In his second, Rocky would endure more than he could ever have imagined.

* * *

It was the third week of the season and Andy Fairman, laptop under arm, marched into the common room where I had taken up temporary residence. Ryan Allsop was a step or two behind him. The goalkeeping coach and his most important asset had some finer points of performance to mull over.

I stayed for a few minutes before they realised I was within earshot and asked if I'd mind giving them a bit of privacy. I said of course, but that what they said so far was intriguing and I hoped they didn't mind that I'd made a note of it. Both said that was fine.

The specific moment they discussed was Fleetwood Town's equaliser two minutes from time at the Highbury Stadium when the ball skied into the Wycombe area, there was a headed touch that bounced from Rocky's grasp and Paddy Madden swept the ball in. Two points gone.

RA, 'I know it looks shit to the untrained eye but I was trying to stop the thing going through my fucking legs.' AF, 'I've looked at it 30 times and often it didn't look nice.' RA, 'At the time I thought that's not going to look nice but it's a fucking reaction. It's come quick, I've tried to get my knees down and my hands as well. I thought, "It's going to go through my fucking legs."'

AF, 'what happened was that last little stride meant you had no alternative as all your body weight was going a different way.' RA, 'I didn't know he was going to smash it there. Dobbo said a load of errors preceded it, bad marking at a throw-in, letting the player get a cross in the first place. The defence should have got higher quicker.'

In the pre-match warm-up, a couple of Wycombe players said they felt Rocky wasn't quite himself. Fairman put that to him. 'As long as I know in myself that I'm doing everything right, we move on. I think last season it would have festered but I don't feel like it's affecting me now.' AF, 'You've been brilliant this season but it's about consistency.' RA, 'There's no doubt in my mind that I can do two games in a week.'

A goalkeeper more than any other player in the squad would need a constant, caring management. I would find that during the season I had more interaction with Rocky than any player, be it at the breakfast table on away trips, at the training ground or after matches when I felt it was appropriate to break his contemplative mood.

Maybe because my best friend and best man Sean Rafter had played in goal for Southend, Leicester and Leyton Orient before a serious back injury curtailed his career, I felt an affinity with goalkeepers more than players in any other position. I knew a little of the mental horrors they went through.

'Keepers made mistakes, it happened. I wasn't a robot. I felt that people often formed an opinion of you based on what other people told them and often a small amount of people made a lot of noise, but if you asked them about last season and could they have named a game where I was horrendous, or made a mistake, 90 per cent wouldn't be able to tell you one. I could tell you [the Luton, Sunderland, Scunthorpe threesome].

'Fleetwood, I didn't class that as a mistake. I know how it looked on the basic highlights, as if I tried to gather it in but people don't understand goalkeeping. That wasn't a header I could have held onto – it was a reaction save. And sometimes you couldn't control where the ball was going to go. I don't think commentators in this country have helped goalkeepers either because they formed a lot of opinions on what goalkeepers should be doing and doing better. It was never as black and white as they made it out to be.'

Talking of black and white, like many professionals these days Rocky Allsop – the palest player in the squad – had tattoos halfway up one arm. 'I didn't like them and I didn't really like the quote – "learn from yesterday, live for today, hope for tomorrow." I had it when I was 18. I just wanted a tattoo.

'It was a phase when you were growing up. I had roses either side. I liked those. My dad had tattoos when he was younger but he hated them now. He never wanted me to have them, but I was adamant. I had a couple of additions – my boys' initials on my shins. CJ and HJ for Charlie Jacob and Harry Jude.'

The boys came to all the home games with mum Sophie, as did Rocky's parents. They had seen so many matches down the years and remained as supportive as you would expect, especially given the precariousness of the position their son played in.

I remembered Rocky mentioning that when his mum started to read *A Life Too Short* about the German goalkeeper Robert Enke who had committed suicide when the sport became too much for him, she wanted him to change his position. 'If you let it [your performance] fester and get on top of you, it could be a horrendous place to be.

'I started to read the book again on one occasion to get an insight and then I put it down. I talked my game through with my parents and my wife. To be honest, my dad was never pushy or over critical. He preferred to be on his own watching a game, in the corner, standing up but quite liked it now in a box with the kids.

'If I played well, he just said, "You did well today." If I had a bad game, I'd say I should have done this and that but he'd tell me I did something else well. My mum praised me no matter what. Sophie was the same as my dad. I'd say I should have done better with the goal and she'd say, "It happens."'

Did mistakes linger longer than they once had? 'For a weekend yes. On days off until I could get back to training again they annoyed me. I was snappier at home. A lot of the time things could look bad when they weren't as bad as they seemed.

'It was constantly up and down. I don't think people realised the emotions we went through as footballers. If I made a mistake there was no one more annoyed than me. Anyone could swear at you and call you shit but ultimately they weren't as upset as I was. I was in a lot better head space now than I had been in terms of things like that and not letting what other people said get to me. I deleted Twitter the first time I was here because if you read the good you couldn't stop yourself reading the bad.'

* * *

The day Rocky Allsop would make national newspaper headlines started like many others. He tended to be one of the first down to breakfast. I asked to join him a couple of times and he always said yes. We chewed the fat a little before he was into his usual routine: team meeting, preparation, warm down with Andy Fairman and Cameron Yates, then the match itself.

For the first time in the season Wycombe would feature live on television as the Sky Sports cameras were in town for the league match against Tranmere Rovers at Prenton Park. The teams swapped ends after the toss and Rocky would spend the first half defending the goal in front of the noisy bulk of home fans.

Immediately he was aware of a lone raised voice spouting particularly shocking words. 'Honestly every 30 seconds or minute this bloke was calling out. It wasn't the usual "you're shit" or "you're a knob" but he was shouting, "faggot" and "nonce".

'I turned around and he was standing directly behind one of the massive cameras. I said, "Mate, there's a camera there that can pick up every word you're saying. You can't keep saying that."

'He stared me in the face and screamed, "Fuck off, you faggot," like he wanted to kill me.'

Rocky managed to maintain his concentration until half-time. Two goals in a minute before the interval had given Wycombe a deserved lead, Gareth Ainsworth wanted his side to nail down the advantage and was in full flow. The goalkeeper wasn't taking in a word he was saying.

'I was absolutely raging. This guy had really riled me. I kept thinking if I should report what I'd heard. I walked straight into the referee as we came out of the dressing room and said to him, "The amount of homophobic abuse I've been getting from behind the goal is a disgrace."

'After the match I was told to do an instant report with Kelly [Francis] and she said an officer from the Wirral might come and take a statement from me in person but that never happened. I don't even know what happened to the guy who abused me.'

In *The Times* the following Tuesday, Rocky's stand was celebrated by writer Matthew Syed. 'It would have been easy for him to have ignored it and got on with the game. Instead he decided that homophobia is the responsibility of anyone, gay or straight, a scourge we can all play a part in beating. The fan was arrested by Merseyside police and will be examined under due process and should be presumed innocent but this was a watershed moment.

'This was a player, a role model, taking on those who seek to perpetuate hate, to perpetuate stigma and to perpetuate the unease that many experience when they attend football matches. This was a player taking a stand against a blight that characterises not only so much of the rest of the world but bastions of our own society.'

It was a fulsome article with one disfiguring blemish. The paper chose to use a picture of Allsop dressed in a pink kit he hadn't worn for the best part of a year. It wasn't in the club's official 2019/20 colour scheme. There were hundreds of pictures to choose from and *The Times* selected this one. Why? It was almost as if they were making a snide insinuation against the very person Syed championed. Some clever clogs sub-editor obviously thought he was having a laugh.

Gareth Ainsworth was fuming when he saw the illustration, worried about the underlying interpretation. Allsop simply said, 'Yes, I saw the picture,' but wondered if there was an implicit message in it every bit as wicked as the abuse he had not put up with.

'I felt like some of the reporting afterwards was trying to suggest I was gay. There was a desperation in certain sections of the media to find a gay footballer. No one came out and said it but it seemed to me there was an undercurrent in the reporting. The way things were worded.

'If there was a gay footballer who was gay and he wanted to come out he would in his own time. It was up to people to do what they wanted to do, not be forced into anything.

'I had a family, a wife and two children. My wife was fine with it, she laughed a bit, but the reports could have hurt someone who wasn't as strong-minded as she is. It could have been damaging to a relationship.'

There was an extra layer of sensitivity to the story unknown to any reporter. Rocky's wife's sister Sarah had a female partner, Gemma, and they had a baby boy Ralphie. 'It was a subject I was more familiar with than many other people knowing what my sisters-in-law had had to go through. If me standing up for what was right was going to help in any way – and not just them but other people in their position – I was glad I did what I did. I wouldn't want my little nephew growing up and thinking that people speaking in a terrible way about his parents was somehow OK.

'If the guy had called me shit, well I got that every week. People saw words differently. I just felt that the word he used was so derogatory. I'd rather he'd called me a c***. Hands down. He used one of the lowest words you could call a person.

'The situation went far beyond racial abuse, homophobic abuse, abuse in general. I went to work on a Saturday to play football and was abused every week, as were most players, but goalkeepers probably got it worse because of how close they were to the crowd. Just because it was considered normal did that make it right?

'I didn't go to Tesco for my shopping and as the check-out lady pushed my loaf of bread through the scanner said, "You're fucking shit, hurry up." I'd get arrested.

'I heard there were people on social media sticking up for the bloke at Tranmere saying things like they didn't hear it and that I should man up. My first thought was, "How could you not hear it?" because it was so clear.

'And secondly it was more than "manning up" wasn't it? That was such an old-fashioned phrase. People said, "it's just name calling" or "it's just banter". It was more than the words it was the aggressive nature of the people who used them. It was like they wanted a reaction. And we were expected to ignore it.'

I wondered if, in retrospect, Allsop had any second thoughts about getting involved in the first place. There was not a single case of a player in the league during the season reporting such behaviour except him. Surely his was not an isolated incident? The only one.

'I did occasionally wonder if I'd done the right thing. I just didn't want my wife and children to look back on this and be hurt by it, and that people might say derogatory things to them.

'When we played Tranmere at home later on I heard a few comments. Someone called me a grass. Playground stuff really. These were grown men, not kids, men with families who had come to the football – well, just come and watch then. You didn't have to abuse someone for doing their job. I understood people were passionate but you shouldn't be allowed to go around thinking you can say whatever you want to people.

'If they saw me doing my shopping or walking the dog would they have the bollocks to say the same to my face?'

* * *

A very different ton of bricks landed on Rocky Allsop when he was dropped for the Blackpool game on Tuesday, 28 January, an evening that would enter Wycombe folklore for so many heart-rending reasons. Gareth Ainsworth announced the team at the training ground the previous day and David Stockdale immediately put his arm across the shoulders of the man he was replacing. It didn't do an awful lot to ease the hurt.

No goalkeeper was immune to a dip in form, be it his own edginess or the cumulative effect of players in front of him engaged in collective floundering. Between mid-December and mid-January, Rocky may have let his positioning, kicking, decisiveness and thus confidence slide. He was the only one who would really know. We could only stand on the side-lines and finger-point.

He had played in the first 27 first-team fixtures and conceded 31 goals, of which 17 arrived in a flurry in the last seven. The manager was concerned that across the board his players weren't winning enough aerial duels. The facts bore him out and Rocky's reluctance to impose himself in his own area was reckoned to have been exacerbating the problem.

The arrival of Stockdale on loan from Birmingham City was a real jolt to his system. Every squad needed shaking up now and again and the fact that Wycombe had played three matches without a reserve goalkeeper after Cameron Yates was injured at Bisham Abbey in a training routine required a decisive remedy.

What blindsided Allsop was Stockdale replacing him in the first team before he had shaken hands with everyone in the place. He was straight into the side and back into the fans' affections. 'Stocko' gave the coaches a double fist-pump as he walked past their room at the training ground to finalise the detail on his loan period for the rest of the season.

The hiatus would last two matches against Blackpool and MK Dons when Stockdale was beaten three times, twice down to his right-hand side. Allsop was restored for the home game against Bristol Rovers. Even after a few weeks of contemplation, he hurt.

'Do you want me to be completely honest?' I replied I'd rather he was.

'I got told Stocko was coming in and I didn't feel like he had to fight for it. I hadn't put a foot wrong, I was having the season of my life, I had kept the most clean sheets in the league, and what more could I have done? I trained hard every day, did all my gym work and had been a good professional. It wasn't down to me that we started to concede goals, there was a massive picture involved.

'It very much felt like I was being shouldered with the blame. Whether or not it was the case it was how I felt. I disagreed with the decision as anyone in my position would have.

'No one knew I was going to come back into the team because you didn't expect Stocko to make those errors. To my mind I was out of the team and wasn't getting my place back because of his quality. My predicament was I was dropped for no reason. The gaffer and I had a chat about it and I wasn't saying anything to you I didn't say to him, but he was the manager, it was his decision. Whether I agreed or not, whether I felt it was right or wrong, ultimately it wasn't my decision.

'I'd been happy with my performances. Maybe team-wise it hadn't gone as well as we'd have liked in recent matches but that was the way of football.

'I wasn't understood by everyone here. They couldn't read me. For a goalkeeper confidence was massive, and all I wanted was assurance that when I'd done well it would be noted. Someone would say, "You did that really well." I think things got taken for granted when you were a goalkeeper. You made good saves and it was my job. When Bayo scored a worldie, it was, "Fucking lovely Bayo." That was his job, how was that different?

'I didn't make it easy for people when I came out of the team but why should I? I hadn't jeopardised anything in the team, I backed Stocko, I did all I needed to do, training-wise, gym-wise, I was good with the lads so why should I then have been nicey-nicey about something I *strongly* disagreed with.

'As much as I was off with it in the first place, as much as it angered me, the gaffer put me back in when he could have been stubborn and not recalled me. He could have made it easier for himself by sticking with his decision and only have one annoyed goalkeeper.

'It wasn't easy for Stocko to be taken out of the team so quickly and for him to be so supportive said a lot about him as a person – a great guy, jokey and very caring. He was good to have around.'

* * *

The goalkeeping coach was a belated phenomenon. Gordon Banks didn't have one, neither did Peter Shilton nor Bob Wilson. That wasn't to decry their value but to wonder what had made goalkeepers so important they required specialist advice. Once one club employed one – much like a kid's toy – everyone had to have one.

In Andy Fairman, Wycombe had a man who served at every conceivable level except playing professionally. He had been employed in the UK and the USA, set up his own coaching business, worked with a number of brilliant members of his ilk, survived for a while at Blackpool under the wretched Oyston dynasty, been a trusted team member for personalities as varied as Ian Holloway, Roberto Martinez and Sam Allardyce and had not wasted a moment perfecting his craft.

He was denied a professional career because though he was a big lad at 12, by the time he was 16 – having spent time at Blackburn and Blackpool – most of the kids he knew had shot past him height-wise. He was getting battered every week in non-league football and wondered why he should have to put up with physical intimidation when there might be better money to earn in a slightly less bone-breaking atmosphere.

Fairman's initiative called Super Soccer coaching for seven to 11 year olds in Lancashire was followed by a period in Chicago, where he delivered summer soccer camps and offered private tuition for aspiring goalkeepers before the catastrophe of the 9/11 attacks and his lack of a working visa meant he had to come home and pick up the threads in Lancashire. In between stacking shelves at his local Sainsbury's, he set up a goalkeeper coaching business in Leyland and had enough success coaching young girls that he was invited to join Blackburn Rovers' Centre of Excellence.

His professional break came when he moved back to Blackpool to run the CoE, from where two graduates made the first team, and when Holloway was appointed manager in 2009 and the club were promoted to the Premier League, the goalkeepers asked if the manager would consider a full-time goalkeeping coach and raved about Fairman's sessions. He became a full-time member of the staff.

'The times with Ian were great, very eccentric and lively and sometimes chaotic. Steve Thompson his assistant and me would have the sessions all planned, Ian would bounce in, rub his hands and say, "Okay guys, off to the greasy spoon on the prom," and we'd all march off to the seafront for fun and games on the beach.

'Though we had a tough season in the Premier [League], Ian always tried to keep things upbeat. I remember Charlie Adam coming in after we'd conceded late in the first half against Liverpool and he began to apologise. Ian gave him a right bollocking: "You never, ever apologise to your team-mates, you've been fantastic, you've made one mistake, you've been awesome this season, keep your head high, you've all been brilliant." There was never any negativity.

'We were relegated in the last game against Manchester United but no one had given us a chance because of our budget, so I'd been in that fight before. I said to Gareth [Ainsworth] a few times, Blackpool were the only dressing room that came anywhere close to the one we had at Wycombe. That season, though, some of the boys who came in the January window started to form little cliques. I think that was the demise of the team.

'At the end of the season we called a meeting and half the boys were in tears. They knew it would never be the same again wherever they went. I'd never been involved in anything like that in terms of how hard it was. Then I had a row with [Karl] Oyston. I was travelling with the first team, looking after the reserves and part of my contract was to do the academy as well.

'I couldn't be with the first team in Newcastle and coaching at the academy at the same time. Oyston said I was ripping him off because I was taking payment for both. He was looking for a loophole to get rid of me. I knew my time was done.'

Fairman contacted a number of clubs but his CV [mostly coaching girls and at grass roots] and no experience as a player at professional level was a distinct disadvantage. Out of the blue, Wigan Athletic offered him a trial and it helped that he spotted Slovak Marko Marosi training at Burnley college and recommended him to the club. Wigan liked what they saw.

From an initial role with the under-18s and 23s, Fairman soon worked hand in glove with Inaki Bergara, Roberto Martinez's first-team goalkeeping coach. The club was relegated from the Premier League but won the FA Cup, where the 33-year-old was a support member of staff on the Wembley bench.

Martinez was being tempted by the manager's position at Goodison Park and had spoken to Fairman about joining his staff there as under-23 coach and supporting the first team. On the same day as that conversation, a call came from Matt Gilks, a goalkeeper who worked with him at Blackpool, saying that the Tangerines' new boss Paul Ince was interested in taking Fairman to Bloomfield Road as first-team goalkeeping coach. He said yes to Everton.

'I loved every minute working there. Tim Howard was the number one and I saw how he worked with Bergara. It was quite a golden period for the under-23s, lads like Ryan Ledson, Matt Pennington, and Luke Garbett. A young goalkeeper called Jordan Pickford from Sunderland arrived on the scene.

'David Unsworth coached the under-23s, old school, very demanding, high expectations. If you fell short he let you know. Then Roberto left and Ronald Koeman was appointed. I covered for Patrick Lodewijks, his first-team goalkeeping coach who had a medical condition. Then Sam Allardyce came in and brought Martin Margetson as his goalkeeping coach.

'I'd done my [UEFA] B Licence with Martin a few years before and when we were re-introduced, he said, "I remember your crossing session from that course, it was one of the real highlights." And there was I a nobody.' By March 2018 with the political situation at Goodison worsening, Fairman departed. Allardyce and Margetson left two months later.

* * *

Wycombe Wanderers had advertised for a goalkeeping coach in early 2018 when Barry Richardson moved to Hull City. Andy Fairman applied and there was no immediate response. He was on a caravan holiday in the south of France with his wife, parents, his two sets of twins and with intermittent access to his emails. One suddenly popped off the screen, inviting him to an interview at Adams Park a couple of days later.

Wondering if he could make it back in time, Fairman asked if a skype interview might be okay but received a negative response. A postponement? Gareth Ainsworth had a family holiday booked. Fairman could not let the opportunity slide, so left his kids with the grandparents and drove the caravan back through France, via the Eurotunnel and on to Buckinghamshire.

Fairman recalled a 'real grilling' from chairman Andrew Howard in the company of Ainsworth, Richard Dobson and secretary Kelly Francis. 'I came out of the room absolutely buzzing, went to Frankie and Benny's with my missus and said I really wanted the job. It felt so right.'

Then he discovered one of his best friends, Billy Stewart, had been interviewed. 'Billy was more experienced than me, had worked at international level and when we spoke he said his interview had gone really well and said, "Yeah I've got it." I was so dejected. I put it out of my mind.'

A week later Fairman learned that Stewart's celebration had been premature. 'Gareth called me. I think he was at Cian O'Doherty's wedding in Ireland. He said he wanted me to join his staff.'

The Rock and the Glue

THE Red Lion opposite Wokingham Town Hall was about to bounce on Friday, 13 December. In one cranny sat Sir Vince Cable, the former leader of the Liberal Democrats, and the party's candidate for the constituency Dr Phillip Lee plotting to try to turn over the incumbent Sir John Redwood and his significant majority (they failed but gave a decent account of themselves).

In another corner of the pub was Gareth Ainsworth preparing to break into his version of 'The Wanderer', though this one wasn't going anywhere. A bit like Sir John.

The Cold-Blooded Hearts – Gareth's latest musical incarnation – had remixed the 1961 Dion classic, formally released it as a single that day and to which the acclaim was such that the BBC gave the story a three-minute plug on *Football Focus*. The Beeb rarely soiled their hands with anything as base as League One.

Ainsworth clasped the mike on its stand with both hands and belted out the strains in the no-holds-barred style that mirrored his touchline urgings. The Lib Dems had gone by this time, but the remaining clientele lapped it up, especially when they discovered the full-time occupation of the evening's guest lead. The lady from Wakefield I danced with said she didn't know anything about football but 'your friend's a bit of alright'.

Wycombe's manager was lost in his 'rock 'n' roll baby' element. His best Aussie mate Pauly Zarb, a fellow INXS tribute band member and highly accomplished musician, played keyboards, guitar and flute as backing for the nearest thing to a hell-raiser Wokingham was likely to see. The heat generated from the music and dancing was such that it was soon impossible to see the world outside, so much condensation had formed on the windows.

Ainsworth had invited his staff for an evening of songs, silly games and shots (I had downed my fourth before I got the remotest hang of the table-tapping game) for a mutual appreciation of what they had achieved together as the halfway stage of the season approached.

The close-knit nature of the backroom team was ever evident. Richard Dobson, Andy Fairman – who drove five hours from Preston not to miss the fun – Dave Wates, Josh Hart and Aly Vogelzang squeezed into a nook of the pub. If this had been Ipswich's staff party they would have needed an entire lounge bar and probably spilled into the snug.

Dobbo's abundant talent at games was such that a shot hadn't passed his lips until we bounded to a second inn, The Redan, where the manager lined up a full quota of cleansing tequilas. The Wycombe number two wasn't a dancer or singer, he was happy sitting quietly in a corner, occasionally glancing at his phone on which were probably screenshots of how Burton Albion – the club's next opponents – defended at corners. But he did join in as his boss belted out 'Sweet Caroline' and we chorused: 'So good, so good, so good!'

If not engrossed in tactical nuances, Dobbo would have been checking the social media trail of his players who – with the luxury of a weekend hiatus after their FA Cup exit and with Bury's EFL expulsion freeing up a second consecutive Saturday – seized the chance to ransack their air-miles.

Adebayo Akinfenwa was in Houston, Texas, to develop his burgeoning fascination with everything NFL, Jack Grimmer flew to Majorca hoping he might tan rather than turn red, Darius Charles and Josh Parker relaxed in Marrakech with their children and Jacob Gardiner-Smith was meeting old friends in Kiev, Ukraine, where a suntan was not a consideration.

While the lads were playing away and their boss sang his heart out, the assistant manager was going through a mental checklist – videos to review, systems to perfect, charts to be updated, training routines to be worked on and, of course, matches to be prepped for.

Downtime and Dobbo weren't best buddies.

* * *

In the autumn of 2019 the manager's job at a respectable club some distance north and east of Wycombe became available. Ainsworth was the prime target, official permission to talk was sought, granted and the post offered – a deal that on paper was too good to refuse, especially as Richard Dobson, Dave Wates and medical chief Cian O'Doherty were all included in the package.

For Dobbo the prospect of more time away from home than he already spent was unappealing, but the opportunity to earn two and half times his salary at Adams Park was enough to make even his head turn, appreciably.

He was snagged on the horns of a terrible dilemma. No one looked that amount of money in the eye and said no without serious deliberation. But the up-with-the-lark 5.30am starts from his home in the New Forest to reach Wycombe's training ground by 8am would extend to who knew what. He'd rarely get home in time to spend those precious post-school hours with his children, Harrison, 11, and Daisy, seven.

The Dobsons had more recently lived in Staines from where the commute to Wycombe was typically stress-free. Dobbo's parents lived in Brockenhurst, slap bang in the middle of the forest, where ponies roamed, greenery was abundant and the air was fresh (with the exception of pony poo). He felt this was the perfect place to raise a family, his wife Caroline concurred and on a single day of house hunting they visited 14 properties and fell in love with one.

'Caroline said, "Ooh, this is lovely," and the kids were super excited. If we hadn't got this one, we wouldn't have wanted to move. It happened that the selling couple were moving to Mexico and wanted to get it done. They were in the taxi on the way to the airport and agreed the sale there and then. We'd seen the house in March, we were in by June.'

Across the road from their new home was an outstanding school that received applications from miles around but in which every spare desk was taken. Within a couple of days of the Dobsons receiving the keys, a family with children of precisely the same age moved away and the spaces were allocated to Harrison and Daisy.

Caroline, a teacher, volunteered to help out on a part-time basis in the school's PE department. Before she knew it, the regular teacher decided to take the retirement she had long promised herself and recommended Caroline to the head teacher. A part-time post was offered and accepted. Everything had fallen perfectly into place.

Now the prospect of a major upheaval loomed. 'The club that came in had done their homework, they knew a lot about our staff and the culture. It wasn't just one of us, but the four. Gaz told me what the offer was. I drove home, walked through the door, told Caroline and her initial reaction was, "You can't say no."

'My mind was racing. Daisy was in bed. I went into her room and had to get really close to see if she was awake. I thought she was asleep but, as I got closer, she opened her eyes, grabbed me, kissed me on the cheek and said, "I love you Dad", rolled over and went back to sleep. I said right there, "I can't go, I can't go." She killed me with one sentence. I know too many people in football who've said, "I missed my kids growing up." Your kids are number one. You can't be so dedicated to football you miss your kids growing up.'

The deal was dead, not to be revived. Might there come a day when Ainsworth and Dobson went their separate ways? 'I'm realistic enough to know that if Blackburn, Gaz's childhood club, came knocking and I was to say this isn't for me, he would go on his own. That would be his call.'

* * *

Richard Dobson joined Wycombe Wanderers in 2007 to manage the Centre of Excellence. A serious knee injury had terminated his playing career at the age of 25, and he initially worked for Brentford in youth development before being tempted to Adams Park.

He had trained as a biochemist. One day in the coaches' room we got on to hair colouring – don't ask me how – and Dobbo remarked he'd once helped in the manufacture of the product which required him to don full protective clothing. 'Why anyone would put that stuff on their hair beats me.' We couldn't quite hear what the manager was saying.

When Dobson first arrived at Wycombe the club wasn't in need of much touching-up. Paul Lambert was the manager who directed the team to the sunlit uplands of a semi-final of the League Cup with successes over Fulham and Charlton and a promotion push in League Two regarded as the herald of better times.

It was clear that for the club to sustain their presence in the league hierarchy, a consistent stream of young talent was an imperative and Dobson's role would be pivotal. Gary Karsa was the head of youth, but when Lambert upped sticks and left after a loss in the League Two play-offs Karsa went with him, and within a few months Dobson had been upgraded to head of youth with a full-time staff and a hale and hearty programme to sustain.

Peter Taylor, the former Spurs and England winger, was next into the manager's chair and led the club to a nine-point lead in the League Two table at Christmas. A late season falter did not prevent Wycombe earning promotion by a single goal from Bury.

The stumble continued into the start of the 2008/09 campaign. Taylor was dismissed in October – Dobson stepped into the breach for one match – and was replaced by the ex-Republic of Ireland international Gary Waddock. Wycombe were relegated that season, rebounded but went down once more in the tumultuous trust takeover year of 2012.

The first team lived a Tigger-like existence but the hand on the developmental tiller was reliably steady. Indeed, such was the importance of a flow of young players that Steve Hayes, the club's owner in a fitful period, called a gathering of the staff to lay down the law.

Dobbo said, 'We were producing excellent players like Jordan Ibe, Kadeem Harris, Matty Phillips and Anthony Stewart and the club thought they could make genuinely good money out of them. Steve was committed to youth development and sat us down at Adams Park. He said, "It doesn't matter how many burgers we sell or advertising hoardings we put up, they will never make the club the amount of money this guy" – pointing at me – "can make bringing young players through so I want you all focussed on helping him." It was a dramatic moment.'

Not quite as dramatic as the day in the spring of 2011 when Waddock's assistant manager Martin Kuhl was involved in a physical altercation as the team returned from an away game, to which the manager – seated at the opposite end of the coach and initially unaware – was swiftly alerted. The consequence of Kuhl's dismissal from his post would mark a significant overhaul of Dobson's career.

There were half a dozen matches of the season to play and a now isolated Waddock asked Dobbo if he would step into the breach. Wycombe won three and drew three of the six matches and were back in League One once more.

Hayes insisted Waddock appointed a permanent assistant, and after a range of interviews the manager was strengthened in his initial belief in Dobson. Hayes was anxious that disruption at youth level would have a negative impact on Wycombe's future prosperity. Waddock argued that the club shouldn't stand in the way of Dobson's desire to better himself.

'I'd been here four years and felt it was a good time to move up. I'd probably outgrown the youth as a sole responsibility and said I'd do the number-two job but only if I retained control of the youth department. They agreed, and to be honest doing both nearly killed me.'

By this time Gareth Ainsworth had become an established and popular player at Adams Park, having joined initially on a month-long loan from Queen's Park Rangers in November 2009 that rolled into the three-year contract he signed six months later.

Waddock, an ex-Ranger himself, soon spotted managerial qualities in Ainsworth and in late 2012, when he was on his way out of the club, made the judgement call that would have a profound effect on Wanderers' future.

There weren't many managers who were dismissed from their post by a chairman caked in sweat and masquerading in an ill-fitting club shirt. Don Woodward was the first chairman when the supporters' trust took effective control in the summer of 2012 and had cut a bit of a divisive figure.

He enjoyed the trappings of office and the kudos generated from sitting in the high-chair at first-team matches. He tossed former chairman then president Ivor Beeks out of his usual seat in the director's box with a cheery "'That's mine now.'

It was only three months since the trust had moved in and, after three successive defeats left Wycombe just above the bottom two in League Two, Woodward and his cohorts determined it was time for a change.

Waddock pulled Ainsworth to one side and said the job was made for him. 'It's too soon,' the player said. 'Don't be an idiot Gaz, this is your job now,' the ex-manager replied.

* * *

The Wycombe supporters' trust's plan was 'to work to a break-even model to secure a sound financial footing.' It was the holding company with control over two separate entities, the football club and Frank Adams Legacy Limited (named after the former captain turned benefactor who bought the old Loakes Park ground for the club), which was responsible for Adams Park, the training ground and protecting the club's heritage.

The budget-balancing conundrum soon became as awkward for the trust as handling a bed of live eels. The choice was to slash as many fripperies as possible to show what judicious sound-money people they were. Unfortunately, scandalously, youth development was burned on the altar of penny-pinching.

Richard Dobson watched in despair as a lighted match was put to the programme to which he'd given his heart and soul. 'Before it [the trust] had moved in and as the deal was still being done for Steve Hayes's departure, there was no one running the club. I couldn't go to anybody, I couldn't speak to anybody. Trying to get hold of Don Woodward was almost impossible.

'We had to renew all the registrations before the deadline and one of the parents, who was a bright business fella, and I came up with an idea to run the youth programme like its own trust through charitable donations and retain the funding from the Football League to keep it alive.

'The league ratified it, the parents wanted to go forward, they each put in £500, which meant we had £52,000 straight away. Woodward said if we could come up with three months of funding he'd allow us to do it [keep the academy open]. We needed £200,000 and we were well on the way.

'One parent pledged £50,000, two others £20,000, but then Woodward disappeared until the confirmation date had gone by and once that happened we didn't have a hold on a single player. An email was sent out from the trust to say the department would be discontinued.

'A member of my staff phoned and asked what was happening. He said, "I thought we'd saved it." I didn't know what he was on about and then my phone went ballistic. No one at the club had spoken to me and I couldn't get hold of Woodward. Steve Hayes had already gone.

'When the trust took over they had no idea what was going on inside the academy. They had never been to the training ground and seen any of the sessions. Woodward just had the idea that he would do things his way, he'd scrap something that would save £200,000 and it was gone, finished.'

Dobson's head was spinning. 'When we'd sold all the good young players, the trust said, "What are we going to do now, all of our saleable assets have gone?" I said, 'I told you this when you were getting rid of the youth department.' It was the most backward thinking ever.

'Look at Kortney Hause who went on to play for the England under-21s and broke into Aston Villa's first team this season. He was a £500,000 player. We sold Jordon Ibe for £500,000 plus add-ons and Kortney was every bit as good but not as sexy because he wasn't a forward. I told the trust he'd play for England at youth level and insisted, "Whatever you do, don't sell him for less than half a million." They accepted less than half of that from Wolves.

'His agent rang to apologise and said it wasn't his doing, but Wycombe were so desperate. I thought, "Oh God, we're giving this kid away." Within a week of him moving, their head of recruitment phoned and said he was head and shoulders better than anything they had at the club.

'We let Josh Scowen and Matt Ingram go to QPR and Charles Dunne to Motherwell. All these boys came through here and one by one they went. When Dunne was sold, the trust said they had to do it or the club were finished. Jordon Ibe's move paid off the debt to Steve Hayes.

'For Wycombe, any sale prolonged the life of the club, paid a debt, an electricity bill, a wage, anything to keep us going.'

* * *

Trevor Stroud once asked Richard Dobson to define his role. It was not meant as a catch. The newest chairman was keen to hear from the horse's mouth what Dobbo felt he brought to the party. He said he was the rock and the glue.

The rock was the person to whom a player could cling to if he was struggling in choppy waters, either with form or in his personal life. The glue was what held everyone in the club together. But Dobson was not simply a problem solver, he thrived on improving the players' aptitude, resilience and intelligence.

He figured in a book *Gold Dust* by David and Keith Mayer published in late 2019 that explored the critical fundamentals of coaching in sport. Keith Mayer had first approached Dobbo when he was working at Brentford, noticing a young coach's ease and eloquence when the sensitive subject of psychology was raised.

Mayer, an FA 'A level' coach, included him in a group with a keen interest in mind over matter for a seminar at Keele University. 'Keith talked about the use of words because with them you could either send people to sleep or keep them alive. I thought he was a genius, telling one story about the day he climbed a rock face which could have been boring but the way he told it was totally riveting. He used language that connected.

'I called him on the way home and said, "OK, you've got me." I was in charge of the youth department and we'd speak late in the evening when he set me tests on emotional control and quality of technical delivery. I'd pick myself apart after every match. Sometimes we'd be on email at two in the morning but it forced me to look at myself and be super self-critical. It made me understand who I was.'

When he was taking his advanced coaching levels, Dobson was introduced to psychologist Misia Gervis, who wrote *The Coach's Guide to Mind-Mapping* and was happy to help set up a programme at Wycombe that became a model for the English game.

'We put on a presentation about what we were doing at the club and the head of psychology at the FA said, "You do realise this is the biggest sports psychology programme of its kind of any club in Europe. There's only Valencia in Spain doing anything anywhere near the same scale."'

* * *

Richard Dobson was one of the first 25 coaches to earn the FA's psychology diploma. He relished the chance to enhance a player's mental capacity as much as how he might improve kicking with their wrong foot.

In the maelstrom of the 2019/20 season, as Wycombe reached historic heights and the stresses of such an experience would potentially overwhelm a few, he and Misia spent a deal of time working on an individual basis with squad members. Some opened their souls, others were more reluctant. He didn't force it either way.

The defining difference in Wycombe's assault on a place in the Championship would be how resilient the players could remain both in mind and body. It was about installing good habits and trusting them. Ask Jordon Ibe, Kortney Hause, Josh Scowen or Luke O'Nien who had moved on to 'better' places what or who had made the most significant impact on their careers.

Dobson cast his mind back to the academy days and the habits he wanted taught day in and day out. 'We'd have resilience workshops to teach our coaches what it meant and looked like in practical terms. We began looking closely at the players' resilience, those who would never give up, would have a shot, miss and then have another shot a couple of minutes later, or those who would take a whack and pick themselves up and get on with it.

'We took kids from Reading's development centre who were deemed not good enough at nine, and four years later we were beating their academy teams with the same players. We had made them more resilient. These kids wanted to keep finding a way and they came through.

'Our psychologists examined communications with the coach they were working with without letting the coach know, and at the end of that month they gave them feedback about how they were communicating with their players. If we had a ladder system where number one was the best player and number 15 was the weakest, we found that the number one was spoken to four times more than number 15. Seventy-five per cent of the communication with the number one was positive and 75 per cent with the weaker player was negative. The coaches' reaction was, "Oh my God I never realised that."

Then the roof fell in when the trust decided that the academy had run its course. 'People were falling over themselves to get into our system and it was all taken away. I loved working on development, I still do, it's my ethos. I don't think you get to a point where football is all about winning. The way I coach, I present players with a problem and ask how they are going to solve it.

'Some of my best coaching has been sat in a mini-bus. I recall dropping Anthony Stewart back at his digs when he was an academy boy here. I'd have ten minutes' one to one posing questions and he probably didn't even realise what I was doing. I dropped in little things like, "What do you think when that happened?" or, "How do you think you could have done that better?" Some learn quicker when you're having chats with them than out on the grass and they're thinking about other things.'

As we talked about the need to keep learning, Wycombe had collected 42 points, were second in the table and everyone was rosy-cheeked. Dobson recalled when the side was ninth the previous season and apparently comfortable before its habitual Christmas spiral.

'I said, "Don't pat yourselves on the back, there's nothing for being ninth in December." We ended up in a relegation battle. We are where we are and the number of points we have now would get us relegated. Until we passed the first target of 50, we weren't even going to start to talk about anything else. We dealt with the next game and the next and if we got to 50 we'd evaluate what our next target could be.

'The management of expectation is something that works in our favour. If we were Sunderland, the fans would be saying, "this is where we should be." Wycombe fans are saying, "This is brilliant". I was talking with Pete Couhig this week and said, "You've come in and all you've seen is win, win, win, top three." There will be a downturn, we might have three defeats on the spin and that's something we'd have to deal with and we would. There'd be no panic, just a conversation – "This is what we haven't done so well, this is what we need to get back to doing and it will be dealt with calmly."

This was no time for the management to lose their head, especially as that was happening just about everywhere else in the town. Something might set off a spark that could ruin the whole thing.

'We played Rochdale away last season and if we'd won four, no one would have complained. We battered them. They scored ten minutes from time, parked the bus and we couldn't score. In the dressing room Bayo was going, "We've cracked, why can't we keep a clean sheet?"

'We had a reserve goalkeeper Yves Mac-Kalambay – about the only person who had a more powerful physique than Bayo – who began screaming, "How many chances do you need? We haven't scored and that's why we lost." Very rarely did I raise my voice, but I shouted, "Enough, boys. These are the cracks that appear in relegation teams. We're not getting relegated. Sit yourself down."

'Our culture was more important than if we were relegated or stayed up. If we went down and the culture stayed intact, we'd continue to move forward. But if we stayed up and our culture crumbled, we'd be in a worse place because there was only one way we'd go. We had to protect the culture first and foremost.

'I said to the pair of them, "These things happen and, for what it's worth, you're both right. We didn't score enough when we had the chances and we conceded against a side that didn't warrant scoring against us. See the bigger picture and stay positive." Then we had a good little run towards the end of the season and got through it.

'But that's where emotions can cloud judgements or effect behaviours. It's about keeping on top of those emotions and being in a good place.

'That's so much a part of my job and not necessarily with the players who are in the team.

'Take someone like Alex Pattison. I keep saying to Patto, "We think you're a really good player but you need to accept there are players who've been here for a while who've done really well for the club, they're fit and well and at the moment they're ahead. That doesn't mean to say you're not going to follow Dom Gape's pathway. When he came here he was in and out and then he got in and stayed in. You can do the same."'

Dobbo was tirelessly watching, anticipating, challenging, considering and developing. Anyone who would reach a training ground after a two-hour drive and then kip in his car until the players started to arrive was worth his weight in the pay rise that had been declined him in the summer.

He was a demolisher of barriers and a raiser of hopes. 'David Wheeler interested Misia who had worked with him at QPR. Chris Ramsay [from the QPR coaching staff] said Wheels was their best trainer and when he arrived seeing players high-fiving and hugging each other and the staff, you could see him trying to work us out. Slowly the shields came down and he'd start seeking you out and chatting about what he watched on TV the previous night.

'It was like speed-dating, how you got to know people in the shortest amount of time and to use every available moment. Getting into Nnamdi [Ofoborh] was hard work – he had this south London attitude of "I'm not letting you in", and then suddenly, one day, he was right into the mix. That's how it worked here.'

* * *

The relationship between Gareth Ainsworth and Richard Dobson reminded me so much of that forged at the FA when Terry Venables appointed Don Howe as his assistant and the pair worked marvels for England in the two and a half years from late 1993 to the 'Football's Coming Home' European Championships of 1996.

Gareth was Terry, all eager inspiration, love for his players mutually returned, tactically astute, able to get his message across simply and effectively, beloved of the media for his easy-going persona and pally backslaps.

When it came to organisational niceties, Terry would often hand across to Don, as Gareth would demur to Dobbo. Defend from a free kick? Don had the plan. Work together as a back four? That was Don's forte. Perfect a tactical shape? Over to you Don. Have a quiet word. You knew who to turn to.

The rock and the glue.

Red, White, Black, Yellow and Cerise

AS Wycombe's players drew back the curtains on the morning of Saturday, 11 January 2020 the illogical nature of their status as leaders of League One was in unobstructed view. Across the street was the Stadium of Light, early day sunshine reflecting off its red-tinged facade.

To this imposing testament to Sunderland's receding glories (the password for the media wi-fi was Stokoe1973), the table-toppers arrived hoping their renowned solidarity and a piece of magic here and there would suffice against a side getting closer to the desired style of – yes that man again – Phil Parkinson.

The people of the city remained unconvinced by their team's manager – Parkinson was Sunderland's 12th including caretakers since Gareth Ainsworth became Wycombe's boss – and were increasingly dismayed at those who had appointed him. I took four taxi rides in the space of 18 hours on Friday evening and match day itself, and each cabbie lamented dire football on the field topped by appalling ownership off it.

The experiences were a cameo of *Sunderland 'Til I Die*, the Netflix series that spent a while in taxis but showed not a single dressing-room scene recording the club's ill-fated attempt to recover the Premier League status they lost in May 2017. The documentaries were lovingly filmed but the deputy head chef was the most quoted and watchable character and her football insight was somewhat limited.

The producers had dared to hope for an uplift in Sunderland's fortunes, but instead we witnessed their descent on football's helter-skelter without padding to soften the fall. In the two years of filming the club changed one owner – the haughty American Elliot Short cashed in his chips – and three managers.

Simon Grayson was the club's shortest-lived boss, Chris Coleman got a few months more and almost looked the part before the new executive arrived and appointed Jack Ross from St Mirren, who led them to the League One play-off final in May 2019 (Sunderland lost to Charlton) before he was shown the door five months later to make way for Parkinson.

One of my drivers suggested they should tear the place down and start over. 'There's a cancer in there,' he said as an unquestionably magnificent stadium came into view. They all asked – in varying shades of plain language – whether Gareth Ainsworth was any good as a manager. I suggested they glanced at the league table.

For the afternoon's football, the locals had the sense of irony to stick Wycombe's fans – many of whom paid £100 for the round-trip – in the 'nosebleeds' behind one of the goals, from where the subliminal message was evidently 'don't look down'.

The eve-of-match-day talking point was Darius Charles – a 32-year-old with a dickey hip – signing an 18-month contract extension. Club and player agreed it was a balanced outcome given the doubts over Charles's roadworthiness. A lot needed to be considered and a year and half was decent compromise.

Sunderland's first flutter in the transfer window was on Northern Ireland striker Kyle Lafferty, who had played largely for Rangers and most recently abroad for Italian Serie A side Palermo. When selling him, the Palermo chairman described Lafferty as 'an out-of-control womaniser – a man without rules.' Quite a tribute from a Sicilian.

Lafferty was not fit to play and so Charles became the focus of unflattering attention. Wearside hadn't forgotten what he had said after his winning goal at Adams Park in October, highlighting Sunderland's conceited sense of superiority. They were eager for their boys to run him ragged. The wait wouldn't be long.

The week on Wearside had been consumed by disquiet at Sunderland's ownership. *The Times* led its back page with a story that smooth-operating chief executive Charlie Methven had departed after injudiciously informing Sunderland's 'fan engagement committee' that northerners lacked decent business sense as opposed to those from the south.

The Old Etonian was being pressed on a £10m investment he was attempting to conclude and raised his voice as he often had when he knew the documentary cameras were trained on him. The charm that initially wooed the supporters had become as faded as his chinos.

He went just before Christmas with Sunderland in 14th (their lowest-ever league standing) and left Stewart Donald, his ally and owner, to face the music. A statement by Donald issued the week Wycombe arrived confirmed the club was for sale and startled the locals by suggesting that a lack of supporter co-operation was forcing his hand.

It was well known around the north-east – and confirmed on Netflix – that Donald had been wooing new investors for the best part of a year. As the months ahead passed, the plight of Donald and his stewardship would by investigated under an increasingly unforgiving spotlight.

By contrast, with the Couhig deal about to be finally, finally formalised after months of bartering between sets of lawyers, accountants and the EFL, Wycombe was in solid shape.

Now the team needed to find one *on* the pitch to defy an opposition with the bit more firmly fixed between their teeth, whatever the dishevelled state of the club administration.

* * *

Wycombe's squad had been permitted a pre-Christmas night out after a two-goal victory over Burton Albion, the highlight of which was Matt Bloomfield's delirious, armband-kissing celebration of the second goal. Rather than chase the West End lights or the hotspots of Aylesbury or Oxford, the boys took the coach to Cardiff.

This was the first time they had let their hair down all season, the consequence of which was that results went tits up.

Going into Christmas one shape and coming out of it another was a ritual for many of us. Down the years a lot of football players glanced at the league table ten days before 'O Come All Ye Faithful!' only to hold it up to the light the morning after 'Auld Lang Syne' and wonder what on earth happened.

Wycombe played four matches in 12 days – against Oxford, Portsmouth, Coventry and Ipswich – for the sparse return of one draw, three losses, two goals scored and eight conceded. It was a period without respite and one in which, habitually, the club's form seized up. No one could work out why.

The familiar pattern played out, though this time to a different background noise. There was little light or shade in the supporters' reaction to the results. Wycombe's one-time leadership of the league by seven points had obviously gone to some heads like a second glass of port after the Queen's Speech.

The excess of grief at no wins from four games rather overlooked the mad fact that the club was where it had been for four months. Top. Of. The. League.

True, whereas Wanderers had been a reasonably solid block for much of that time, fissures had begun to show. Ainsworth was forever urging his players to win a match with individual brilliance. We had seen too little of that; instead individual errors had become the norm and the brilliance was coming from those in opposition shirts. The impact players weren't impacting.

A goal here or there sufficed when the defence was at its most robust, but recent lapses and the lack of a consistent goalscorer

– two would have been better – meant that when Wycombe conceded first, dismay quickly descended.

Taller, stronger, more adept teams had begun to flourish. In truth, a sense of reality had been restored to the league's results. It was as plain as the nose on Santa's face that Wycombe's early season consistency couldn't last forever. An objective look at the superior quality and (especially) quantity of the squads around them indicated a team vastly overachieving.

Sunderland provided another startling contrast with their mass of players with experience at higher levels who took home comparatively thumping great wages. Before the season started they had banked the third and last £15.5m chunk of the £90m from Premier League parachute payments designed to soften the fall of ex-members of the hierarchy.

The Black Cats' form ducked and weaved. Stewart Donald had become panicked by the necessity for promotion and threw discretion to the four winds by paying a League One record £3m for Wigan Athletic striker Will Grigg in the final five minutes of the January 2019 transfer window. It hadn't worked.

Grigg was on the substitutes' bench against Wycombe. Fellow striker Aiden McGeady, who cost Spartak Moscow £10m when he moved to Russia from Glasgow Celtic a decade before, had fallen from Parkinson's favour. That said, the squad was strong on paper, decent in depth and had a significant advantage over Wycombe in miles under the belt above League One.

Of those in the away team not on loan, Rocky Allsop (Bournemouth), David Wheeler (QPR) and Joe Jacobson (Cardiff City) combined for 22 appearances in the league above their present status.

There was another barebones look to Wycombe's squad. We knew – though the fans were reduced to constant conjecture – that Jack Grimmer was to miss another two months with a pelvic strain, an injury that could not be rushed, as Gareth Ainsworth and Matt Bloomfield explained to him from awful personal experience.

Fred Onyedinma had a similar injury and, though he looked strong of limb and happy of disposition at the training ground, he remained achingly short of full fitness. Maybe Fred would be ready for Rochdale, or Peterborough, likely Blackpool, perhaps MK Dons, surely Bristol Rovers. The weeks were being ticked off and still no sign of the lad.

The day before the Sunderland match, Cameron Yates, the number-two goalkeeper, was on crutches. The day's practice session had been moved to Bisham Abbey because the Wycombe training ground resembled a bog and it was thought the risk of injury was too great. Yates had hyperextended his right leg on far more forgiving ground. Such was life.

The club in the league's pole position now had one available goalkeeper, which placed extra emphasis on enhancing the squad during the January bargain hunt. But Ainsworth had only microscopic room for manoeuvre.

The Football League's salary cap management protocol (SCMP) had been brought in to prevent clubs living beyond their means. The by-laws stipulated that a League One club's 'player-related expenditure' should not exceed '60 per cent of relevant turnover' and '100 per cent of football fortune income' over a specified period. The term 'football fortune' included revenue streams such as the FA Cup, EFL Cup and Trophy prize money distributions, league parachute payments and net transfer income.

Each club sent the EFL its SCMP returns, from which the finance department delivered an analysis of the figures as a benchmarking tool. A club would be assigned a number so that they could compare their performance against others in the division while not knowing – decent guesswork usually did the trick – which number represented which other club.

On the ratio of player cost to income, Wycombe had reached 99.8 of their SCMP 'headroom', meaning they couldn't spend a penny without tripping the wire triggering potential fines they couldn't afford. They were one of four clubs with less than £4m in 'total income' from such elements as matchday revenue (their most significant source], commercial activity and a meagre slice of the Premier League's 'solidarity' funding.

The annual, average player basic wage for League One in the 2019/20 season was £113,000, down from £153,000 two years earlier. Wycombe ranked third from bottom. The average player costs were £3.5m, down from £3.8m in 2018. Wycombe were fifth from bottom. There was one club far ahead on all counts, which everyone knew was Sunderland. Now was the time to get to grips with the fallen once mighty again.

The journey north was plain sailing, six hours on the road and, bar the usual stop at the M6 toll-road services, Scott Boylin's braking technique was barely required until we reached the outskirts of the city – pretty amazing for a Friday afternoon.

The board games were as keenly fought as always, marked by a record-breaking triumph for me and Dave Wates at In One Word. We needed only ten clue words to complete the five answers. Our opponents were too stunned to jeer.

* * *

At noon on Saturday, the team-talk was brief and to the point, interrupted by a fire alarm that felt like a dismal harbinger of doom. Richard Dobson illustrated Sunderland's potential danger and shortcomings at set pieces, before the manager's final reminder of how he wanted his side to set up.

Ainsworth preferred to play first into the howling gale that sent anything not screwed down flying across the hotel foyer each time someone stepped into its revolving door. At half-time it would probably be the moment to unleash Adebayo Akinfenwa and put some more wind up the opposition.

The manager was keen to emphasise unity. Momentum and composure were vital but unity was the imperative. 'We walk in together and we walk out together irrespective of the result. Southend went in and came out through the side door, we won't be doing that. We're Wycombe. We're not inferior.'

A grey-shirted squad gathered outside the hotel and embarked on the five-minute stroll to the ground. Security was left, right and centre, which seemed a little OTT as only a few stragglers were at the ground by one o'clock. The local pubs were still doing healthy business.

Wycombe's players did all walk in together, but five hours later the idea of walking out as a group had been blurred by the outcome. In truth, most of them looked shell-shocked.

* * *

The teams entered the field of play to the strains of Elvis Presley, 'Wise men say, only fools rush in.' There could be no playing the fool this afternoon. From tight tiny grounds with row upon row of empty seats to the Stadium of Light and nearly 30,000 patrons, this was a rarefied alternative to Wycombe's normal weekend experience.

Among those finding their seats were Matt Bloomfield's grandfather John, father Steve and brother Joe, who had ventured north from Suffolk. Six of Jack Grimmer's relations had travelled from Aberdeen despite knowing he was not in the side. Ten minutes had gone before it felt like wasted effort and expenditure. By the time half an hour had passed, so had Wycombe's hope of keeping the score within range.

In no match thus far had so many crosses flashed through the Wycombe penalty area with such little confident defending or decisive intent to intercept them. The side wasn't at sixes and sevens – more like nines and tens.

Anthony Stewart, an ever-present bastion of steadiness, gave away a daft penalty and the free kick from which Chris Maguire scored the final goal in a 4-0 victory – after which he gleefully taunted Rocky Allsop remembering the goalkeeper's slap across his cheek after Sunderland's loss at Adams Park.

Darius Charles was mocked every time he touched the ball and few of those touches were his best. Giles Phillips, playing at right-back where he wasn't comfortable, was taken off after half an hour. Those clean sheets seemed an awful long time ago.

The absence of any spark in the team when it emerged for the second half was a real concern. It was probably a lost cause at 3-0 down, but the players looked listless, sapped of energy and confidence. I'd not seen that before whatever the state of a match. The constant swirl of paper cups, plastic bags and other detritus around Ainsworth on the touchline underscored the depressingly aimless nature of the day.

'Imagine what it felt like for me, 3-0 down after half an hour, standing there and wondering what might happen in the next 60 minutes. That's when I could appreciate that the job had never been everything in my life.'

Whether that was Phil Parkinson's philosophy, he could at least relish a first win in three attempts against Wycombe. In the tunnel after the match, there were quite a few 'fuck you' exchanges between the players. Forgiveness for October was unforthcoming. The enjoyment of delivering such a thrashing gave Sunderland's players a platform they weren't going to kick away.

Parkinson said, 'They [Wycombe] always do the basic things you have to do. And playing the top of the league side, it's important to make a statement. They are not there by magic, they've earned it. Today's was the best atmosphere in the ground since I've been here.'

'Get us home,' Ainsworth called out to Scott the driver. The post-mortem was swiftly underway. Richard Dobson had the match on his MacBook screen before we'd hit the A19. 'Oh fucking hell,' he said as the first goal was reprised.

Matt Bloomfield asked for my impression. 'I don't think anyone did themselves justice.' The captain went up to the front to sit with the management duo. They talked uninterrupted for a good hour.

* * *

Halfway back, on the coach, a debate about Raheem Sterling, the reigning Footballer of the Year, was gathering a decent head of steam among the black players. There was implicit admiration for the way Sterling had stood up to racism from terrace louts, as encapsulated by his appalling treatment at Chelsea the previous season.

The Manchester City and England forward was being lauded as a model pro, though it was tough for the Wycombe guys to relate completely given the extremity of his wage packet and lifestyle compared to those surviving on a tiny fraction of his income.

I moved nearer and asked if I might join the conversation. Adebayo Akinfenwa beckoned me to the seat across from him and Josh Parker. Over the aisle sat Darius Charles, Rolando Aarons and Nnamdi Ofoborh. What did I think of Sterling? I suggested he overplayed the self-justification and pressed himself to work harder because of the colour of his skin.

I might as well have said, 'Isn't Sunderland a long way from Wycombe?' The depths of the lads' dismay at the standards to which they were consistently judged, the indignities they suffered and their anger at the ignorance at the heart of so much of the general football discourse on racism was striking. They would always feel the need to have to prove themselves more.

Bayo reminded us that when he was 18 and playing for his first professional club, FK Atlantas in Lithuania, his *own* fans greeted his home debut chanting, 'Zigger, zigger, zigger, shoot the fucking nigger.' Here he was, almost two decades later, unrelenting and throwing himself with all his zeal at his football.

Most of the stuff he heard at grounds now was tame in comparison to his first experience, but he knew, they *all* knew, that racism seeped through the country's pores despite many fine words spoken and campaigns promoted. Instead of No Room for Racism, the Premier League's campaign, there was plenty.

I was challenged (politely) as we discussed dreams, children, upbringing, fashion, relationships, sports writing and skin colour. 'This should be on TV. Imagine the reaction,' said Parker, the most pointed of the group. 'It would help people understand what we face all the time.

'If we brought this into the public domain it would be a game changer. Conversations like this may go on at some clubs but I know we have the cleverest changing room in the country.'

Rolando Aarons was picked up for saying he had to have the best designer clothes, regardless of cost. It got a little heated. Rolando asked if I'd ever walked into a store and known I was being watched. That every time I leant forward to select an item the security guards inched that little bit closer. I said I had never had that sense. He said it always happened to him.

On reaching the training ground to help unload the kit, collect our cars and head home, Rolando reached for a hug and said goodbye. His loan spell from Newcastle had expired and he wasn't staying. I hadn't known until that moment.

To be honest, Wycombe hadn't seen the best of him because he was injured in his first appearance and his skills flickered only sporadically, but when they did he was irresistible. The winner against Shrewsbury had been the most precious moment.

He was on his way back to Manchester to see his son and then on to the north-east. The next thing we knew, he was heading even further north to Motherwell of the Scottish Premiership, on loan until the end of the season.

Wherever he went there would always be a part of Rolando that was Wycombe.

* * *

The main reception at Adams Park before the visit of Rochdale was replete with smiley people wearing purple bibs and shaking coin containers. The cause was the Chiltern Samaritans' 'Anything But Blue' campaign as we approached Blue Monday when depression spread its ugly tentacles into the lives of so many families.

The third Monday in January was the day Christmas credit-card bills landed with a thud onto carpets covered with faded tinsel and drooping mistletoe. The suicide rate among men the average age of those about to run out for a football match historically accelerated at this time of year.

Rochdale, bless 'em, joined Wycombe in doing football's bit: two teams whose club colour was blue wore their away strips – Rochdale's a fetching cerise and Wycombe's vibrant yellow. David Bottomley, the Rochdale CEO, arrived with a pocketful of cerise ties as back-up and Wycombe chairman Trevor Stroud donned matching yellow tie, socks and belt.

Gareth Ainsworth chose to wear a black leather jacket and red patent leather crocodile shoes. One of Rochdale's staff asked if he'd come on his Harley Davidson. 'Yeah, didn't you see it parked outside,' the manager said as he rolled his eyes.

This made for a vivid backdrop that was wholly supported by a match vivid in so many ways. A depression-lifting face had reappeared at Adams Park. Jason McCarthy, having made only five appearances for Millwall since his move to the New Den in July, returned for a third spell, on loan until the end of the season, ostensibly as cover both at right-back and centre-back. It was a spark the team needed.

Josh Parker was making his full league debut. He had been a persistent presence on the substitutes' bench, sitting through the season waiting for a gesture in his direction. It always seemed to go to someone else. This was professional purgatory.

Parker had taken the bull by the horns and sought out the manager to tell him that, though he wasn't wanting to cause a fuss, he believed he was worthy of his chance and when it arrived he knew he'd come good. His chance had come.

At least Parker was not the man holding the pistol when Wycombe shot themselves in the foot after 18 minutes. A mis-firing, cross-field pass forced McCarthy back towards his own goal from where he nudged the ball into the penalty area.

Rocky Allsop wanted to buy himself a yard with a controlling touch, but Rochdale's Ian Henderson, closing quicker than he imagined, stuck out a right foot and deflected his clearance into the net. Then Rocky fumbled a mis-hit shot that Calvin Andrew ought to have converted.

Allsop had heard in the week that the club was eyeing a high-class goalkeeper to sign as back-up, a decision which made eminent sense given Cameron Yates's leg injury but had an unsettling effect on the season's ever-present. He was struggling to clear his head of all the talk.

In the context of the season, a loss at home to Rochdale would have been horrid. McCarthy epitomised urgency. He took possession on the right-hand angle of the penalty area and instead of picking out Adebayo Akinfenwa with his cross he picked out the back of the net.

He raced off in the direction of nowhere in particular, raised two arms to the heavens, kissed his badge and knew the last time he had been this delirious was when his son George had been born eight months earlier.

'Before the game I was worried because I thought I'd be unfit, but as soon as I got out there all the doubts disappeared. If I'd scored that goal for any other club I wouldn't have had the same level of emotion, but the fact that it was Wycombe, I really felt I could let it out.'

McCarthy had to be involved in the deciding goal in the fourth minute of added time. His 20-yard pass found Paul Smyth, who'd been brought on for fresh, attacking legs. Smyth ran at Luke Matheson, the 17-year-old who preferred playing the game at the other end of the field.

Smyth cut outside and Matheson made a tackle kids make. A stonewall penalty. A lot of people looked away, Joe Jacobson kept his eye on the ball, ran forward and tucked it low into the corner.

The ground went nuts, Matheson wept, the game re-started and the whistle blew.

Poor Luke couldn't be consoled. Akinfenwa went across and hugged the kid who had pulled his cerise shirt over his head. As he reached the tunnel, Ainsworth stopped him. 'I told him he was going to have a career full of high moments and to appreciate those he needed to experience the bad ones as well.'

Still on the pitch, match-winner Jacobson donned announcer Michael Kenny's eye-catching multi-coloured jacket for his lap of honour – *JJ and his Amazing On-Loan Technicolour Dreamcoat.* For Wycombe, any dream would do.

McCarthy hadn't showered, the sweat, grass and mud was stuck to his shirt and limbs as he undertook the sponsorship rounds. He wallowed in his love of the club and what it meant for him to be home. The warmth he generated would have been useful before the match when the under-soil heating system failed to ignite. Adams Park was now fully aglow.

'We needed that,' chorused just about everyone with a Wycombe affiliation as they marched off into the night. Luke Matheson, head down and obviously in turmoil, climbed onto the coach for a five-hour journey home. He looked as if he needed to call the Samaritans.

Two weeks later, tears turned to wide-eyed wonder when the kid signed for Wolverhampton Wanderers for £1m and was loaned back to Rochdale for the rest of the season. The career full of high moments Ainsworth said he would have would likely arrive sooner than Wycombe's manager had anticipated.

* * *

The purple people were still counting the donations when Wycombe's re-match with Peterborough offered the chance to reach the magical 50-point line, the first team in the league to do so. The fact that Posh had won only once in eight games – against marooned Bolton – served to make the timing of the match particularly appealing.

For his second match in succession, Giles Phillips was to see the dressing room interior before half-time, only at the Weston Home Stadium it was because of another of the utterly incredulous refereeing decisions that littered the lower leagues.

When he saw Charles Breakspear was the match official, Richard Dobson let out an, 'Oh no!' His exclamation was something far stronger when Breakspear showed Phillips a straight red and awarded Peterborough a penalty after 18 minutes without a goal.

A cross from the right was headed back across goal by Ivan Toney, whose striking partner Sammie Szmodics lunged at it, missed and landed in the back of the net. Phillips was the nearest defender and the two may have brushed shirts. Szmodics theatrically threw his arms into the air.

Breakspear did not blow at once. Players were turning away to re-start. A linesman shouted in the referee's ear. Then he blew. Phillips was dismissed and the match pivoted decisively in Peterborough's favour. Word on the referee's grapevine was that Breakspear hadn't been looking forward to the appointment. Why, we wouldn't know.

Ainsworth's tactical re-shuffle didn't stem the flow of goals, a flurry of personnel alterations at half-time (the referee shook hands with home striker Ivan Toney as the teams walked off) proved no better. Posh won 4-0, the third team to score four against Wycombe in five matches. A high tide was unrelenting and potentially overwhelming.

For the first time in the league season Ainsworth bit his lip. He was not going 'to compound a miserable night' by saying what he really thought about the penalty decision. He was a notoriously tough adjudicator of referees. Breakspear would do well to get a two.

The Disciples

'This is the victory that has
overcome the world – our faith.'

1 John: Chapter 5

'WHERE does the power come from to see the race to its end? From within.' In the Academy Award-winning movie *Chariots of Fire* the quote attributed to Scotland's Olympian evangelist Eric Liddell was the witness of a man whose core was a devotion to God set above all earthly trials.

Liddell's faith was life-affirming. He heard His word and lived it, trusting completely that the reward would be greater than any gold around his neck.

Almost a century on from Liddell's daring deeds at the Paris Olympiad, those willing to stand and speak God's truth to sporting endeavour were a rare breed. The multi-faith make-up of professional football in Britain in the 21st century was evident more in gestures than words.

When player after player crossed himself as he walked onto the pitch, touched the grass and cast his eyes heaven-ward, we hoped these were not throwaway gestures for the cameras but rather a sincere ratification of faith. Few spoke openly about their religion, whether through individual sensitivity or the threat of ridicule from team-mates and the terraces if His word got out, we could only surmise. Alex Samuel was a refreshing bucker of the trend. He gave all the glory to God.

When he yearned for direction in his footballing life – *any* facet of his life – prayer was a two-way conversation and so it was in the spring of 2018 when he was in the living room of his latest temporary home in Stevenage with wife Rachael and pastor Ali Loaker asking what was to happen next in his career.

'I'd just found out I was being released by Stevenage but I'd been injured since January and had no idea what was wrong. Given my circumstance, no club was interested and the injury had prevented me from impressing other teams. I was in a dire situation. So we prayed, asking God what was going on. I saw a vision of the Wycombe Wanderers badge. It came right out of the blue, no pun intended.

'I knew that Akinfenwa played for them, but apart from that I didn't know anyone there.

'It was just too random and so I realised that God was revealing what He had in store for me. At the time I thought, "Have I eaten too much cheese?" I looked at the League Two table. Wycombe were doing well and as I was injured, there was no chance that they would be interested in me. But that was human logic.

'A week later my agent called and said that a club might be keen. I asked who and he said Wycombe. It just so happened that, despite a very disappointing season at Stevenage, the game against Wycombe was one of the few I'd started. I suppose I'd made an impression. I rushed over to Rachael and said, "God spoke, it's incredible!"'

Then it went completely quiet for months.

* * *

Alex Samuel had run a committed race for years, intermittently interrupted by the setbacks that befell and often derailed many a would-be professional footballer. His home-town of

Aberystwyth in coastal mid-Wales wasn't a regular tent-pitch for professional scouts. He recalled their football pitches pitted with molehills, where trying to trap the ball and then run with it tested the hardiest kid.

At 12 he was signed to Swansea City's youth programme. His parents had recently divorced and his mother Karen drove the hour and 45 minutes to Swansea while, in the back seat, Samuel tended to the needs of his disabled younger brother Nikolas.

Alex would make sure Nikolas was comforted and fed, the car arrived, he leapt out, changed into his football kit, trained and then prepared for the homeward journey where once again he'd be there for his brother.

He impressed enough to be signed to Swansea's centre of excellence, only to discover, as he was about to make his debut, he couldn't play because under FA of Wales rules he lived too far away from the mother club. There was also a sniff of interest from Cardiff City, but any such move was hoist by the same regulations. It was back to Aberystwyth and those damn molehills.

'When I was 15, the club set up a reserve team and that became my next step. We often played against 30 to 40 year olds with massive bellies – it was crazy. Finally, I made it to the first team, but still faced complications. Two weeks before my 16th birthday I had my chance to come on as a sub against Llanelli but we'd broken the age rules and were docked points.

'Once I turned 16, I started coming on for a few minutes here and there. Playing in the Welsh Premier helped me enormously. It forced me to learn what the real game was about and I quickly figured out how to defend myself against massive men. If you thought I got battered now, you should have seen me in those days.'

Samuel was selected for the Welsh schoolboys under-18s and an FA of Wales semi-professional team, but life remained a strain for a lad from the outreaches. Blond and slight, he didn't fit in with those from the principality's grander spots.

'I was different to the other footballers in the team. I didn't share the same interests and the other players were far from welcoming. I read books, which was deemed strange. My food was stolen. Although nobody knew me, I was determined that it wouldn't stop me from doing well on the pitch.

'I will never forget my first game with them. It was against Northern Ireland. We were 1-0 down with 20 minutes to go. I had been on the bench and was brought on as a sub. Then in the last minute I scored the winner. There was a sense of "who is this kid?" It was one of the best nights because for the first time my dream of being a professional footballer seemed possible. The goal was one of the best headers I'd ever scored.'

Samuel's progress awoke more clubs to the potential of the kid from the coast. Manchester United came calling, Newcastle United, too. Karen Samuel took it upon herself to be agent and protector. 'We had been through a lot as a family and those types of experiences are humbling. When my mum spoke to the scouts, she was real with them and people liked that about her. They would go out of their way to be helpful.'

He had a single trial match for Manchester United that re-alerted Swansea to his skill set. 'It was like, "How is this boy from Aberystwyth having a trial at Man United and we haven't had a look in?" Swansea offered me a two-year scholarship and, to be honest, it was an easy decision to make. Swansea had always been my dream team, plus I would be close to family since my dad lived there. So I signed the contract, moved into digs just before I turned 17 and embarked on the next stage of my football career.

'During that first year I had to make life-changing decisions. At the start of the season I decided to take a Maths A-level in case football didn't work out. But after six months I quickly realised that it was either/or. So I gave up my education, which had always been important to me, and fully committed to football. It was such a risk. I wrote a note to myself and looked at it every day: "Remember how much you want it."

'Throughout the two years I worked hard, grafted and always pushed my best. But the level of competitiveness was almost overwhelming and this only increased as we approached the end of the scholarship. Thinking back, it was a weird environment for a young lad.

'We were expected to work as a team but were competing against one another for a professional contract that would only be offered to a few of the players. Trialists were also constantly coming in and there was always the worry that they may take your place.

'In fact, just before decision day, Swansea brought in a striker trialist from New Zealand. He was a big lad, played in my position and during his first match did an unbelievable turn against one of our experienced centre-backs. Straight away Swansea offered him a two-year deal. I couldn't help but think, "After all that hard work, is this it for me?" Swansea were flying in the Premier League under Michael Laudrup but for some reason the lad turned the offer down.

'A few weeks later the day eventually arrived that every scholarship player had worked for. One by one our names were called out and we were taken into a separate room. Finally, I was sat before the coaches, I was so nervous. But it was good news. They told me that they wanted to offer me a contract and I was ecstatic!'

Such highs were never forever in any profession, but as a footballer – at the beck and call of coaches and managers with pre-conceived ideas – they couldn't be savoured for long before a low arrived. A lot of footballers don't find peace because there is always something else – another pressure, another stress.

'When the first year of my professional contract began, it felt as though the hard work was only just starting. Now I would have to prove myself in the Swansea under-21s. I hit the ground running, did well and established myself in the team. The next year, when Garry Monk took over as manager, I was chosen to play for the first team against Bournemouth. There I was up front with Nathan Dyer on one wing and Jefferson Montero on the other. Incredible.

'But for the rest of the season, I was back with the 21s. Then the next football year began and two days before the transfer deadline I had a call from my agent who said Greenock Morton wanted to take me on loan.

'I had genuinely never heard of it. I asked where it was and he said, "I think it's in Scotland." I needed some experience and my agent felt that it would be good for me. I left at four the next morning in time to arrive at Morton to sign before the deadline.'

If Samuel had felt isolation as a child in Aberystwyth, a similar sensation overtook him in Greenock, especially as he'd just entered a relationship with Rachael and was immediately going to leave her behind and head off on his own for a new adventure. These were testing times for young loves.

The football club owner was Millions, a company famed for its 'tiny, tasty chewy sweets'. The ground, Cappielow Park, like Adams Park, was in the midst of an industrial estate and a bugger to get to. The official directions for those coming from the south read, 'Head north on the A78, follow the road past IBM, and continue to the second set of lights. Turn right into Dunlop Street. Follow this road until it turns sharp left and goes downhill. Follow the road through the junction until you reach the traffic lights. You should now be facing the river [Clyde]. Turn right. Follow the main road through two roundabouts and continue until you reach the Cappielow Industrial Estate. The ground is on the right.'

What it didn't say is where you went if you *weren't* facing the river.

* * *

Greenock Morton's owners couldn't have been more accom-modating to the new signing. 'They provided me with a flat, duvet and top-of-the-range saucepan. In fact, it's so good that I've still got it. For the first couple of weeks I had the ambition to discover the "top chef" in me but I soon lost interest considering every night was a meal for one.

'It was a really well-run club and the whole experience was a fantastic learning curve. I had two five-month loan spells, played against Rangers at Ibrox – an incredible experience – and then returned to Swansea. I was raring to go, but unfortunately wasn't being selected for the under-23s. With just one year of my contract left, I felt nowhere near to the first team. Instead, on my 21st birthday I played with the under-17s against Afan Lido, a humbling pill to swallow.'

Swansea had now appointed American Bob Bradley as their manager. One of his first games in charge was in the Checkatrade Trophy tie against Newport County. The Swansea squad was down in numbers and Samuel was picked. He played on the left wing, scored and was told to report for first-team training the next day. 'I was flying. Everything changed so quickly.'

The expectation was that he would play the following weekend's Premier League match at Stoke but Bradley preferred Daniel James (who joined Manchester United at the start of the 2019/20 season) and he never got a sniff of the first team again.

Alex's agent had seen the writing on the wall and told his client he should consider another loan. Wrexham would take him, there was always Aberystwyth, and Newport, who were bottom of League Two and the width of the Bristol Channel from safety (11 points adrift with 12 games to play), said they were keen. 'I told my agent that as long as I was still in the Football League, I would do it. So I went to Newport.'

'When I first joined the team in the January, Graham Westley was the manager. Although people have differing views, I really liked him. He was a multi-millionaire and a fascinating man, with interesting tactics for getting a reaction out of the players. But the team was too close to relegation and Michael Flynn took over as manager. He was excellent with the team and his passion for Newport inspired us. He saw me as a striker and gave me the opportunity to play regularly in that position. Amazingly,

Newport managed the great escape, winning eight games out of 12 and surviving the drop on the last day of the season.

'In the penultimate game, Carlisle away, we were winning 1-0. But at one point I went for the ball, got kicked on the foot and my hamstring popped. I came off and we lost 2-1. I was utterly disappointed and had to watch the last match from the stands. But what a day! Newport beat Notts County 2-1 and the atmosphere was incredible. We had achieved the impossible and the fans were jubilant. I had only joined in the January, but was awarded Player of the Season and felt so honoured. I will always have a heart for Newport.

'Despite my performance at Newport, Swansea decided to release me. There was interest from Stevenage, but Rachael and I were due to marry in three weeks' time. It was a tough decision, as both of us would be uprooting our lives for my football. But in this game, you have to take any opportunity. So Stevenage it was.'

* * * *

Nikolas Samuel turned 14 in 2020. He suffered with Pitt-Hopkins syndrome, a condition that affected barely a handful of the world's population. Nikolas's particular strain was even rarer. Pitt-Hopkins syndrome was characterised by 'intellectual disability and developmental delay, breathing problems and recurrent seizures'. It was said that people with Pitt-Hopkins 'typically do not learn to develop speech, some may learn to say a few words'. Nikolas Samuel never spoke.

Alex, almost ten years his brother's senior, spent months educating himself about chromosomes and splice site mutations, eager to know as much as he could about the condition, so he could do his bit to help his brother whenever he wasn't running around trying to make his living as a footballer.

'I had a tough upbringing. Nikolas needed constant care, so when my dad left, my sister and I had to help more than ever. We were only children ourselves and yet Nikolas looked to me as the father figure. Pitt-Hopkins affects the gene in chromosome

18 and, just because of a small change, he is unable to talk. But Nikolas has a certain splice [a splicing of the messenger RNA, ribonucleic acid, can lead to a gene mutation], making him the only one in the world with this type of Pitt-Hopkins. It also means that he is a lot better than some.

'We have met people who suffer from worse symptoms, and although Nikolas has seizures they are minor, often exhibited in a trance. He is just so incredible. I have such a love for him. Currently my mum and sister look after him full time. But my sister and I often wonder about the future. It's a journey.'

As had been Alex's connection with God. His parents separated when he was ten and later divorced. He would go to his bedroom and cry, immediately sensing arms around him. 'My godparents went to a church called Church on the Move and that's where I truly developed a relationship with God,' he said.

'It was also where I met my future wife. The church was an incredibly expressive place of worship and I first noticed Rachael when she was dancing. I could only see her from behind, but liked what I saw. When we chatted after the meeting, I felt God tell me, "She will be your wife."'

From Swansea to Greenock, back to Swansea and on to Newport, they stuck together, though these were not easy times for young people who would have given anything for a settled lifestyle. When Samuel landed at Stevenage, the situation was about to get tougher and their reliance on spiritual strength more imperative.

The strain of injury and disaffection with football almost broke them.

'Stevenage was the toughest year of my life. I wasn't featuring much, but when I did have game time I played well and scored goals. In the January I kicked the ball during training and my ankle flared up. I knew that something was wrong. But Stevenage kept telling me to "wait" because they thought it was just bone bruising.

'Three months later, I had a vivid dream where I was on an operating table. At first, the physiotherapist from Swansea City was assessing me, followed by surgeons who removed a stone from my ankle. The stone was black and hot to touch, but eventually turned into a precious, pink jewel. In reality, at the time, having surgery wasn't even considered! Stevenage were still treating the injury as though it was just bruising. Although I was being transferred from doctor to doctor, no one could tell me what was wrong, until God showed me in the dream.

'As I looked into the meaning of the dream, I had hoped that the surgery was just symbolic! But one thing I knew for certain – the black horrible stone becoming a jewel was a promise that my situation would become my testimony. A month later, a consultant suggested administering a steroid injection. But God spoke to Rachael and she felt very strongly that this wasn't right. If they had given me an injection, it would have kept me out for weeks, without the certainty that it would even work. As we sat in hospital, awaiting the injection, we prayed that God would give the doctor revelation of what was wrong to stop the procedure. When the radiologist called us in, he said, "I've looked over it and I can see that there's a chip in your ankle. So you will not be having an injection."

'From that moment, the events occurred exactly as I had dreamt. Bizarrely, Stevenage asked for guidance from Swansea's physiotherapist, who consequently arranged the surgery in Wales. Afterwards, when they showed me the bone, it was the same colour as in my dream – pink – a reminder of the testimony that I had been promised. So something that was meant to harm would turn into my favour.'

What would happen to Samuel next? Stevenage hadn't worked out. Newport and Yeovil sent positive signals. God told him there was something better that didn't involve either of these clubs. He remembered the Wycombe badge but nothing had come of it. It was time for a real leap of faith.

'Turning down Newport's offer was a tough decision, because I had loved my time at the club. I have a good relationship with their manager, Michael Flynn. So we spoke and I thanked him for the opportunity, but explained that I couldn't help but feel that I needed another direction. He completely understood. It was a "jump off the cliff" moment.

'The next few weeks were silent, with no interest from any clubs. Although Stevenage had released me, I trained with their youth team to help recover from my ankle surgery. I was running and swimming every day, trying to rebuild my strength. But I hadn't played for eight months. In the end, the only option was a trial match at Yeovil.

'I couldn't understand what was happening. I knew that God had shown me the Wycombe badge but I was heading in the opposite direction. I was ready to play again, was able to strike the ball pretty well, but was breaking down emotionally. The night before the trial at Yeovil, I cried out to God asking Him to make a way. Then my agent sent a message with the Wycombe address. They had asked me to go on trial.'

Gareth Ainsworth and Richard Dobson had been monitoring Samuel's progress because he had played well against them for Stevenage and moments like that always stuck in their minds. They welcomed the 22-year-old to assess his character as much as his skill set. By his own admission, Samuel was awful in training – he could barely run and was completely unfit. He was preparing himself for the big 'thanks, but no thanks'.

'I was really struggling. But for some reason, each Friday the gaffer would say, "We'll keep you for another week." Over that time, I began to build my strength and was feeling fitter. To my amazement, three weeks later I was offered a six-month contract. I knew that this was God's plan, but financially it was tough. The money was limited, so Rachael and I could only afford to rent a room. But we were so happy that I was at Wycombe. It was worth it.

'Gradually, I felt stronger every week. I played in the Checkatrade games, scored against Fulham and finally got my chance to play in the league. During a home game against Rochdale, we won 3-0 and I made a goal for Fred [Onyedinma]. The next game was Walsall away, I came on as a substitute and scored. But one of my favourite memories at Wycombe came shortly after. In two consecutive games I scored the winner against Shrewsbury and the next week, snatched the winner against Accrington. This laid the foundation for my place in the team.'

* * *

On 5 September 2019 Alex Samuel signed a three-year deal with Wycombe. Gareth Ainsworth described him as an outstanding professional. He was a throwback, a fiercely committed forward, full of open-hearted toil, willing to throw himself at and after the ball, cut down a defender's time, the epitome of the manager's demand that no opposition player be allowed ten yards of space before it was filled. Richard Dobson said he reminded him of Morph – the cartoon character that could bend and blend its plasticine-like form into a myriad of shapes.

Samuel was not the tallest, not the strongest and not a prolific scorer, though he got his share. But he was the personification of the team player.

He was also the one to whom any team-mate could go if they needed a word of joy. Matt Bloomfield was the dressing-room prefect and Bayo Akinfenwa the boisterous lifter of spirits to whom Ainsworth and Dobson looked when new players embarked on a Wycombe career or needed to be reminded of the club's ethos and expectations. Samuel could spot a tortured soul a mile off.

'I am truly blessed to be at Wycombe. The gaffer and Dobbo are two of the most humble, amazing people I've met. Every player is respected and made to feel that they belong. These two factors bring out the best in us. It's why we thrive individually and as a team.

'There is such a unified, team environment on and off the pitch. We are encouraged to be ourselves and I never feel as though I have to hide my faith at this club.

'Looking back, God has brought me through the difficult times and has strengthened me because of them. Right from my childhood He's been there. Through the challenges of my brother's disability and my parent's divorce. He guided my football journey even from those days at Aberystwyth. Then, miraculously, to Swansea, where he dared me to believe that football was not just a throwaway dream and it allowed me to meet my wife, who I continued this journey with.

'Every loan has shaped my character for the better. Even Stevenage, which was one of the toughest years of my life, helped me to trust God beyond reason. Finally, He brought me to Wycombe, which has become the jewel of that testimony, proving that He will always make a way.'

* * *

Jason McCarthy was driving to the swimming pool one summer morning in 2018 listening to a gospel song sent to him by Ben Frempah, who trained with Wycombe though he wasn't on formal terms with the club.

Such was Frempah's uplifting presence and commitment, the manager paid his expenses to and from South London and the training ground.

The music wasn't McCarthy's regular choice of sing-a-long but something drew him to a particular track. From nowhere, he sensed a 'great heat across my whole body'. At the same time he heard the words, 'Son, I love you'.

The voice was so distinct he immediately looked across his shoulder to make sure no-one had climbed into the back seat when he wasn't paying attention. There was no human form there. He had to pull to the side of the road.

At the instant of that expression of love, a peace had come over McCarthy that he had never felt before. Even as he told the story that sense of peace returned just as he had to Adams Park in the third week of January.

Jason McCarthy came to Christ the day he was told he was loved. He had not been a regular churchgoer in his youth, the only time he remembered attending a religious service was an uncle's funeral. His parents had not been devotional. He knew there was something missing from his life, but he didn't understand what it was. Now the void was filled.

During his six months at Millwall, where his hope of a substantial Championship run was nipped in the bud by an injury within weeks of his move, he was back in an empty space, professionally and spiritually.

McCarthy had been signed by Neil Harris, liked the plans the Millwall boss had for him and appreciated he'd be in a contest with Mahlon Romeo for the right-back spot. He got Harris's nod but was stopped in his tracks with what the medical staff initially believed was a contusion to the sole of his right foot.

'I thought it was pretty innocuous but then I tried explosive movements and it was really painful. The medics gave me a steroid injection, I played a reserve game, it started to blow up, they re-scanned and found damage to the sesamoid bone [under the big toe]. That was eight weeks out.'

During that period, Harris left Millwall for Cardiff City, their fellow Championship side. Gary Rowett moved into the New Den and McCarthy wasn't in his planning. The player got wind of communication between the club and two prominent League One promotion challengers, neither of which were Wycombe.

Millwall preferred a permanent move but the demands were too high. When a loan was mooted, the clubs who expressed an interest ducked out and Gareth Ainsworth was on the phone daily to check the defender's situation. The move he wanted above all others fell into place. He signed on loan until the end of the season.

A fortnight after McCarthy departed Wycombe in July – 'the gaffer told me I had to go and take my chance in the

Championship' – he learned of the potential Couhig takeover. 'All the lads had talked about in pre-season was if we could stay up. Suddenly it all changed and I knew what the team was capable of with a couple of new faces.'

Though he was playing for Millwall, he talked to his former team-mates as much as to his current ones. 'Alex [Samuel] is one of my best friends, we spoke three times a week, Gapey, B [Akinfenwa], Cam Yates, Anthony Stewart, pretty much everyone. With my former clubs there may be two or three I kept in touch with, but with Wycombe there were so many. That's really rare. It is difficult to detach yourself from a club like this.

'God is everywhere but I see His hand massively on Wycombe. I spent half a season at a club this season that didn't even have a chaplain. No one else in the dressing room had faith and often I felt quite alone.

'At my former club Barnsley, when I was out of the side, everything was getting on top of me. One of the players there, George Moncur, shared how God had a plan for me. It was appealing but it wasn't enough. I don't know why, but it wasn't. When I first came back here [in August, 2018] I met Alex and Ben Frempah and there was something about the way they carried themselves I really liked.

'They opened a whole new avenue. It was difficult at first. I was 22 years old and no one had really shared the Bible with me. What I perceived as church was a man behind an altar wearing a collar and just really boring. I saw God as this big man in the sky, far far away.

'Then I went to Alex's church, in Windsor, My Church, and there were people dancing, singing and joyful and I realised my perception was completely wrong. For my wife Zara to hear that I believed in God and had this crazy experience, she thought I was a bit crazy too.

'I was baptised. I told Zara I wasn't going to try to persuade anybody else but as time went on she would see that I was a better person. It took about six months, she preferred the man I had become and from that she set out on her own journey, she was baptised, God is the foundation of our lives and we see things from an entirely new perspective.

'Football can be a tough calling. Being a player may seem bright and shiny from the outside and it can be amazing, but it can be a lonely place, you can have a lot of time on your hands. I've seen players who have lost their way with no solid foundation, a rock you know is there and that God will never let you down, He'll never forsake you, He's always with you.

'God has given me that shield. It would be awesome to see more and more players come to the faith. I really don't think it's something to be ashamed about, you should be proud of it and you stand for something you genuinely believe in in a world where there are so many different options and other things get shoved in your face.

'It's really cool we can have this at this club. I don't think you would find it anywhere else.'

On Thursday afternoons a group of Wycombe players would meet in the local Costa coffee shop to share the experiences of the week, talk through their lives, and pray together.

McCarthy and Samuel were joined by Nick Freeman, 20-year-olds Nnamdi Ofoborh and Cameron Yates, along with Frempah. All were devout, wholly and utterly committed to God's word. 'We go through each person and say, "How's your week been, where is your heart at, how are you feeling, are you struggling?"' Samuel said, 'It's a space for people to be open. Last season we were praying for the club and for certain team-mates who were going through rough times.

'The team knows that they can come to us and we will be there to help. This is not a clique. This is family. Church isn't just on a Sunday, it's anytime people want to come together. We laugh, joke, cry, and do life together.'

* * *

Sir Alex Ferguson was just plain Alex when, in 1992, he agreed that John Boyers should become chaplain to Manchester United. It was a spiritual epiphany. The club was about to enter a period of domestic dominance and European glory that shone like a beacon, and God only knew whether the two events were related. Boyers would go on to found SCORE, serving sport through excellence in chaplaincy.

One of the members of Sports Chaplaincy UK was Benedict Musola, once a semi-professional goalkeeper in his home city of Nairobi, Kenya, and now very much the paternal pastor to Wycombe Wanderers. Throughout a working week, Benedict would minister to the social needs of Hazelmere where he was lay chaplain at Holy Trinity Church. His Fridays were given up voluntarily to offer what he could for Wycombe's players and staff. On Saturdays he was usually to be found in the director's box, ever watchful.

A football chaplain was a safe haven, an ear in which to pour any vexations, someone who noticed a personality change, sought out an injured or side-lined player, comforted a bereaved one, cherished a new father, who was proactive in the pastoral sense and reactive in the spiritual one.

'I am an option the players had if they wanted to use it. The challenge in football was that all the players are trying to prove to the manager that they should play in the team next weekend and so you didn't want to show any chinks in your armour.

'And yet the chinks might be there and issues going on. Sometimes people needed a safe space to discuss it and that's where I came in.

'Depending on the nature of the issue, sometimes I was obliged to bring it to Gareth's attention. My role was not spiritual or religious, I wasn't here to promote religion but to help Gareth and his team at a pastoral level. That said, if players wanted to discuss matters of faith or any issues around that we did it but that wasn't my primary focus. I had a player here once who wanted to read the Bible and asked, "Where do I start?" That one shocked me a bit.'

Musola joined Wycombe a year into Ainsworth's period as manager. Given the manager's faith and the chaplain's open, warm personality, the trust between them was immediate and instinctive. Musola learned quickly when it was OK for him to step in and offer a comforting word and when it was better to stay silent.

'In chaplaincy we talk about presence, about being there for people. During a difficulty, some will want you to interact, others may not but just want you in the vicinity so you're an option. There are players here I know I can challenge. We sometimes even talk about football and how they played. My support is there in whatever way they want, to help them actualise their potential.

'Alex [Samuel] is very open about his faith, which is so good. I was here the week we signed him and Gareth was saying, "You must speak with Alex, you need to speak with him." Alex has even offered to pray with the manager.'

Though individual cases had to remain private, Musola had seen the benefits of his work in myriad forms. 'I was there to have the right conversations, to keep people positive and that whatever happened stayed within the ethos of the club.

'Gareth made certain decisions that impacted players, some were more open talking about that than others. I helped to deal with frustration, heartache, and, if necessary, to pick up the pieces. On a match day when I was in the stand I was looking at the dynamic between players, when a player came off, the body language, interaction, an insight into what might be going on underneath.

Before the home match against Tranmere in late February, the next at Adams Park after the death of Mark Bird, Musola suggested that a prayer on the pitch would be apt. Alex Samuel, Jason McCarthy, Nnamdi Ofoborh and Anthony Stewart stood heads bowed in a small circle. 'We prayed for everyone's safety, aware that it was more than a football game, for good health, and that it would be a good experience for everyone who came.'

A 3-1 victory for Wycombe was entirely coincidental.

The following day Benedict was back to the day job, supporting local families in a difficult place, dealing with social workers, the police and anyone in need. There had been four stabbings in Buckinghamshire in two months, one mother had recently been over-dosing on 50 ibuprofen a day, he had helped talk someone from leaping from a bridge into the River Thames.

There were troubled people everywhere. We all needed a small mercy once in a while. And to be reminded that there was something infinitely more important in life than three points on a Saturday afternoon.

The Kashket Chronicles

JOE Jacobson rang the training ground bell, a summons that prompted everyone to drop what they were doing and congregate at the nearest pitch. Even the staff's daily post-training contest that involved striking the ball from one corner quadrant to the next – a form of footballing darts – pulled up in mid-flow. It had to be hard-core stuff to drag them away from that.

As Gareth Ainsworth had chosen to play Giles Phillips in a back three at Rochdale in September rather than stick with a preferred four, Jamie Mascoll was concerned about a lack of confidence in him as Jacobson's understudy.

He didn't say so out loud to anyone, but Ainsworth was a past master at reading minds and was determined to nip what he instinctively knew was Mascoll's unease in the bud. He pulled the lad to one side before he festered any longer. There was a long way to go in the season and all would have a part to play.

Jamie was thus in a buoyant mood and content that he mattered. In a previous training session Scott Kashket felt he'd been impeded trying to reach a pass and Mascoll sped onto it, which led to an exchange of views and a challenge to determine who was the quicker. When Jamie saw Scott peeling his boots off and dared him to put them back on for a race, competitive spirits were aroused. Kashket had to re-tape a blister but he wasn't going to let this one pass.

The showdown would be across half the length of a pitch after training. The rest of the squad dashed for their iPhones and, of course, Adebayo Akinfenwa was keener than most to show the race and plug it to his following on Instagram, complete with introduction and whispered running commentary.

I was reminded of the quad scene from *Chariots of Fire*, and not simply because, like the fabled 1920s sprinter Harold Abrahams, Kashket was a Jew and along with Jacobson were the only two who played the game professionally in England, another distinct marker that set Wycombe apart.

Maybe like Abrahams, Kashket felt a desire to prove himself for reasons other than speed of foot, though he confessed he wasn't an orthodox practitioner of the faith like his mother, Cheryl. This was just a bit of banter though it had an edge.

The first running of the race ended after two strides when Mascoll fell flat on his face, forgetting that the track was taking at least a spike and possibly a long stud. Seeing his challenger stumble, Kashket had his shirt peeled and was swirling it over his head halfway down the track. In the spirit of fair competition, a re-run was called for.

The second dash was desperately close, Kashket winning by a whisker as his supporters tried to catch up to his disappearing form, and Akinfenwa pursued Mascoll to the changing rooms, iPhone to the fore. 'What you gonna say cuz, what you gonna say? Stick your chest out, come back with something.'

* * *

Scott Kashket was on the payroll at Leyton Orient during the deplorable regime of the Italian/Albanian Francesco Becchetti, a waste-management magnate who proved beyond all doubt to be a prolific waster of managers.

One afternoon, as Kashket was about to come as a substitute, a Becchetti henchman approached manager Andy Hessenthaler

– that week's east London plaything – and said that under no circumstances was he to be allowed to play.

For over two years Becchetti ruled Orient, taking them from League One to the National League, a kind of reverse saviour. At one stage during this lunatic fringe of an ownership, he marched down the side of the pitch waving his jacket around his head and aimed a kick at Hessenthaler, an act for which he was banned for six months.

Kashket was walking next to his manager at the time and his initial thought was that a demented fan had dashed on and lashed out. Instead, when he turned around, there was the abominable chairman with what was noted as a distinct whiff of alcohol on his breath and a very expensive watch half dangling from his wrist.

Perhaps Becchetti's hatred of Kashket stemmed from his witnessing this attack, but ask the player why he thought the Italian had it in for him and his implied answer rather gave the game away: 'Only he would know if he was anti-Semitic.'

For an article in thesefootballtimes.com published in February 2019, Sam Wilson traced the beginning of the end of Orient's 112 years as a Football League club to the insanity of Becchetti's tenure, highlighted by the 2016/17 season that ended with the club's innards torn out and relegation to the National League. The single mention of Kashket in the article said the owner 'mistreated' him, though there was no explanation as to what form this mistreatment took.

Scott said, 'We won our first few matches when he took over and he seemed fine, then we lost a few and it was as though he just wanted to hate everybody.'

Whatever Kashket may have felt in his heart of hearts, he couldn't prove whether Becchetti's treatment of him was based on religious hatred. 'The only possible explanation from my point of view was that he held anti-Semitic views. People from my family spoke to those in Italy about him and the evidence was pretty powerful.

'Remember I was an 18-year-old boy. It wasn't as if I was a big earner and he wanted to get me off the wage bill. It was really confusing for a teenager to try to deal with it. It was so different to me.'

* * *

The 2019/20 version of Scott Kashket was alive and kicking – ball not man. He had been at Wycombe for the best part of three years and as the new season got its skates on he signed for a further three, the longest contract of his career.

He was hard to pigeon hole, a slight-framed, darting figure who could slot into any position in the front line, play wide, go through the middle, the trademark socks halfway up the shin *a la* Jack Grealish that exposed his legs to defenders and demonstrated an unflinching courage to put himself where it hurt with a greater chance of actually getting battered and bruised.

Kashket was knocked around, got up, chased the ball down, had an instinct for goal and an especially sweet left foot (size six and a half, the same as his right). He would not be everyone's first choice and as the season progressed he would have to become used to not being Gareth Ainsworth's either. Whether right or wrong, he had been tested so much in his teenage years it had become water off a duck's back.

From the age of 13 Scott had dealt with less than robust ankles and heels to the extent he decided to stop playing 'big kid's football' and take up the more intricate game of futsal, a version of five-a-side that rewarded close-quarters technique and was blossoming in popularity. He represented Britain in the Maccabi Games – notionally the Jewish Olympics – at the age of 15, demonstrating an instinct for control and precision that became well noted.

Leyton Orient were among the clubs that recognised a young, slight boy with potential. At that same time, they signed on a short-term contract the Tunisian Syam Habib Ben Youssef, a defender who had broken into the national team but landed in east London bereft of the knowledge of local customs or friendly faces.

The Kashket family took in a Muslim boarder without a second thought. Russell and Cheryl Kashket more or less adopted Ben Youssef at the same time as the middle of their five sons was grappling with his GCSEs and trying to find his feet in the sport. Ben Youssef filmed Scott playing futsal and sent his work off to a number of clubs, among which was Spain's Hercules of Alicante. They immediately asked Kashket to come for a trial.

He flew on a Tuesday, played half a match on Wednesday, after which Hercules offered him a five-year contract and returned to England a day later to sit another exam. He had only just turned 16 and the thought of such an extended stay in a foreign land away from family and friends was unnerving and exciting at the same time.

Scott's parents did not want him to regret not giving it a shot and so he departed, staying in a university residence, hating the solitude and suffering severe homesickness. The family asked the Spaniards if he could sign for one year and the club said 'si' but if he impressed enough for them to offer him a new contract the minimum stay was three years.

There were technical details to sort out – the club played fast and loose with the rules and in trying to secure his international clearance upped his age by 18 months, forging his contract to make him appear 18 when he was only 16. In the midst of all these shenanigans, he was involved in a car crash along with four team-mates as they took a sharp bend near the campus and struck a lamppost.

Remarkably, considering Kashket was in the middle of the back seat – usually the most precarious spot – he escaped with the odd scratch and residual whiplash. Hercules sent him home for a few days to recuperate in his own environment and when he returned, in one of his first training sessions, landed awkwardly trying to bring a high ball under control and felt his left knee give way.

'The Spaniards wanted to operate immediately, but I called home and spoke to my mum who demanded a second opinion. The thought was I'd partially torn my ACL and in England they didn't want to operate considering my age. I had five months out. Hercules still wanted to sign me but I'd be out for the rest of that season. While I was at home, Leyton Orient allowed me to train with them. I hadn't really intended to play for them, just get my fitness levels up.'

At this stage, he received a call from Wingate & Finchley who asked if he'd sign so he could play in the FA Youth Cup even though the official forms suggested he was too old. Kashket convinced the club he was 17 and when Orient discovered this possible conflict of opportunity they re-doubled their efforts to attract him.

The following week Kashket signed for the Os, played in the youth cup and scored twice against Southend. Now Maccabi of Tel Aviv was showing interest and he flew to Israel. That trial lasted little more than a month before he was back in east London.

There was conflict everywhere he turned – different clubs wanting to sign him and contrasting opinions about the extent of his injuries. He signed on a scholarship with Orient, played at Stoke in the youth cup, came off with cramp and the team lost on penalties.

His ankle hurt, the club told him to think nothing of it, he went down in matches and was accused of exaggerating. He told Orient's medical staff he thought he'd broken his ankle because the pain was so bad and was finally sent for an MRI. The news came back that he had a syndesmotic fracture which involved disruption to one or more of the ligaments. To that day there was floating bone in his left ankle.

But if he thought that a bit of bone was causing him pain, the treatment he received from the people who ran the club was increasingly grievous. Within half a dozen games of the Italians arriving, Russell Slade, the manager, was excoriated in front of the squad and two weeks later had gone. Fabio Liverani, a former midfield player for Lazio of Rome and Palermo in Sicily, had been the coach of Genoa for seven matches and was sacked after winning once. It was hardly a record of distinction, but Becchetti hired him for Orient in December 2014.

Liverani told the squad that everyone would be judged on performances. Kashket was on the bench for one of his early matches and the manager brought on a 16-year-old substitute instead. A month went by before Scott went into the manager's office with a translator to ask where he stood and was told he'd never play for Orient while Liverani was in charge. The manager was gone in weeks.

Ian Hendon replaced him and staggered Kashket by telling him, 'I've heard a lot about you,' and that he was regarded as a disruptive influence. 'I don't care, I'm going to judge you by what I see,' Hendon told him. A couple of weeks later, Hendon pulled Kashket and said he hadn't seen anything bad and wanted to offer him a new deal. Then Hendon was out.

'I was 18 at the time, Ian was up front and tried to help a lot. We were sixth in the league and they got rid of him. Kevin Nolan arrived as player-manager, Andy Hessenthaler was his assistant and then Nolan went and Andy was promoted. He said he knew what was going on with me, and in one game I was meant to be coming on at half-time and one of the chairman's cronies came down and said I wasn't allowed on.

'The next pre-season a tour was arranged but no one told me anything about it and I was stranded at home. I spent pre-season training with the youth team. A lot of National League clubs had been interested in me in the past but that summer there was nothing.

'I had a trial with MK Dons and after about ten minutes I was throwing up from both ends. They sent me back to Orient ,who said there had been a bug going around and 21 of their

24 players had caught it. MK told me to stay away. I went to Gillingham for a few days and played one match, but Justin Edinburgh*[1], the manager, said he wasn't looking at forward options so I was back at Orient.'

Just as Kashket thought he must be jinxed, a call from his agent said that Wycombe Wanderers were interested and might be keen to sign him. Richard Dobson's long-time friend, Lee Harrison, the goalkeeper coach at Orient, had suggested he might like a player 'who has a knack of coming on and making things happen'. Dobson and Ainsworth watched footage of Kashket and agreed it was worth taking a chance on him.

It was the final day of the transfer window; Scott agreed a short-term contract but was inwardly troubled. His body hurt and the mental scars had not healed. Orient was a rotten club. They owed Harrison £5,000 at the end of his contract and refused to pay. Lee told the Italians he'd donate the money to the Great Ormond Street Hospital where his son was receiving treatment for cancer, but if it didn't show up he'd tell the world about it. The cheque arrived later that day and was instantly sent to GOSH.

The first period of Kashket's time at Adams Park was trial and error, not least that he was suffering a bout of glandular fever and didn't know it. He'd play a match then fall ill and tried to disguise how he was feeling inside, fearing it would appear a weakness. His first match was at Hartlepool, where he played on the right of a front three with Paul Hayes and Adebayo Akinfenwa and scored both goals in a 2-0 win.

The following weekend, in an FA Cup first-round tie at Chesterfield, Kashket scored a hat-trick as Wycombe won 5-0. 'The day before the tie I signed a contract for another two and a half years, and everything I seemed to touch went in.'

He was having more trouble with his joints. He rolled his left ankle in training, started to develop pains in his groin and

---

1 Justin Edinburgh, then the manager of Leyton Orient, died in June 2019 after suffering a cardiac arrest. He was 49 years old. The football nation mourned.

spent most of the time isolated in the gym. He was fit to play against Tottenham Hotspur at White Hart Lane in the FA Cup fourth-round tie in January 2017, an epic battle that Wycombe led 2-0 and then 3-2 with a minute of the match to go, before being stung 4-3 by a winner from Son Heung-min in the seventh minute of added time.

Tears filled Wycombe eyes that afternoon and a fortnight later, at Crewe, Kashket would be crying too, but for a very different reason. 'Something was wrong and though I didn't know what, I sensed it was bad. It was the pain.' Medical chief Cian O'Doherty improvised with strapping across the top of Scott's legs 'like I was wearing a big nappy'. He would play only a handful of matches that season as the club felt he should rest as much as possible and return refreshed for 2017/18.

'I tried to train on the first day but couldn't. I didn't get back on the pitch until February. In 12 months, I played three or four games, and coming into Christmas 2017 the pain hadn't changed, an internal pain, I couldn't really explain it but it was awful.'

Ainsworth and Matt Bloomfield had had similar groin injuries, and though it meant spending extended time on the side-lines it didn't end either career. 'The gaffer kept saying I'd be fine but I didn't know if I would. I thought it was over. Then one day I did an exercise I'd been really struggling with and I could do it. Very quickly I improved and tried to get back training, but in my first running session with Watesy [head of sports science Dave Wates] I tried to turn and couldn't. I said to him, "My leg won't stay straight. I can't do it, I can't run."

'Cian had to tape one of my legs to get me back into a rhythm and moving in a straight line. I tried some finishing but I'd forgotten how to strike a ball properly. Then the feeling began to come back and the technique as well. Even today I don't move as I used to, but I've adjusted. I'd rather have had the injury when I was younger because now I'm in a better frame of mind, I know what I have to do, I can't be complacent, so I come in [training] earlier, I do all my core work, eat healthier and live better.'

* * *

When Prince William married Catherine Middleton at Westminster Abbey on Saturday, 29 April 2011 he wore the red tunic of an officer of the Irish Guards. The jacket had been made by Scott Kashket's father Russell, a tailor all his working life, who produced a magnificent piece of craftsmanship displayed to billions across the globe.

There was as much pride from a son to his father as there always had been from the father to the middle of his five sons. Scott recalled that the times he was injured his dad would be at a loss to know what to do with his Saturdays as they had always been spent watching him play.

'I'm sure he missed it more than me sometimes, but mum and dad were always urging me to keep looking ahead and not give up on anything. They said I should never quit.'

The message was drummed into all five of the Kashket boys: Brett, Reiss, Scott, Nathan and Zack. They were a typically close Jewish family and their parents were insistent when they were younger that they brought their friends around to the family home as often as possible.

On many occasions there were 30 or 40 people in the house plus assorted pets. Scott's mum Cheryl was kosher and the family respected all the festivals and rituals, though fasting for a footballer was a bit of a chore. 'I couldn't abide strictly, football could make it too difficult to fast. I tried but I needed to drink in the hot weather when fluids were essential.'

The fascination with Russell Kashket's role in the royal wedding did not abate and a call in its aftermath from one of the glossy glamour magazines delivered a multi-page feature on the Kashkets from Loughton, along with family photographs and inside stories.

The requests began to multiply, one TV company believing Kashkets could become the British version of the Kardashians – five sons, dogs, cats, a lovely house in the Essex suburbs, friends around all the time, just perfect for the inter-action, potential feuding, non-stop discourse, noise and clutter that had turned the Kardashians into multi-millionaires.

At 14 years of age and seeing the potential future benefits of super-stardom, Scott Kashket thought it was a terrific idea. His parents wouldn't hear of it.

* * *

Barry Fry was pointed to his place in the Adams Park director's box overflow and for once he couldn't think of quite what to say. There was a pigeon hanging from the back of his seat, dangling at an angle as if its claws had become entangled with the operating mechanism and the poor thing had starved to death. Kelvin Hammond, the ever-accommodating doorman, arrived with a plastic bag and removed the bird.

Fry was director of football at Peterborough United, a club from a bit of a no-man's land in the country but to which Darren Ferguson – Sir Alex's boy – had been lured for a third time with a budget far out of Wycombe's aspect to construct a team expected to mount a serious challenge for the Championship.

Ainsworth was expecting his toughest match of the season as Posh possessed power and purpose epitomised in the heavily tattooed talents of Marcus Maddison, who cost £250,000 when he moved from Gateshead, then in the old Conference Premier, in August 2014.

Maddison may well have been the player on whom Fry bet to finish the league's top scorer the previous season, with a bit more on top for Peterborough to be promoted. The FA found Fry guilty of breaching betting rules, fined him £35,000 and handed down a four-month ban with three suspended for two years. To be honest, it was always good to see Barry around, because mischief was never far away.

Maddison looked as if he was a bit of a lad and would need appropriate attention. Thus, Curtis Thompson's first home outing of the season came with the designated task of getting as close to him as his tattooist. 'It's one v one and ten v ten,' was Ainsworth's shout.

Thompson stuck like a limpet to his man, having to mind his every step after a caution when Maddison wriggled free in the first few minutes, but the ten v ten part was a desperate struggle. Wycombe conceded their first set-piece goal of the season, trailed 2-0 and were frankly all over the shop. Even Dominic Gape gave the ball away playing across his own area for the first Posh goal – a once-in-a-blue-moon indiscretion.

Rolando Aarons – awaiting a full start – came on just before half-time for Fred Onyedinma and his electricity galvanised his reorganised side. Adebayo Akinfenwa was outnumbered five to one in the area when he headed home Gape's free kick, and then Wycombe scored their classiest goal of the season to date, a move that began with an interception by Gape on the edge of his own area before he contributed twice more in a dozen passes, from which Jack Grimmer's tempting cross was diverted by Frankie Kent into his own net. Wycombe one-dimensional? Pull the other one.

Peterborough, endowed with the best front three in the league, drew ahead when the ball bobbled free from a corner and Ivan Toney thrashed it into the net.

On either side of this, Maddison had been substituted – he didn't take to that – and Thompson was shown the red card for a second bookable tackle. Down to ten men, surely this was too much to ask of Wycombe, but the spirit remained willing and, three minutes into added time, Scott Kashket was clattered in the area.

Here, Posh showed a distinct un-Posh-like side, scuffing at the penalty spot, delaying and dithering, arguing with referee and linesman, anything to try to disrupt the spot-kick. Marking his 150th appearance, Akinfenwa strolled up, saw the goalkeeper lean to his right and rolled the ball to his left.

'I took the decision myself [to take the penalty] it was the right time and the right call,' he told the audience in the sponsor's lounge at the heady conclusion of a 3-3 draw. 'I did it the same against Portsmouth, that was a different game again but I made the decision.'

The entire Peterborough squad came back on to the pitch, wandered around for about five minutes then sat in a circle, not a word passing between them. Ferguson said, 'We needed to manage the game a lot better than we did but this is the one team in the league that, regardless of the situation, will keep going and going.'

Alan Parry, Wycombe fan, TV commentator and long-time friend, accosted me on the steps of the directors' box. 'There are teams in this league with more talent, who are bigger and stronger, but I tell you what this lot have got more of than any of the rest and it's this.' AP thumped his chest so hard I feared he might do himself a mischief.

* * *

The return game against Peterborough would be played on Tuesday, 21 January 2020. Scott Kashket was sat in the director's box at London Road trying to take in the match and at the same time make sense of his day.

On the evening of Wycombe's loss at home to Tranmere in the FA Cup in November, most people wanted to be out of the ground as quickly as possible. Kashket was among a number of players denied by the irrepressible goalkeeping of Scott Davies. He was getting changed when told he couldn't leave without speaking to club secretary Kelly Francis.

Together with Gareth Ainsworth, Francis told him Wycombe had been informed of potential charges by the Football Association relating to gambling on matches when he was at Leyton Orient.

The Kashket family contacted Nick De Marco ('the QC who really packs a punch' according to Britain's world heavyweight champion boxer Tyson Fury) and the two talked with the FA's lawyers about the circumstances of Scott's career at the time he had made his bets, his state of mind and all other relevant details. He accepted the details of the charge without equivocation.

The FA said they would get back to Kashket's team as soon as possible, and on Christmas Eve (lovely timing) they released the news that the striker would be charged with misconduct under its rule E1(b) in respect of, '183 bets placed on football matches between 3 September 2014 and 22 August 2016'.

'My initial thought was that this happened so long ago, it had completely gone from my mind and I never thought anything would come of it. At Orient without a doubt it [his shocking personal situation with the club] affected my behaviour in everything. My head wasn't clear, even in training, I had no confidence.

'I was betting online, sitting in the stands and playing with my mobile phone thinking, "Oh, I'll have a tenner on the next goal, the other team to score first, not Orient to score," that kind of thing. I wanted to get out of the club and they were making it hard for me to get out. I hated it. It wasn't as if I had any insight. I was more or less in isolation there.

'The betting would start, I'd win, bet a bit bigger, the money would go up, then I'd lose a bit and want to try to win it back. I don't really remember what was going through my head at the time, it was more to amuse myself. I never minded the occasional bet but that's when it got out of control, I didn't really care. I was just chucking around some of my money.'

The FA said Kashket had until 30 December to answer the charge, but that was such a critical period with match upon match a delay was requested and the date was pushed back until 10 January. Gareth Ainsworth provided a witness statement, as did Andy Hessenthaler, the Orient assistant manager at the time, Leon Braithwaite, an MSc in applied sports psychology and long-time friend of Scott's, and Errol McKellar, who had worked at Orient in various coaching roles.

The letters amounted to a plea for leniency, but the FA was resolute and Kashket was banned for six months, in effect the rest of the season. The FA's performance in this was the very essence of hypocrisy. While happily sitting by and watching money pour into the game from betting companies, they wanted to ramrod any player in whatever circumstance they believed offended the game's 'good' name.

Kashket had been in a vulnerable place, unable to play because of a bully of a chairman who allowed personal prejudice to outweigh fairness and decency. Clearly he'd bet more than he should more often than he should, as a kid with no idea of the potential consequences, but six months? Really? Was this by any measure a punishment that fit the crime?

Mr Di Marco told Cheryl Kashket the news and she passed it on to her son. Scott called his manager and Ainsworth – in consultation with chairman Trevor Stroud – said the club would appeal. A three-person commission appointed by the FA whizzed through the processes and reduced the penalty to a two-month ban with a further four months suspended.

* * *

Wycombe were in the midst of their preparations to play at Peterborough the following night and Gareth Ainsworth had told Kashket he couldn't risk his plans being tossed into the air. He would have to leave him out, but he could remain with the squad until the club knew the extent of the sanction.

Scott didn't have his phone with him, so it was left to Kelly Francis and the manager to inform him of the FA's new punishment. Permission was granted for Scott to watch the Peterborough match but he wasn't allowed to travel on the team coach (Francis gave him a lift to the ground). He sat in the director's box in his player's tracksuit, shivering with the cold and the sense of injustice, reduced sentence or not.

It was decided between the family and their lawyer not to appeal, fearing the FA might react angrily and restore the six-month ban they had been so desperate to impose. The commission's report, even in precis form, made sobering reading.

'In the 2014/15 season, SK staked £14,456.85 on 170 bets, for a return of £13,389.10 – a loss of £1,067.75. Of those bets, 75 were on games in competitions in which LOFC participated: 32 were single bets and 43 multiple bets. The competitions involved were matches in EFL League One, FA Cup and one EFL cup tie. SK staked £2,773.55 on competitions in which LOFC participated, his return from these bets was £4,311.44, amounting to a profit of £1,537.89.

'A total of 19 bets were on LOFC, nine single bets and ten multiple bets; ten against the club. One was a spot bet on a particular LOFC player to score the first goal. SK staked £922.37 on LOFC and his return was £1,868.50, for a profit of £946.13 betting on LOFC, that included bets against the team.

'In the 2015/16 season, SK placed 12 bets in total, none of which were on competitions in which LOFC participated and no bets were on LOFC. SK staked £310, his return was £250, and therefore he lost £60. In the 2016/17 season, SK placed a single bet on football – not in a competition in which LOFC participated and not on LOFC. He staked £40 and lost it.

'In total, from his 183 bets across approximately two years, SK staked £14,086.85 and lost £1,167.75.'

Under the sub-title 'perception of impact of bets on game integrity', the commission added, 'There is no suggestion in this case that a) SK was match fixing or b) SK was betting with the benefit of any particular inside information or c) there was any suspicious activity or betting patterns around SK's betting. Indeed, one of the factors that led SK to begin betting was the fact that he was prevented from playing in or training with the first team at LOFC or having any interaction with the first team at LOFC.

'However, one important factor to be considered is perception. As the sanction guidelines make clear, *"A key aspect is whether the offence creates the perception that the result or any other element of the match may have been affected by the bet, for example because the participant has bet against himself or his club, or on the contrivance of a particular occurrence within the match. Such conduct will be a serious aggravating factor in all cases."*

'It is plainly a serious aggravating feature in this case that a) SK bet against LOFC on multiple occasions, and b) SK "spot bet" on one occasion on an occurrence within a match in which LOFC was involved.

'While we acknowledge that there are factors which mitigate to a degree against the gravity of such matters in this case, there is no getting away from the fact that betting against a participant's own club and/or on an occurrence within a match involving the participant's own club undoubtedly aggravates a breach of FA rule E8.

'The fact that SK might in practice have had only limited contact with the first team during the period when the bets were placed only mollifies that perception to a very limited degree.'

The commission did acknowledge the distressing space Kashket was in at Orient 'and the consequences of those difficulties that are described in the witness statements that were provided to us. We have deliberately "sanitised" the evidence before us in that regard and not set it out in detail in this decision and written reasons. That is for two principal reasons:

'a) First, we are conscious that the evidence contains material that is sensitive and personal to SK. There is nothing to be gained from publicising that material in detail, particularly when it appears that SK has done an admirable job of moving on from his time at LOFC. We confirm, however, that we have read that evidence with care and taken it fully into account when determining sanction.

'b) Secondly, the evidence contains allegations – including certain serious allegations – about the manner in which certain third parties treated SK at LOFC and the alleged motivation for that treatment. That evidence and those allegations are, however, untested, and those third parties have been given no opportunity to respond to them. In such circumstances it would be wrong for us to detail such matters in these written reasons.'

* * *

It was mid-February 2020 and Wycombe remained in the thick of the League One promotion battle. The team was warming up for its home match against Tranmere, the fourth time the sides had met in the season.

As the players dashed for final instructions, a familiar figure stood at the head of the tunnel. Scott Kashket was careful not to place a toe inside the line lest he fell foul of his sanction.

Each player in turn gave him an enormous hug, exchanged the odd word, then disappeared. Scott walked around the ground and sat in the Frank Adams Stand with his girlfriend Claudia, who normally only came to Adams Park if he was playing.

This was anguish of the highest order for a professional footballer. When the FA announced that he was banned from all football activity, they really meant what they said. He thought he might help coach a few young players in his area to keep in shape and help improve their talent, but he couldn't. He hoped he might be allowed into the inner confines of Adams Park, but he wasn't. He could talk to his team-mates on the phone but that was it. The days were a drudgery, late to sleep, late to rise, lacking a singular purpose, missing the dressing-room banter.

His manager thought the penalty ridiculously severe. 'Scott was being punished now for something that happened a long time ago, and to take him away from football altogether was so harsh. I'm not sure the punishment fit at all, because it was in these periods of solitude when he got into trouble in the first place. He needed to be around football.'

The home games he attended were a half-decent distraction. Scott and I sat together for the Bristol Rovers match at the back of the stand. He had his scarf pulled up over his mouth and hat yanked down as far as it would go. He tried to engage with the match but it was tough, despite the encouraging result.

'I presumed I wouldn't be allowed to go to games but they [the FA] said I could attend as a spectator. I bought a ticket, went through the turnstiles and watched like a normal fan.

'I missed being with the boys. I missed them all so much, going in and doing what I was used to. It was all I really knew. The days became very repetitive, which I found weird and hard.

'Some players would be happy to be at the training ground for a minimum amount of time, but I generally spent the hours of 8am until 3pm there. I was one of those loud characters around the place, always up for a laugh, loving the banter, and to take that away was very difficult. Just being at home, as lovely as it was spending a lot of time with my girlfriend, it just wasn't the same.

'It wrecked my body clock. I was going to bed late, getting restless. I would wake up at midday or one in the afternoon. I was never a good sleeper, when I travelled with the lads I was always awake at six, you ask Dominic [Gape]. To be at the training ground for 8am meant leaving Loughton at 6.30 in the morning to make sure I beat the traffic.'

Instead he would be watching season after season of *Vampire* on Netflix.

* * *

In the first week of his enforced absence from the sport that was his life, Scott Kashket couldn't be bothered to pick up his fitness routines. 'I had to get everything out of my system.' From there, he dedicated as much time as he could to making sure that when he was called back in late March he would be ready from the first opportunity.

'I was in better shape at the end of February than I was when I was playing. I was stronger and thinking quicker, I was doing a lot of fitness work at my local David Lloyd club and running up hills, which I'd never done. My routine at the training ground was always slightly different to everyone else's. I did a lot of core work and after the suspension I was experimenting with different weights. I was feeling very happy with my body as the time came closer to play again. But all I could do with the ball was a few tricks to keep myself occupied.'

Joe Jacobson was one of those who worried how Kashket would fare being away from the squad for so long. 'Scott got bored very quickly, you have seen him around the place, you see what he's like.

'I remember when he first signed for the club Dobbo pulled me and said, "We've got another Jewish boy coming in, he's really quiet, he's got a speech impediment and we don't know if he'll come out of his shell." And he was quiet for about a month. Then it was "Who is this kid?" He became the loud, crazy one.

'He spoke to Dom Gape a few times and needed to be assured that the boys were missing him and the training ground was too quiet. He loved being that guy, the noisy one. I tried to think how I'd cope not being around the squad. I'd find it really difficult.'

All Scott Kashket could do was wait and worry. When he was available for selection again, Wycombe would have eight matches to play from which four wins was going to be the minimum requirement to stay in the promotion race. He would be as eager as a newcomer to make an impression.

To use him, where and how, would be among the manager's more critical late-season calls.

A Matter of Life and Death

BOB Rickwood was unable to drive for two months during the winter of 2019, which was purgatory for any scout but for one who once ran his own taxi company – Farnham's finest as he recounted it – it felt like double jeopardy. Especially as he now had his pick of two parking spaces.

Wycombe's chief scout had been asked to double as kit manager when Nathan Lugg, previously in change of shirts, shorts, socks, boots and jock straps, departed the post to deal with health issues he acknowledged required time and space to heal. Luggy lived for his laundry and was grateful to be back on the beat for Brentwood Town in the New Year.

Rickwood's spell in the world of soap suds and spin cycles ended when he went arse over lather on the pitch at Rotherham and snapped ligaments in his left wrist, which was worse given that he was left-handed. His wife Linda said he could quickly learn to use the vacuum with his right hand. Bob needed to be back on the touchline and fast.

Rickwood, bald and bustling, was old school and at 67 was never likely to pass up his black book for a scouting app. His note taking was as precise as a 1960s bobby on the beat. A day in his working life usually involved two matches at diverse, often unsheltered venues where if the heavens opened he was a bout of flu in the making. Being an ex-cabbie, he loved to drive and chat, regaling his passengers with stories like the time he gave Ferenc Puskas a lift through Wolverhampton, after which they chatted football until 1am (though Puskas apparently spoke very little English).

Bob got the job at Wycombe via a circuitous route formed when he ran Heath End Wanderers, a junior club in Hampshire that beat all comers including a Reading FC side with such a complete performance that the league club asked him to contemplate helping to run its youth section.

He was preparing his move to the Madejski Stadium when he was tipped off that Mark McGhee and Colin Lee, the Reading management team, were about to head to Leicester City. Bob bided his time and went to the Midlands where he then subsequently decamped with McGhee and Lee at Wolverhampton Wanderers.

Lee was the manager at Walsall when Bob – its chief scout by then – recommended he sign Gareth Ainsworth on loan from AFC Wimbledon, a move that was a boon for both sides. The pair kept in touch and when Ainsworth became Wycombe's manager in 2012 he called to offer Rickwood a scouting post he gleefully accepted.

From that day to the January transfer window of 2019/20, getting on for eight years, Wycombe had not paid a single red cent in transfer fees for a player. That fact alone was utterly remarkable.

Rickwood's position had been earned through years of hard labour now getting appreciably harder. The job was lonely and collegiate – much in the mould of football reporting. You travelled around with the same people, happily socialised and became friends but protected from your companions the secrets that the club invested in you to unearth.

Bob said his fellow scouts were increasingly regarded as second-class citizens and clubs in the cash-soaked Premier League who resented something for nothing had begun to herd them into corners of their training grounds as if they were sheep. Tea and biscuits were no longer a given.

Wycombe had played just the two matches in the season proper, but Rickwood had already watched at least 30. He was never happier than chalking up the miles, eager to spot that talent who could make all the difference.

The one player who stood out for him in the two matches we watched together in an afternoon was a terrier-like Brighton forward named Aaron Connolly. I'd follow his progress. Connolly's limitless unselfishness fitted perfectly with Bob's insistence that I watched for what a player did off the ball as much as when he had it.

As the season moved on, Wycombe would have fewer minutes in possession than any team in the league and I would increasingly appreciate how much this basic element of the game was fundamental to the team making the most of its talents.

It was what you did when you had possession (or didn't) rather than how often you had it, that made all the difference.

When Bob returned to full fitness in December the following month's transfer window cluttered minds and how many (or few) players were enticed could have profound impact on a club's position at the end of the season. Rickwood needed to be alert to changes in the manager's whim.

Wycombe were stymied by the EFL's rulebook more than most. The time the club spent in the top two positions in the league had, paradoxically, diminished their room for manoeuvre. There was reduced oxygen at the peak and little breathing space for expenditure. Wycombe had been paying bonuses of £250 per player to those playing each time a result meant the club was either first or second in the table, which took outlay to the permissible limit.

By being as irrepressible as it had in the first five months of the season, the club was more or less stuck with what it had for the remaining five. Ainsworth knew the side's limitations more than any man but couldn't do anything about it.

There were increasing strains. After the traumatic loss to Peterborough, the manager was prowling, searching for proof of subsidence and how he might address it. How was it a side once resolute as rock had become so porous? How many balls they had once won were now being lost?

Was it an increase in aerial inferiority at the back, the goalkeeper's starting position being too closely attached to his line, or maybe failure of the front two sections to close the ten yards so imperative to the team's strategic plans?

The perception that Wycombe had begun to lose challenges in the air prompted Ainsworth to mutter aloud about 6ft 4in centre-backs. Almost without a second thought, Rickwood started to plough through 'available' giants. None fit the bill or would cost far too much to add to it.

By the window's close, Wycombe ranked lowest but one in League One in combined players in and out. A modest three – defender Jason McCarthy from Millwall and goalkeeper David Stockdale from Birmingham arrived on loan and striker Rolando Aarons returned to St James's Park, Newcastle. Coventry City were bottom of the table but they already had 50 professionals, so one in, one out made very little difference.

Top of the 'window league' was Blackpool, with nine arrivals and eight departures, soon to be followed by manager Simon Grayson. Blackpool were next to bring its multi-changed squad to Adams Park. The club's media team stopped trying to guess the team after a quarter of an hour of metaphorical head-banging.

Ainsworth had announced his XI at the training ground the day before. Stockdale was straight in. The new keeper put his arm across the shoulders of Ryan Allsop, who was first off the field and sat silently in the canteen opposite Alex Pattison – the housemates who were generally a roguish pair. Rocky was paler than usual.

* * *

The home dressing room was its usual fevered bustle an hour and a half before kick-off against Blackpool. Some players were reflective, others talked bollocks to pass the time. The manager told me to be in there at 6.10pm. 'I need everyone,' he said. This felt critical.

'I want us all to remember this moment,' Ainsworth said as the players took the seats beneath where their match shirts hung. 'No matter what happens [for the rest of the season] you've given yourself a right chance. There's no getting away from it now. People have been saying all season, "How the fuck are Wycombe doing this?" and we're there still.

'I want to go for this now. I really do. I want us to get promoted out of this league.

'Some of you in this room will be feeling great because you know you're starting tonight and some of you will be angry with me because you're not, but I guarantee now if anyone came here and had a go, I'd be fucking there for you, I'd stick up for you, no matter what. I'd be there because you're my boys.

'The team is my decision but as a collective, everybody, we will succeed. We haven't succeeded yet but we can do this. I want to show you something I believe will give you an edge.'

The screen on a wall flickered into life. 'Listen carefully and take this with you. There are two types of warrior, the samurai warrior and the zen warrior. The samurai is the one with the sword, the one who lives or dies by it, everything he does is bravado, everything is linked to the result, the victory.'

The badges of Ipswich, Portsmouth, Sunderland, Oxford, Peterborough and Fleetwood were displayed. 'All these clubs need to get promoted this season, they *must* get promoted. They are spending too much money, buying too many players, everything is attached to results.

'The zen warrior is about the mind. They may lose the small contests but they never lose the fatal battle. Every time you lose a small contest, you learn, you grow. We are the zen warriors, strength comes from learning and adapting and constantly improving performance and finding a way to succeed.

'Whether it is in a tackle, a header, whether at home, at the training ground, or on the pitch, we're trying to succeed and to better ourselves. We have 17 battles to go, we'll attack every single one focussing on performances and learning from each experience.

'We may not win every one of those 17 but we will not be about results, we will constantly be about performance. The samurais will suffer, their demand to get results means some will crumble. Not everyone can be promoted. The mind is mightier than the sword. You've got to believe that.

'We are going to stay in control of our emotions, performance based, we remain above the line. That doesn't mean you don't demand from each other but that happens in the right way. Below the line is not in control, result fearful, scared of losing. We will not be the loser at the end of the day, we stay above that line – 17 battles to go. You've given yourself a chance. I want us to do this in true zen warrior style.'

It was a shame that the roar from Wycombe's dressing room as Ainsworth closed the door behind him wouldn't reach to the opposite side of the ground where most of the patrons were already behind glass, raising theirs.

Mark Bird was having a pint with his mates amid the usual banter, probably about the need for the team to buck themselves up a little bit after the Peterborough result and how many points Wycombe would need to pull off Gareth Ainsworth's zen desires.

One moment Mark was talking, laughing, bantering, the next he was on the ground. These were terrifying seconds amid the realisation something was seriously wrong. The nearest St John's Ambulance crew were summoned, staff were notified, club doctor Bob Sangar and chaplain Benedict Musola dashed across the pitch. The Thames Valley air ambulance was requested. Everything was happening in a blur. Those players preparing to play were shooed down the tunnel.

Two days from the death of the Los Angeles Lakers basketball legend Kobe Bryant, his 13-year-old daughter and seven other souls in a helicopter crash in California, we held our collective breath as a red chopper, with the help of a single arc-light, negotiated the trees surrounding Adams Park. It landed plumb inside the centre circle.

The crew raced across to the Woodland suite where Mark was being comforted as best as humanly possible. It was decided, in consultation with the ground controllers, managers and the referee (our old chum Trevor Kettle), the match should go ahead with an 8.50pm kick-off. By 8.58pm Wycombe were two goals to the good, Nick Freeman with a left-footed volley and Alex Samuel, bursting on to an instinctive pass from David Wheeler, side-footing a second.

No one on the pitch was to know that as the match unfolded into a gratifying 2-1 win for Wycombe the idea of kicking a ball around had taken on a meaningless hue. Mark Bird had died on his way to Wexham Park Hospital in Slough. He was 62 years old.

It was doubtful if there had been a more sombre day at Adams Park, putting aside the match result. An hour prior to the opening of the Woodland suite to accept guests for the visit of Blackpool, it had been the venue for a gathering to celebrate the life and mourn the untimely death of Oliver Darlington.

* * *

Oliver was 13 years old. He had missed a month of football at the end of 2019 with a form of Osgood-Schlatter in his knees and was preparing to make his comeback for Downley Dynamos at the start of the new year. His favourite at Wycombe was every teenage Chairboys idol Adebayo Akinfenwa, though young Ollie was more a wide player in the mould of Fred Onyedinma, who loved to take on his defender and get to the by-line, a provider rather than a scorer.

As a Christmas treat, he had been on holiday in New York with his mum Rachel and sister Holly. Though he had been suffering with a sniffle and was taking cold medication, he behaved like any precocious kid his age would, running through Central Park, ice-skating, lapping up the sights and sounds of a magical city.

On Monday, 30 December he landed back at Heathrow after a sleepless overnight flight with a bout of the shivers. His father Tom collected him and took him home, where there were more presents to be opened, before the lad said he was tired and wanted to head to bed. It was around 8.30pm.

By four the next morning he was calling out for his parents. Something was clearly very wrong. Two hours later he was in Stoke Mandeville Hospital and seriously ill. The Darlingtons were told their son needed to be transferred to Southampton General Hospital, 100 miles away. They heard the word 'sepsis' being used.

Slowly Oliver's organs began to fail and, though there was a momentary boost of hope, by the 3 January the CT scans were showing that his brain had been seriously damaged. Tom and Rachel took the heart-breaking decision to agree that his life-support machine should be turned off.

Ollie had been a regular at Adams Park with his dad, who first watched Wycombe in 1991/92 and became a season-ticket holder on the terracing behind the goal. Father and son usually walked the 15 minutes from Downley to the ground. They had been at Torquay the day of the 2014 great escape where Tom remembered Ollie saying to him, 'Dad you're crying,' after Wycombe's incredible survival.

They were at Adams Park on the day Akinfenwa signed and Ollie had his picture taken with the new star. They went to Wembley when the side lost in the League Two play-off final to Southend. They had planned to be on the terraces for the visit of Ipswich on New Year's Day.

By March 2020 Tom Darlington was living day to day, lost without his eldest son, in a swirl of varying emotions. He couldn't understand why Ollie had been taken so abruptly. 'The doctors said it was an extreme septic reaction. Lots of people got the disease but in most cases the symptoms were mild and the reaction a lot slower.

'There was a lot unknown about sepsis, why a body would turn on itself. The doctors knew it was an infection but they didn't know what caused it. There were those who had an underlying health condition which weakened their immune system. Ollie hadn't shown any sign of a chest infection, flu or meningitis, all those tests came back negative. Something just attacked his body. It could happen. In the western world, with our modern hygiene, we thought we could understand most things but this one we would never know.'

A couple of friends of the Darlingtons contacted the club to let them know that one of its younger fans had passed in tragic circumstances. 'The first I knew was when a story appeared on the Wycombe FC website,' Tom said. 'I'd never been that deeply involved with the club as work and family commitments prevented it.

'Pete Couhig then got in contact and asked if we could meet. Pete was very emotional about it, he had kids of the same age. It had been planned that Downley Dynamos would be at the Bristol Rovers game for an outing and Pete said they wanted to use the match to celebrate Ollie. We thought it was a fantastic idea.'

In the 13th minute Gareth Ainsworth started to applaud, players from both sides began to applaud, as did the referee, as did those inside the ground, everyone was rising to their feet. There was a momentary lapse in the game, the players weren't sure whether to keep playing or not.

The scene was captured on a video that Tom would play to himself on a regular basis. 'I was trying to hold it all together during the applause, it was so very touching.' He would often look at a picture he had of his son with Ainsworth before a kids' match involving Ollie and the Wycombe manager's 13-year-old son Kane. It offered him consolation.

On 11 January at the Stadium of Light there was a similar reaction in the 13th minute. It was the first match after Ollie's death, the supporters of Sunderland had rallied to the story and wanted to show their appreciation. Not everyone in the ground realised what the clapping was for but joined in anyway. 'Imagine, at a stadium like that, 30,000 people chanting Ollie's name. In years to come we could look back and really appreciate how much that meant to us,' said Tom.

'There cannot be an easy way to lose a child, the suddenness of it all. I think we struggled with how quickly it happened, there was no one to blame, it wasn't an accident, he was a perfectly healthy young kid.

'We worried for his siblings. Ollie's stepbrother Ryan was almost ten, Holly eight and Jack three. Holly and Ryan were up and down. Ollie was a very caring big brother and they all looked up to him. He and Ryan would be out in the garden kicking a ball around or playing Xbox together and then Ryan became the elder brother. He said he wanted Ollie back. We had 13 and a half years of great memories, we did a lot with him, of course we wanted more but we had a sense of pride in everything he did.'

Tom Darlington was a level one FA coach, he took charge of most of the games Ollie played in and realised that because of his immersion in the tactics, he hadn't stepped back and taken enough footage of his son. He kicked himself for that.

'Ollie didn't score as many goals as he should have done, he used to hit the woodwork all the time, almost every game. He was a pacey, direct, wide player. Like Fred [Onyedinma]. He loved to scare defenders, he was good with the ball at his feet. Not clinical enough in front of goal possibly but he was leading scorer a couple of seasons.

'He was the life and soul of the team, a character. He was big, boisterous, energetic, caring and fun. A lovely lad.'

* * *

The day after the transfer window closed, Wycombe travelled to the north of the county to play MK Dons, or 'the fucking franchise' as it was romantically known. The Dons had muscled in to Buckinghamshire a few years back which really pissed off the Wycombe fraternity and meant there was little love lost.

The Dons stadium was quite something, an add-on to the Doubletree Hotel, where you walked into reception, up one flight of stairs and there was the pitch. The place was packed to the rafters the previous July for a German rock band called Rammstein. One of the stewards described the scene as akin to the Nuremburg rallies of the 1930s, all thunderous din and weird salutes.

For the football, empty spaces were in abundance. The Wycombe fans had been stacked in a corner segment and were decidedly peeved that rigorously enforced numbered seating in a seven-tenths empty arena meant that when younger fans at the front stood up the older ones behind them couldn't see. Actually, the Dons might have done them a favour, for this was as impotent as Wycombe had been all season against a side that was nothing to write home about.

Mark Palmer, who introduced the Couhig family to Wycombe but disappeared in a puff of smoke before the deal completed, was a guest of MK Dons owner Peter Winkelman who on his own was worth ten of Wycombe according to the latest issue of *Company Check*.

Quite what brought this association about we could only surmise, but Palmer had fallen out of favour with Wycombe's hierarchy before getting his feet under the table as a director. The club didn't think he'd delivered enough in terms of the deals they had expected.

The result – a 2-0 victory for the FF – it was a nasty jolt for Ainsworth, not least the concession of the second goal that beat David Stockdale down to his right in much the manner of Blackpool's late consolation in his first match. A lot of thinking about the goalkeepers needed to be done.

This seventh loss of the season felt more strange because the previous week the team had indulged in a character-building development day where, rather than draw inspiration from an outside source, they talked among themselves and about themselves.

The format was that defenders, midfield players and forwards split into their respective positional groups and spent an hour and a half forming a presentation on what it was about the other elements of the side they most appreciated. Those chosen as spokesmen would then stand in front of entire squad and staff and speak about the subject.

'No harm can come from today,' said Richard Dobson. 'It's about your fellow players leaving the training ground feeling ten feet tall. Telling them what they do that makes you feel better. You walk away knowing how much your team-mates think of you and rely on you.'

The midfield group decided to illustrate the team's strength by depicting it as a tree; the roots, some long, others shorter, representing the resilience of the defence; the stump as the midfield, solid and uncompromising, and the strikers were the greenery, which flowered and bloomed if root and branch did its job properly. The defenders drew a human body, in which all the parts required sustenance for the greater whole to function, the brains and the brawn, the eyes and ears and, if they didn't mind me saying so, the balls.

The forwards, being the slightly cockier group, chose a different route, with lookalikes of the rest of the squad shown on the screen with a single word to describe each player. Some were pretty close to the mark – Peter Kay as David Stockdale drew the greatest ribaldry.

Tin-Tin for Jack Grimmer, the oldest player in the world for Matt Bloomfield and a Bull Mastiff for Curtis Thompson were the least defamatory of the remainder.

* * *

The entire staff wore 'Mark Bird – One Of Our Own' t-shirts under their official attire at MK Dons, and in the 62nd minute, the number that marked his age, came a resounding minute's applause. Tom Darlington stood in the midst of the tribute.

Four matches had elapsed since Mark's death to his funeral in Amersham on Friday, 28 February, by which time Wycombe were third, a point behind the joint leaders Rotherham and Coventry. Still no side had been able to fashion a decisive break from the ever-enlarging pack.

A 'Mark 62' quartered Wycombe shirt was draped across the lectern from where the funeral service was led. The celebrant read from legendary 19th-century American short-story writer Washington Irving, best known for *The Legend of Sleepy Hollow*. 'There is a sacredness in tears. They are not the mark of weakness but of power. They speak more eloquently than ten thousand tongues.'

Mark's son Luke – also in a Wycombe shirt – eulogised about growing up and falling in love with football, telling how his dad attended every match he played, usually driving the team in his transit van from where the teenagers would often moon at the cars behind. One driver once cut the van up, forcing Mark to slam on the brakes and demand he make the occupants behave. He simply said, 'It's boys being boys.'

Which was how it had been the night Mark Bird passed. 'Conforming was not his style,' Luke said. 'He was having a beer with his mates and went out with a bang. I just wished we could have wound the clock forward 20 years, that would have been perfect. He worshipped his four grandchildren more than anything and would never see them grow up.

'Actually, I think he loved Gareth Ainsworth first, then his family and then his mates.'

In the last but one row of the congregation the Wycombe manager dipped his head.

Mr Barton's Boys

TREVOR Stroud was woken by Storm Ciara whistling through Buckinghamshire and a recurring image of the roof having blown off the main stand at Adams Park. On the eve of what was likely to be his final match as Wycombe's chairman – though he couldn't be absolutely sure – he did not want this to be a portentous legacy.

Structurally, the arena had remained intact, which was a blessing for all concerned. There were decent-sized chunks of bark, branches, the odd tin can and coffee cups spinning around the car park. And paper, lots and lots of paper.

Probably about the same amount as had been back and forth between Wycombe and Preston in the previous three months as the club and Football League tried to draw a line under an agreement for Rob Couhig's company, Feliciana EFL Ltd, to assume majority control of Wycombe Wanderers Football Club.

This had been a long-winded process, interrupted by legal minutiae, cross-checking, endless to-ing and fro-ing and finally a need for delay as the prospective boss needed to undergo an operation in New Orleans on the hip that had made regular transatlantic flights increasingly unbearable.

Rob tweeted a picture of the Wycombe flag draped above his hospital bed before the anaesthetic kicked in. Where might the club be when he came around? As the takeover conversations extended so had a pre-occupation with the football team and its status come mid-May. Its long-term residence in the top two in League One inevitably cast minds, even some saner ones, to what might be if *it* should happen.

Stroud could not be caught sitting on his hands. He had begun the process of applying to the local council for planning permission for the floodlight upgrade necessary should Wycombe by some miracle end up in the Championship. There was no point being promoted and not being able to see when playing at night.

The current lights flickered into life on the evening of Tuesday, 11 February 2020. The pylons had remained upright after the weekend hammering but staff were battening down the rest of the hatches. A new system called Dennis was gathering pace in the Atlantic Ocean and the perfect human storm of Cyclone Joey had made landfall outside the main entrance.

Fleetwood Town were the form team of League One with only a single defeat in 12 matches supplemented by decent transfer-window energy, and so it was no surprise that Joey Barton's boys skipped off the coach looking every inch a group determined to put some more wind up Adams Park.

Fleetwood worked with triple Wycombe's budget, they had travelled to AFC Wimbledon by train three days earlier, then won there without ripping up too many trees, returned via rail to Lancashire, ventured south by road on Monday, then stayed overnight and fizzed into the ground.

Chairman Andrew Pilley forked out money so his players could have a session in a cryogenic machine to aid their recovery. 'We're trying to do everything in a very professional manner,' Barton said. 'It's the little things like this that can make all the difference in a season.' For more reasons than one, they looked a cool side.

Wycombe's penultimate midweek fixture of the season left Gareth Ainsworth once again re-jigging furiously, unable to use regular first choices Matt Bloomfield, Curtis Thompson or Darius Charles at all and Adebayo Akinfenwa only as a threat from the bench. Blooms, Bayo and Darius had each scored against Bristol Rovers three days earlier for the 3-1 victory that kept those who would invade the automatic promotion spots at a short-arm's length a while longer.

Ainsworth was more than pissed that Rovers' novice manager Ben Garner – who had not won any of his first 11 matches in charge – moaned about Wycombe's time-wasting and general play to the press but was as pleasant as pie in the managers' post-match social. It felt like being ticked off by the work-experience kid.

The Rovers gathering was genteel as opposed to the hubbub generated when Barton bounded in around 10.30pm. His side had won 1-0 and the air in the room was thick with scouse. The supply of Moretti in Ainsworth's fridge had run dry before Barton joined his coaching staff. 'Where've you been?' the Wycombe boss asked, greeting him with a bear-hug of genuine warmth.

Ainsworth should have been able to smell the smoke rising from the referee's room, where the ears of Kevin Johnson, his linesmen and the fourth official were still burning.

* * *

In his best-selling autobiography *No Nonsense,* Joey Barton recounted the year he spent at Burnley in 2015, the twilight of his pyrotechnic playing career, during which the squad underwent psychometric testing. 'Our so-called insight profiles gave us an external assessment of our aptitudes and attitudes.

'The manager [Sean Dyche] wanted us to share the results but most lads took them home, as though they contained deep and dark secrets. I stuck mine on my locker, so everyone knew what, or who, they were dealing with. This is me, as a person. It is spot on.'

Elements of Barton's 'Behavioural Style Overview' were reported as 'communications style is direct, straightforward, and no-nonsense, perhaps blunt. Can seem thin-skinned, often fussy and dissatisfied. Emphasis is on bottom-line results. May be seen as demanding and tough. Good ability to cut through facades and get to the heart of the matter. Can be defensive when criticised and censured by others. Not easily impressed. Questions information and wants proof.'

This night he definitely wanted proof. A minute from the end of his side inflicting Wycombe's second home league defeat of the season, Barton was sent from the touchline after fourth official Stuart Butler – the man who had been stalked by Accrington's coaching staff earlier in the season – told referee Johnson he had been targeted by shocking language.

Butler had been under the cosh all night. Fleetwood's coaches had taken it in turns to shadow and verbally molest him – one would step forward and give him a mouthful, who was then tugged on the sleeve by a second with a freshly unscented choice of words, before Barton decided he needed a go. Richard Dobson, arms outstretched, requested Butler do something about it. In the end he did.

The occurrence became a classic case of 'he said/she said'. Butler was adamant he heard the words 'cheating c***' directed at the referee. Barton told me he hadn't used the word 'c***' since being sent off at Bristol Rovers in December 2018 for calling the referee 'a cheating c***'. Barton insisted he had used the word 'dog' not 'c***' towards Johnson.

Several witnesses in the tunnel, where Fleetwood's manager was escorted after watching for a few seconds in the main stand, distinctly heard the words 'cheating' and 'c***', though it may have been him repeating to an empty space what he was alleged to have shouted at the referee.

In Ainsworth's office, Barton was disarmingly angel-faced. We chatted for ten minutes about the match – 'we really showcased our authority' – his lack of enthusiasm for playing

Sunday League football at 38 for fear of attracting every two-bit punk who'd like a bit of him, about not wanting to coach his eight-year-old son and the hardy, perennial shit refereeing. We clinked beer bottles and wondered if we might meet again at the Wembley play-off final.

It would be a raucous journey back to the Lancashire seaside. Fleetwood had been superior in every respect, reducing the home side to a single telling shot, a lashing right-footer by Josh Parker that goalkeeper Alex Cairns finger-tipped on to the crossbar and over it. As his defenders thumped Cairns on the back, the referee awarded a goal kick.

It just had the feeling of a night when reality – encapsulated by the sound and fury of the league's most notorious character – seeped into Wycombe's notion of promotion like the February chill. One result ne'er a season decided and I hoped I was horribly wrong, but for a lot of folk transfused with light and blue blood this evening had a sense of the beginning of the end of the fun.

Parker's shot was the only one of ten Wycombe mustered all night that hit its target, taking the number of direct hits to a grand total of ten from 45 attempts in their four most recent defeats. The lack of a forward with a sense of direction was doing the supporters' heads in.

The back looked creaky too. In the third minute Rocky Allsop side-footed an attempted clearance straight to the feet of Fleetwood's centre-forward Ched Evans. The goalkeeper somehow unscrambled his brain before Evans and blocked his strike. Danny Andrew's shot was pushed onto the crossbar, Harry Souttar, a young 6ft 6in defender, headed wide of an open goal and Lewis Gibson, on loan from Everton, thudded the bar. Then Evans was sent off for an elbow that caught Jason McCarthy above the right eye.

As happened against Tranmere in the FA Cup, Wycombe could not make the man-advantage count; indeed, the team played with such brittle confidence that Fleetwood's flourished and after 74 minutes they scored the decisive goal.

Barrie McKay had signed on loan on the final day of the transfer window, a forward who started his career at Glasgow Rangers before a move to Championship side Swansea City, where he was increasingly restless. Barton couldn't believe his fortune, describing McKay as 'the best player in this league without a doubt'.

He had indeed been elusive all night and it was to his decisive pass into the six-yard area that Paddy Madden applied a slight touch that tricked Allsop and the defence, who stood in a line and admired it.

Callum Chambers of Fleetwood had his nose broken in a messy conclusion that had Dobson in an uncommon rage. He was stewing about the officiating and Fleetwood's touchline antics, marched down the tunnel mouthing to himself, took one of his long showers and was nowhere to be found when late-night drinks were taken. He was already halfway to the New Forest.

Rocky Allsop had to endure being named man of the match and tried to make small talk to the sponsors when he felt like crap. 'Nice to get the shirt back ... important we don't get carried away ... tick the matches off one by one ... keep things in perspective ...' It wasn't his fault that half the room had tuned out.

Fleetwood won the following weekend, extending their success to four in a row by defeating Peterborough for the Posh's first loss after six consecutive victories. Wycombe were at Bolton, a repeat of the first day of the season that seemed like both a lifetime ago yet only yesterday. The August heatwave had been replaced by Storm Dennis, with its buffeting winds and soaking rains.

Fred Onyedinma, who had appeared for a few minutes against Fleetwood, was back for his first full start since the opening week of October, and Paul Smyth offered balancing width on the right. We had wanted to see them in positive tandem, taking on the full-back, stretching a defence, getting beyond the back line.

Keith Hill, the canny manager who replaced Phil Parkinson, had acquired some older heads in the transfer window and early on Bolton knocked the ball around with discouraging purpose. Wycombe reorganised, fully engaged and took the lead when Smyth spun away from his marker, darted into the area and had a shot parried.

The ball landed at the feet of Jason McCarthy, tucked in by the touchline. In attempting to clear his cross, Aristoto Nsiala, Bolton's Congolese defender, volleyed the ball into his own face and over the line.

When Onyedinma skipped clear of the Bolton defence and was brought down inside the penalty area by goalkeeper Remi Matthews, there was a demand for his dismissal in expressive tones from the row behind me.

Alan Parry was ever exuberant where Wycombe were concerned. He felt sure the goalkeeper should be sent off, though a change of rules in 2016 deemed a yellow card sufficient if the foul was accidental rather than malicious. AP was still arguing the toss when the whistle blew for the penalty to be taken.

Joe Jacobson, thankfully deaf to the on-going furore in the director's box, slid the penalty into the bottom corner.

They Think It's All Over

ON leap year day Saturday, 29 February 2020, Wycombe closed fourth in the table after a 3-1 defeat at the Keepmoat Stadium, home of Doncaster Rovers. Adebayo Akinfenwa scored his 54th league goal in the quartered colours to become the club's all-time leading scorer in the competition. It ought to have been an occasion to crack open the bubbly.

There were those who had regarded Akinfenwa's signing in the summer of 2016 as a publicity stunt, especially when he burst on to the stage in one of Adams Park's suites like an entrant on *Britain's Got Talent*. 'What do you do?' 'I'm a football player.' 'Yeah right.'

Here he was, a record-setting footballer still. Yet the big chap couldn't enjoy the goal that should have been the platform for a point at least against one of his many former clubs. 'The fact we lost trumps any positive emotions. We should have seen the game out.' The three goals Wycombe conceded were all distinctly sloppy.

The team were three points off the lead but with two dormant weeks ahead – by dint of the loss of the Bury home fixture and though a rest was undoubtedly welcome – they might return for the trip to Burton Albion outside the top six to lend the remainder of the season an entirely uncharacteristic complexion.

'The players are gutted because they're better than this,' Gareth Ainsworth said. 'Ten games to go and fourth place though. Brilliant.' Not everyone agreed. In some quarters Wycombe fans were displaying the levels of entitlement they would regularly mock other clubs for. There was too much premature celebration of where they could be heading rather than a recognition of where they had come from.

If Wycombe's faithful were suffering a mild erosion of faith, their sense of dismay was nowhere near as withering as the acid rain falling on all connected with Ipswich Town. On two days out of four, at the beginning of March, #itfc was trending on Twitter and not in an encouraging way.

An injury-time defeat at Blackpool meant Town were seven points adrift of Wycombe on the same number of games. A single-goal loss at home to buccaneering Fleetwood the following Tuesday night – which meant Ipswich had taken four points from a possible 24 – invoked breakouts of black humour and utter disillusion.

Phil Lown – @lownyp – tweeted, 'On the train and hear the announcement, "if you see anything strange please report it to our staff." Now at Ipswich station showing [Paul] Lambert's team selection to the Greater Anglian ticket collectors but they don't appear to be able to help.'

From @IpswichFanZone, 'There's a whole generation of Town fans who've never seen the club play in the Premier League. The biggest fear now is without serious changes on and off the field there will be a generation of fans who won't see the club at Championship level.'

A generation of Wycombe fans yearned for the chance to see their club in the Championship for the *first* time. They knew this could be their chance. But reality and football fandom didn't always march to the same tune. What made no sense was the 'woe-is-us' reaction to recent form from those who would have given their right arm in August to know the club would play League One football the following season.

There was much gesturing at a troubling statistic, that at Adams Park the team had gathered 42 points from 54 but away from home just 17 from 48. Of Wycombe's last ten matches, six were away.

I had often wondered how the playing group would deal with the unique stresses and strains of being front and centre of an unconsidered promotion contest for so long. On the face of it they remained the upbeat, thought-provoking, hard-working lot they had been all season, but what was happening in their gut? They would now have 14 days, seven without seeing the training ground, to play the last quarter of the season in their heads.

Ipswich's perspective was very different – a feted club fallen on hardship when they had been expected to lay waste to League One. After the Fleetwood defeat (Joey Barton's boys had lost one of 16 matches) Ipswich manager Paul Lambert said, 'It's the expectancy levels on their shoulders, the first time they've had to deal with this sort of pressure, even the older guys. It's totally different expecting to win things than staying in a division or fighting relegation.'

Another of the samurai sides, Coventry City, were soaring. In the lone league game on Sunday, 1 March Coventry defeated Sunderland with a second-minute goal by Matt Godden, who had shattered Wycombe in December. Coventry now led Ainsworth's men by five points and had a game in hand.

Unless the sky fell in on the Sky Blues they would take one of the two automatic promotion places. Could the team that had occupied one of the top-two spots longer than anyone in the season find the strength to get back there again?

* * *

Gareth Ainsworth was scrolling through his mobile phone one morning in early March when the name Petr Cech popped up and stopped him in his tracks. Ainsworth was still attempting to recover from his socks being blown off when the legendary US rock band KISS sent him a personal accolade on his ten years at Wycombe. I doubted a FaceTime message from Sir Alex Ferguson would have gone down any better.

Cech, the former Arsenal and Chelsea goalkeeper, was now technical and performance advisor at Stamford Bridge. The two men had never met and attached to the message was an image of Cech playing the drums. Tidily as it happened.

He sent it in the hope the pair might get together for a gig. The Wycombe manager said he'd love to and Cech's response was to invite him to the FA Cup fifth-round tie against Liverpool at the Bridge.

Ainsworth was not normally one for attending non-Wycombe evening matches as they would impinge on the family time he so fiercely protected, but in this was an irresistible opportunity. The pair agreed to hook up sometime when their diaries were less congested.

For as long as Ainsworth could remember, music had been a huge part of his life. His mum Christine had sung with the big bands of the north in the 1960s and he acquired her love of and aptitude for a song.

The family was a resilient epitome of the 60s and 70s, dad Bill was a factory clerk and driving instructor which meant he was rarely at home and Christine worked in a hospital fracture clinic and doubled up as a dinner lady. The Queen's Park area of Blackburn where they lived was 'not tough necessarily, but northern,' Gareth said.

'Though you didn't know it at the time, you were building a resilience. No one gave you anything in Blackburn, everyone grafted. We had a very stable family life as well, despite a few moves of home.'

The first of these took the Ainsworths to a corner plot on Goodshaw Avenue with a garden big enough for Bill and his two sons Gareth and Liam, the junior by 18 months, to kick a ball about. The brothers were allowed to go to a nearby field

– 'it sounds crazy now letting seven and eight year olds walk unsupervised for 15 minutes' – through estates and ginnels, playing football with their mates until the sun went down, when one of the local mums would shout at them to make their way home.

At Holy Souls RC school, Gareth was top of the class when it came to sporting prowess and hoped to be rewarded with a trial for the town's age-group team but didn't get picked because his schoolwork wasn't considered of high enough quality. At secondary school he made another false start.

'I got a detention for not doing my homework in the first week. It was all new to me because at primary school there was no homework. I got a real ticking off and for a year my confidence was knocked for six. I couldn't settle. Playing for the school team would have meant sticking around the school longer and I just wanted to be out of the place as quickly as I could.'

When he looked around the changing room it was clear he was a late developer in many senses. 'I'd get changed for PE and think bloody hell, some of these lads were big in more ways than one, puberty had hit, these were muscly lads and like men compared to me.

'Dad kept saying, "You'll come through like a train." At 14 I started to grow and since I'd held my own with the bigger lads athletically, suddenly I had this super pace and strength. It was my options year. I never had to see the teacher who gave me that first detention. My confidence levels grew and I started to excel at football, basketball, athletics. I knew I had some sporting talent.'

At 16, Gareth was offered a trial at *his* club, Blackburn Rovers. He was spotted playing the junior leagues in Clitheroe and his trial team contained Jason Wilcox, who would win the Premier League with Rovers in 1995; David May, who joined Manchester United and figured in their treble success in 1999, and Keith Hill who became Bolton's manager in 2019.

Ainsworth scored a hat-trick in a 5-2 win. Jim Furnell, the former Rovers goalkeeper who graduated to the coaching staff, told Bill and Christine the club wanted to offer their son an apprenticeship. 'My dad said it was just what he expected.'

At the end of his apprentice period on 10 May 1991 – Gareth's 18th birthday – Rovers manager Don Mackay called him into his office and told him he was being released. He'd had a big party planned and all his mates were coming. Gareth closed the manager's door behind him, stood outside Ewood Park and sobbed.

* * *

Preston North End were soon in touch offering a three-month trial. Though local lad Lee Ashcroft was on fire on the right wing, they recognised potential in Gareth Ainsworth. After three months, manager Les Chapman told him that Sammy McIlroy, the former Manchester United midfield player now in charge of non-league Northwich Victoria, was keen to have a look and as Preston couldn't offer him anything permanent, suggested he went there.

'I ripped it up in the trial. I always seemed to do well in the high-pressure matches.' Ainsworth was offered a contract but, on his dad's advice, didn't sign it. Bill thought that if his son tied himself to Northwich and a bigger club came in he'd be stuck. All the Vics had to do was cough up the petrol money for his journey to and from Blackburn.

Out of the blue Preston called asking if Ainsworth could play that weekend. They had an injury crisis and there was a space on the right wing against Shrewsbury. He could hardly refuse, had a decent game and was offered a six-month contract he wouldn't have been able to accept if he'd signed one with Northwich.

Once more North End released him before a northern agent called to say he represented Cambridge United and manager John Beck would like Gareth to travel to the Abbey Stadium for a trial.

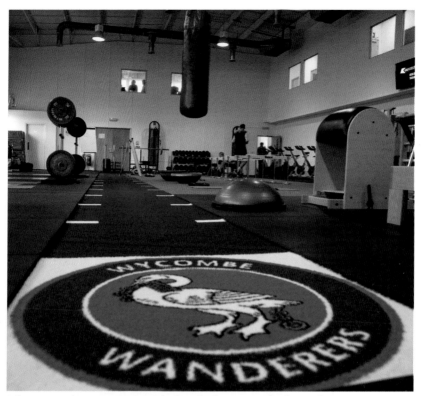

The gym at the training ground where bodies are put back together.

The first day back after ten weeks in lockdown, a delighted Dave Wates, Richard Dobson, Gareth Ainsworth and Josh Hart.

Sterilising the balls. Kit manager Steve Vaux prepares for training after the lockdown.

Author Neil Harman and Gareth Ainsworth on the first day of post-lockdown training.

Darius Charles had a remarkable season when he might have been retired with a damaged hip.

Alex Pattison returned to training looking fitter than he had ever done.

Jack Grimmer, who hadn't played since 26 November, prepares for the play-offs.

Gareth Ainsworth and Richard Dobson run the rule over the team in their final practice match before the play-offs.

Neil Harman [white shirt] refereed the final practice match and joins the squad for a pre-play-off photograph.

Matt Bloomfield [centre, facing camera] urges his players on at half-time during the last practice before Fleetwood.

Wycombe secretary Kelly Francis [far left] joins Gareth Ainsworth and his football staff.

Adams Park from a drone.

The Gaffer and his Generals.

Scott Kashket and Adebayo Akinfenwa in playful mood.

Dominic Gape, Anthony Stewart and Matt Bloomfield stare down the opposition before the play-off semi-final, first leg at Fleetwood.

Nnamdi Ofoborh's dramatic 25-yard strike in the first minute gives Wycombe the lead.

Joe Jacobson scores direct from another corner for Wycombe's second at the Highbury Stadium.

David Wheeler's trademark 'wheels' celebration as his team-mates joyously acclaim the third goal.

Joey Barton and Gareth Ainsworth shake hands at the end of Wycombe's 4-1 first leg success.

Anthony Stewart takes the knee for Black Lives Matter at Adams Park.

The posts at Adams Park are disinfected before the start of the match.

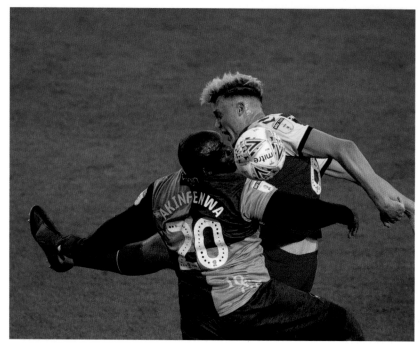

Harry Souttar, Fleetwood's centre-half, finds his hands full with Adebayo Akinfenwa.

Fred Onyedinma's slide-rule finish between the legs of goalkeeper Alex Cairns brings the scores level on the night.

Finishing the job: Onyedinma's precision strike in injury time confirms Wycombe's 6-3 aggregate victory.

Fred about to be mobbed by his ecstatic team-mates as Wycombe's place in the final is secured.

Joy and relief mixed together. In the background are the faces of those fans and former players who have passed away.

A minute's applause before the Wembley final for the late Jack Charlton, an England World Cup winner in 1966.

Anthony Stewart rises at the far post to give Wycombe the lead.

Joe Jacobson scores from the penalty spot to secure Wycombe's victory.

JJ with arms outstretched. An image of happiness.

Faces in the crowd – those Wycombe fans who couldn't be at Wembley in person.

Joy at the final whistle, Matt Bloomfield, David Stockdale, Adebayo Akinfenwa and Giles Phillips celebrate.

Joe Jacobson parades the trophy as the celebrations begin.

Pete Couhig, white cap, joins the players on the Wembley pitch.

Gareth Ainsworth celebrates with his two senior pros, Matt Bloomfield and Bayo Akinfenwa.

One man and his cup. Gareth Ainsworth

A tip was passed on that Beck liked his players to 'put themselves about a bit'. Taking the advice at its word, Gareth put himself about a bit. Cambridge's tactics were rudimentary, more chase, harry and harass than show off delicate ball skills. 'I smashed the full-back a couple of times and after the match John Beck said, "You'll do for me son."'

Cambridge were competing for a place in the first Premier League and it was only after a two-leg play-off semi-final defeat to Leicester City that that particular dream faded, never to return. Ainsworth watched both matches and signed for the First Division club for £175 per week. Beck said he would make him a £1m player.

He moved in with a local family, into a box room with a single bed and the small TV he brought with him from home. That would have been OK but the family's pet cat took an instant dislike to the lodger. If Cambridge's new attraction was sitting on the edge of his bed, the cat would sneak up, scratch him and dart away. One day the feline shit on his pillow. Not just because of cat excrement did Ainsworth almost pack in the move altogether.

'I was a scrapper from my Blackburn and Preston days but emotionally I needed toughening up. Maybe the cat did me a favour. Some kids in our area were sent to work at 16 because they needed the income to help pay their share of the upkeep of the house. I was lucky that it didn't happen with me. My parents had worked so hard.

'I nearly quit Cambridge a couple of times, then Beck put me in the team in a new position. He wanted me in midfield rather than out wide because I battled so hard. My debut was against Bristol City, who had Andy Cole in the side. From an 84th minute corner I scored with a header and we won 2-1. Then there were rumours that Beck had been talking with Preston about the job there. Next week he was sacked.

'Gary Johnson took over at Cambridge and left me out. Then on Christmas Eve John got the Preston job and signed me.

'We were relegated the first year, losing in the last game, but he put me back on the wing and we got to the play-off final where we played Wycombe. I was 21. Wycombe were a good side, my hero Simon Garner from Blackburn played in the side which made the loss more bearable.

'Beck got the sack the following year and went to Lincoln City. Gary Peters took over at Preston and pulled me in one Friday and said he'd brought this lad in from Manchester United on loan and he was going to play him on the right wing. So I was replaced by David Beckham and after that I was a bit surplus.'

For a third time, Beck signed Ainsworth, taking him to Lincoln City. 'John Beck was great for me, made me feel wanted and when someone did that they got the best out of me. I scored 40 odd goals in 90 games.

'My domestic situation was in a bit of upheaval because I took my girlfriend from Blackburn and ended up doing the typical footballer thing and left her for a girl I met in Lincoln. Then I moved to Port Vale. John Rudge, the manager, paid £500,000, which was a big statement and I had a whirlwind year. I felt on top of the world, I really matured.

'I don't think I played a one-two or tried a step over my entire life. But John Rudge re-defined my role to get past the full-back and get crosses in, he worked on my touch and positioning so I could receive the ball better.'

In October 1998 the 25-year-old was the subject of a £2m offer from Premier League Wimbledon, a price that Port Vale were unable to refuse. Gareth Ainsworth was about to become a member of the Crazy Gang.

* * *

If the most vivid years of Wimbledon's craziness had passed – it was a decade from the famous FA Cup final victory over Liverpool – many elements remained undisturbed. During his first training session, the new signing wondered why his team-mates kept going down with nobody near them.

In dribs and drabs, they limped away from the session and the new signing worried if there would be a full complement for the weekend.

When he returned into the dressing room, he realised he'd been done like a kipper. The new suit he'd bought to celebrate his move was in ribbons and his trainers were smouldering in the corner. His first bonus sheet included such perversities as should Wimbledon lose by five goals or more the players had to attend a night at the opera or go to owner Sam Hammam's favourite Lebanese restaurant where they were only allowed to eat his preferred delicacy, the sheep's testicles.

After half a dozen games and not a testicle tasted, Ainsworth had the makings of a serious injury. 'I didn't want to say too much because getting hurt straight away felt like a weakness. I had the pubic overload injury that affects so many players and, rather than three months out, it cost me a year.

'When I came back my ankle was smashed in training and that kept me out for another 12 months. I'd signed to play Premier League and ended up having only a handful of games. One of my proudest moments was scoring twice at St James's Park as a substitute when we were 3-1 down to Newcastle. But I never fulfilled my potential.'

Ainsworth appeared with a constellation of talents and toughs in Lawrie Sanchez – who would become a Wycombe manager – Kenny Cunningham, Chris Perry, Efan Ekoku and Robbie Earle. He had been signed by Joe Kinnear, who wore the term 'character' as a badge of honour, and Hammam was a wonderfully insane owner.

'It was perfect for me,' Ainsworth said. 'I could handle myself by then. I had the "Wild Thing" nickname but I wasn't really wild. I had the rock 'n' roll, I used to push it to the limit, but I had good morals. I might have put *myself* in danger but never anyone else.

'My fiancée Betty and I married towards the end of my Wimbledon days. It seemed the next logical step. We were very young, I was still in party mode a bit and the marriage didn't go right. I had a couple of loan spells at Preston and Walsall and ended up going to Cardiff. Sam Hammam took me there when the club was on a charge and ended up getting promoted at the Millennium [Stadium] against QPR. Lennie Lawrence then said he couldn't guarantee me a place, he released me and Ian Holloway [QPR's manager] came in.'

For Ainsworth, west London was a perfect location to play football and enhance his reputation as a music man with an edge. While at Wimbledon he teamed with Trond Andersen, a Norwegian international signed by Egil Olsen – the former Norway national manager had replaced Kinnear – and Chris Perry (a groundsman not the central defender), who was a drummer with the band Jericho.

They formed APA (Ainsworth, Perry and Andersen) and collaborated on a track called 'Faces' that caught the ear of Pete Winkelman, the entrepreneur instrumental in the relocation of Wimbledon FC to Milton Keynes as MK Dons. Winkelman invited them to his house for a recording session. 'Anastasia was there at the time so it was a bit surreal but we stayed for a week, Chris, Trond myself and a mate Eddie Masters, and recorded three songs, including "Faces".'

The gigs grew and so did Ainsworth's footballing reputation. He loved the time at Loftus Road, though it became a place of persistent upheaval where managers came and went like buses along Wood Lane. 'I had a reputation and name so it was a lot easier to go into that dressing room. I had a great start. We were going for promotion and got it, first year.'

His marriage to Betty was ending and being parted from his daughter Scarlett was hugely demanding. He lost himself in his other twin loves, football and music. And then he met a Venezuelan girl called Donna in a coffee shop. His life was about to *really* change.

* * *

Flavio Briatore was the owner of QPR and not a man with a huge tolerance threshold for losing. In almost three years in charge at Loftus Road, the former Benetton and Renault F1 boss went through ten managers, the longest serving of whom was John Gregory who lasted 376 days. Gareth Ainsworth was the caretaker manager for 50 days, split evenly before and after the five-month spell in charge of the Portuguese Paulo Sousa.

For seven months in the 2007/08 season under Briatore's fellow Italian Luigi De Canio, Ainsworth was both the senior professional and club captain. The two spoke a combination of Italian, English and the pidgin Spanish he was learning to impress Donna. Ainsworth would become part of the inner circle at meetings in Briatore's Knightsbridge offices where Bernie Ecclestone, the owner of F1 and a QPR investor, often lauded it. This was high-octane company.

Ainsworth had not given coaching a consideration. He was taking physiotherapist courses at the FA's Lilleshall outreach but still loved being a player who didn't embellish his game with too many fripperies. 'Kevin Gallen once said to me in the tunnel, "You do know you've got time on the ball Gaz." I said to him, "Time is my worst enemy." I was an instinct player who put in a shift.

'We had a lot of very good tacticians in the side. I'd sit at half-time as they talked about being overloaded in certain positions and thought how are they seeing this? I was just trying to get past my full-back and they'd talk about various systems and tactics.

'We worked out Luigi was going to leave and he pulled me one day and said the boys respected and listened to me and I was a good leader. I should consider taking the [coaching] badges? I'd played with players you could tell knew the game, read the game, studied the game, whereas I played the game, wanted to live life, do the music and the furthest thing for my head was management. I'd always been one of the lads, the one taking it a bit to excess but just loving it.

'I was lucky Luigi saw something in me and Flavio gave me ten games. I didn't change anything, I just let the status quo stand. I had no knowledge. I told Flavio I wasn't ready for management, which I thought was the right decision, and he said, "OK but you're going to find it hard to play for the club again." I said that was fine. It was a relief because I wasn't ready.

'I had a year on my contract. Jim Magilton was sacked as the manager and just before Christmas Gary Waddock, an old QPR mate who was the manager of Wycombe, asked if he could take me on loan. I was 36.'

As a precursor to the life awaiting him, Ainsworth's time at QPR taught him about survival amid upheaval. His initial one-month loan to Wycombe became three and though he became player of the season – his flailing, uncompromising style had not been calmed in his latter 30s – he couldn't single-handedly reverse their slide into League Two.

Named as captain, Ainsworth inspired the side to third place the following season, but, being Wycombe, joy was short-lived and relegation reared its ugly head in 2012 as the trust become the club's custodians. Less than two months into the following campaign, Waddock was dismissed.

'I hadn't expected to be in the side against Wimbledon that turned out to be Gary's last in charge but when he said he wanted me in the side, of course I was there. Dobbo had become the assistant manager and we were both waiting for Gary in his office after the match. The place was really low.

'Don Woodward, the chairman, was in a Wycombe kit, he'd been doing something for charity for the fans at half-time and hadn't changed his clothes. He came in to ask where Gary was and said he needed to speak to him urgently. We knew what was coming. Dobbo and I still joke to this day that if ever a chairman came into the office wearing a football kit, we were obviously both fucked.'

* * *

Gareth left the manager's office and walked straight into Gary Waddock in the corridor outside. 'Gary said, "I'm out. You two – Dobbo and I – are fine. It's your turn. You have to go for it." He knew we might be stepping into his shoes and that he was fine with it. That was the biggest endorsement anyone could have given. It was the mark of him.'

Two days later Woodward offered Ainsworth the position of Wycombe's caretaker manager. 'I'd done a couple of passing sessions and taken the reserves now and again but I was still a player really. Lee Harrison [the goalkeeping coach] was with us, we sat in Gary's office at the training ground and turned the situation over in our minds.'

The supporters' trust had taken over guardianship of the club three months earlier. Everyone was having to learn on the hoof, novice governance and novice management.

The previous owner Steve Hayes had departed but was still owed considerable sums. The trust had to work out how they could pay that back. The new caretaker manager had no clue about the accuracy of the club's financial state except that it seemed to be under a permanent transfer embargo.

'I tried to bring in a left-back on a free but wasn't allowed to. But our form on the field rallied. I attributed that simply to the change. You could have put anyone in charge and I think they would have got an upturn in form because that was what often happened. The crazy things that happened in the world, like Donald Trump getting in or Brexit, people loved a change.'

* * *

The 2013/14 season at Wycombe Wanderers – Gareth Ainsworth's first full campaign as manager – would forever be regarded as the Great Escape, though without the need for a Tom, Dick or a Harry.

The club was living a hand-to-mouth existence with a four-man staff, David Robertson was the director of football with physiotherapist Theo Farley alongside Ainsworth and Dobson after Lee Harrison's move to West Ham. Academy players were sold from under management's nose to foot the bills. The group of players who reached 15th in League Two to complete Ainsworth's initial season had re-signed as the manager hoped 'that with a better start we might go a bit higher'.

Barry Richardson's appointment as goalkeeping coach delivered experience at just the right time because Ainsworth and Dobson were still learning as they went along. 'I felt for those managers who lost their jobs in the first year. I was lucky. I got that period out of the way. But we were still having to turn our hands to all sorts.

'We built the goals at the training ground, I ordered nets off eBay because that way we got them more cheaply. Thinking back I still don't know how we stayed up that season, but that moment, the Torquay moment, made me as a manager.'

From 1 March to 26 April 2014, Wycombe took ten points from a possible 36, and when Bristol Rovers came to Adams Park for the penultimate match of the season the likelihood was a victory, and another at Torquay on the final day were required to remain a league member. There was little doubt that relegation would spell the end of the club as a going concern.

Wycombe and Bristol were on level points, Rovers won 2-1 and celebrated in the dressing room, on the terraces and a few inebriated idiots fought shadows on the pitch as if victory had secured their status and shattered Wycombe's.

'At the end of every season there was a tradition that we walked around the pitch after our last home game to wave to the fans and thank them. I usually took my kids but decided this time to go with Dobbo. The abuse we took was awful. But I could understand it. I'd taken the club to the brink of going out of the EFL and felt responsible. A few people applauded, a few *knew* the situation. That we were really in trouble. It was the first time I was worried that I might have to confront someone outside the ground, but by the time I walked out to the car park that night everyone had gone.

'I drove home a bit erratically and Donna once again put me straight on the important things in life. I made the decision to go in on Monday morning and convince everyone that we were going to stay up.

'The staff had two meetings with Don Woodward that week and he was turning the screw. I remember him saying, "What the hell are you going to do differently?" Don had backed me that season but if he could have afforded to sack me I don't know what his preference would have been.

'Dobbo and I hung motivational pictures on the walls. We bought the frames, the drill and the screws. We had an 11 v 11 at the training ground on the Thursday. Half the boys knew they were leaving at the end of the week, some had chucked the towel in but they beat the team I was going to play at Torquay. How did you work that one out?

'At a meeting in the dressing room the players talked about whether their wages would be paid if we went down. Some on one-year contracts feared the club would declare them null and void. I hoped Torquay [already relegated] didn't finally turn up at the weekend or we were going to be battered.'

Wycombe won 3-0 at Plainmoor. A couple of minutes from the end of the match the news spread through the ground that Bristol Rovers lost 1-0 at home to Mansfield Town, who had been on a west-country jolly. There was magic in the Devon air. Wycombe had indeed 'done it differently'.

* * *

Gareth Ainsworth was entering the second year of his two-year contract and needed to become a manager in more than simply a name on the door. 'I either stepped away or started to do the job properly. The Torquay experience taught me that I had to be better.

'How many managers got so close to absolute disaster and learned from it? Not a lot. But I got to the point where I said to myself, you can't just be this energetic, positive guy, there has to be more.'

A change of leadership at the top of the trust would have an immense bearing on the future. Andrew Howard was big in ice cream and motor sport but had no experience of running a football club. Beechdean Dairies was founded in 1989 by Andrew and his wife Susan and had grown across the following 25 years into one of the most successful independents in the field.

Howard would test the footballing set up like it hadn't been tested in a long time. Ainsworth said the new boss scared the shit out of everyone. 'It was all very nice here, everyone was everyone's friend through to the team and you didn't get a lot done in those situations. We needed someone to come down on everyone to get serious results.'

Howard intended to drive Ainsworth to become a manager whose responsibilities extended beyond training, football and results to understand the practicalities and realities of football economics, even if he himself thought them utterly crackpot. Ainsworth learned to use Microsoft Excel, how to (attempt to) balance a budget and see the fiscal wood from the trees.

'The first day Andrew came in, he took me around all the kiosks and explained why they were so important. I became involved in meetings with sponsors. He was a people person but totally results driven. I felt under pressure when he came in because I had to deliver.'

The team rebuilding took on different guises. In terms of personnel, on the eve of the 2014/15 season Wycombe lost their two central defenders, Gary Doherty and Danny Rowe, and needed stability. Richard Dobson asked around and Mark Warburton, the Brentford manager, had a defender, Alfie Mawson, on loan at Welling United. Wycombe backed a hunch.

Striker Paul Hayes who had been on loan at Adams Park in 2012, arrived on a permanent move from Scunthorpe and Sido Jombati, a Portuguese defender who had done the rounds of west country non-league football, joined from Cheltenham Town.

Left-back Joe Jacobson had been player of the season at Shrewsbury, but new manager Micky Mellon decided he was surplus to requirements. 'I wanted to be based around London and was offered a contract by a couple of clubs but I thought I could do better. I was at Glamorgan for a T20 cricket match, my phone rang and it was the gaffer and Dobbo in a car together,' said Jacobson.

'To be honest, I was worried because they had just survived going out of the league. I didn't want to go to a struggling team and had a good season in League One even though Shrewsbury was relegated.

'I'd spoken to Accrington's manager James Beattie and it was as though he was reading stats off a sheet of paper. He said, "Oh you played 'x' amount of games and scored 'x' number of goals," and I could tell he didn't really have a clue who I was. Maybe the gaffer didn't either but it was the way he spoke that persuaded me.'

With the personnel in place, it was time to build the squad's character. In October, they were taken to the World War One battlefields of the Somme and visited the graveyards of both the Allied and German soldiers which had a profound effect on young men the same age as many who went to fight in France and never returned.

Ainsworth regarded the trip as a pivotal moment in shaping the squad, underscoring the incredible value of *esprit de corps* and what enduring togetherness might mean for success on other, far less bloody, fields.

The target for the season was to reach 55 points. Joe Jacobson recalled, 'We won the first couple of games and had a sense that as a group we were better than we'd thought. The lowest we were that season was fifth and had a feeling that "we can do this". We were flying. You could tell that sides were a little scared of us.

'There was no expectation, no pressure. We got to 55 points in January, had a meeting to re-assess and the message was "we want to go for it". We had a small squad, got to the last ten games and then had a couple of injuries. Our final points tally of 84 [one behind third-placed Bury] would have been enough to be promoted nine out of ten seasons.

'We had a meeting with Andrew Howard on a development day at his factory before the play-offs and he told us he didn't think the club was ready for promotion. Financially, the best thing would be if we stayed in League One and could re-group.'

The loss to Southend at Wembley in the play-off final was a horribly chastening experience whether or not it satisfied the bottom line. Jacobson remembered the team retreating with their families to a room at a hotel in Wembley where the decorations had been removed and they stood around not knowing what to say to one another. 'It was the weirdest atmosphere. It was like "what happens now?" That was it. We said our goodbyes and went on holiday.'

By the time Wycombe were finally promoted at Chesterfield in 2018, Gareth Ainsworth was a serious manager with a serious chairman and the best bunch of lads all eager for their next challenge.

* * *

The team behind the team was increasingly professional, with Dave Wates recruited as the head of sport science – 'We had to sacrifice a player to afford Dave but it was a trade-off that paid off,' the manager said – and Irishman Cian O'Doherty employed to lead the medical department [of one].

Ainsworth was an empowering manager who allowed his staff to do their jobs without peering over their shoulders every five minutes. 'I'm a very live-and-let-live person. I let people get on with it. I don't want them to mess up. In the early days, when you're young, you've got all these hormones flying and you want people to fail because you can look better than them.

'I got to an age where I was OK with everything. I'd had my divorce, Donna came into my life and taught me a lot about what was important. I've got my faith. I have my kids [Scarlett, 16, Kane Presley, 13 and Gabriela, 11]. I have my safety net. There are so many people with much less than I have, but I've worked my socks off for what I have.'

He still had to work to budgets that would have sent most managers around the twist. 'When Andrew Howard came in he made money better, he made the commercial department better, people came back to the club but in all honesty we never turned over enough to make us safe.

'We wouldn't have been in the league if Andrew hadn't brought his drive and investment, but we weren't that much better off when he said he was leaving. We understood why he couldn't stay with his other commitments, the racing cars, his dairy business, and he wasn't someone who could be half-hearted, he was either in it or he wasn't.

'Trevor Stroud became chairman but there was no multi-millionaire in the wings, the club never made the money it needed and to compete was really tough. We'd been in the bottom half a dozen budgets, always, always, no matter what league we were in. We were the 15th biggest budget in League Two when we were promoted.'

In April 2019 Stroud called Ainsworth to the ground and told him that the club were losing so much money and no amount of good works could staunch the flow. The forecast was that Wycombe would endure a £1m deficit and the only way they could survive was to trim the player budget by the best part of a third. 'Trevor said we couldn't cut anywhere else because there wasn't anything else to cut. The budget we had would have put us in the bottom four in League Two, let alone League One.'

At the end of the 2018/19 season ten players were released out of the necessity of a squad trim. Nathan Tyson, Paris Cowan-Hall and Michael Harriman were foremost among those who left – 'though the decision was taken out of my hands,' the manager said. 'Had I known then what I learned two months later when the Couhigs announced their interest, I might not have got rid of so many.

'By that time I was on the phone talking about players nobody had heard of because they were all we could afford. I had a playing budget of just over £1m, the players on the books cost £700,000, so I would have £400,000 to bring ten in. You were talking about £600-a-week players capable of doing a decent job in League One. They weren't easy to find. We scoured the place for loan players who might be available and if they might fit into the way things were done here.'

It was in that period betwixt and between that Ainsworth and I met for our coffee to discuss this project. 'I was staring at the worst season we could ever have. I wasn't sure I wanted that documented but then you said the story was about a smaller club that can't compete and I thought, "You know what let's give this a go."'

We talked about his empathetic nature with his players, a sense that he knew what they were thinking almost as soon as they did. 'I'm able to get inside their heads. There's not a bad one among them. I'd seen what jealousy could do in life, and especially in football how it held people back. We don't have that kind at Wycombe.'

And so here the club was, new American owner, right in the scrap, evergreen players having astonishing seasons, the new ones gelling, a camaraderie second to none, exceptional vibes, living the dream. So many Wycombe teams from the past had been in this dressing room, they had felt the difference, they knew the club was special.

'We survived and this year has been an absolute whirlwind,' the manager said. 'I'd got to know the faces and names of the fans and that what we did meant everything to them. It was all the graft we put in. They knew how much we'd been up against it this season.

'When I first met Rob Couhig he said he wanted to come for no major reason but that he enjoyed football, saw Wycombe was a struggling club, knew the difference he could make and that he liked a challenge. We needed him and he knew we needed him.

'He said he'd get the budget to where it was. The way he was talking about the club and what they could do, I thought it was brilliant, one of my strengths had always been working people out pretty quick and I was excited to work with the family.'

Wycombe were family. To have stayed with one club for as long as he had marked Gareth Ainsworth down as a manager to cherish. There was little he hadn't experienced in life, nor wanted from it. Except to manage a league higher one day.

He was on the cusp. And yet, in a city far away, something was brewing that meant he would have to bide his time a little while longer.

It Is Now

ON Friday, 13 March 2020 football went for a Burton. Unlike Wycombe. The news landed with a sickening thud, the doors were closing, the turnstiles would not turn, pitches would not be taking a stud and terraces would stay bare. The game was up. For how long no one knew.

A particularly virulent contagion had spread quickly across a world of relative unpreparedness. Covid-19, a coronavirus, was taking a lot of people down with the force of an Adebayo Akinfenwa shoulder charge. The difference was that if you saw Bayo coming, you could steel yourself for the impact. There was no sense of this opponent.

The first thing we were told to do that could repel the virus was to wash our hands as many times as we could during the day for the time it took to sing the opening verse of the national anthem. Our local priest said we ought to recite the *Hail Mary* instead. Death was coming, that much was clear.

The day before the shutdown, Gareth Ainsworth had tactically debriefed Wycombe's proposed match at Burton in two separate meetings in the common room so that at least one empty chair separated each player. He was not to know that this would be the last time he'd see his team in the flesh for weeks.

We greeted each other with a touch of elbows and furrowed brows. The usual banter was replaced by a gallows humour regard for our well-being. Matt Bloomfield had a large water bottle in one hand as he balanced on one leg on an upturned BOSU ball saying he'd never felt this weird in his professional life, which was something given his Nureyev-like body shape at the time.

David Stockdale had been to Las Vegas across the two-week break that took in the weekend when Wycombe should have faced Bury. He returned to the training ground in full Wyatt Earp mode from the top of his stetson to the tips of his cowboy boots, though the Yorkshire accent rather destroyed the illusion.

He offered his hand as if fearing he'd be rather less than his new character if we touched elbows. I accepted the gesture and my heart sank the next morning to find him in the common room that was now his isolation chamber. He was running a temperature and Cian O'Doherty insisted he stayed apart from the rest of the squad.

As he left the premises by the back steps, Stockdale stopped for a second to recognise a familiar figure in a car that had pulled right up to the door. The driver had retracted his window by about an inch.

It was David Wheeler, who had been told not to come to the training ground earlier in the week because he'd been feeling a little ropey. 'I didn't sleep at all on Wednesday night, temperature up, sweating quite a bit.'

O'Doherty came through the entrance carrying a mirror and a couple of swabs. 'What are you doing talking there?' he said by way of a rebuke. 'You're a braver man than me.' Stupid again more like, as I had been shaking hands with the goalkeeper two days earlier.

The medical chief asked Wheeler to close the window and gingerly, with gloved hands, passed the swab through the driver's door and his sample was taken.

At about that moment, the EFL announced it was bringing a halt to proceedings. The Premier League followed suit ten minutes later. There would be no football until Friday, 3 April at the earliest.

* * *

People had already begun getting antsy. Some hid frustration better than others, but Paul Smyth was on permanent edge. Though it might be weeks before he pulled his boots back on for real, he was darting around the training ground in perpetual motion, thumping the turf time and again if he missed his target.

Smudger was a jack-in-the-box character who fizzed through life as if he had so much time to make up for, even though he was only 22. He had endured variable highs and lows during the season: a goal on the opening day, kicking a post in training which put him out of first-team contention and a debilitating sense of uselessness when he couldn't shake off the injury.

Richard Dobson was showing particular concern for him and set up a meeting with psychologist Misia Gervis to cover all the bases. Smyth made encouraging progress though it probably helped he had practised amateur psychology on a fellow professional a year earlier.

The last match of Wycombe's season – and who knew when that would be – was scheduled at Accrington Stanley, a club where Smyth had spent a period on loan the previous season. The player said he was pretty sure that after watching him play for Stanley, Bill Ainsworth had recommended him to his son.

In Lancashire, Smyth was not the sprite he had been the minute he walked into Adams Park. He struck up a friendship with Billy Kee, a fellow Northern Irishman, who had been the club's top scorer in the 2017/18 season with 25 goals. Sharp-minded on the pitch, Kee was struggling with a myriad of mental conflictions off it.

Smyth reckoned he kept Kee going through the following season, simply by being there as and when needed. 'Billy said if I hadn't been at Accrington, he wouldn't have been playing football. I was with him every day. His family lived in Leicester, I was in Blackburn and his missus's parents were there too. In a regular week we'd play on a Saturday, he would go to his house in Leicester, come up on Thursday, train, stay at his in-laws' Thursday and Friday and then Saturday after the game he'd drive home.

'But there were times when we didn't get days off, we were stuck in Blackburn, so I'd go to the shops with him to keep him occupied and happy. He had a bad time with gambling and a bad patch of drinking so I'd make sure he was occupied, we'd play darts and pool, no drinking at all, mostly killing time.

'I'd never seen anything like it. He had become totally self-centred and not meaning to be because he was usually a rowdy, loud guy, but he was just so quiet, didn't want to speak, couldn't be bothered with anything.

'There were times when he'd wake up and want to stay in bed all day. Because he had anxiety and depression and it was killing him, he didn't want to leave his house. I'd say, "You're coming out with me, I don't give a shit, I'm coming to pick you up." We'd go somewhere and he was back to himself again.

'In the end he had to give the game up, which was really sad. Football could consume you. One day you felt unbelievable and on top of the world and the next it was as if you had nothing in life. That was how Billy often felt. A key part of football was having a good group around you.'

Smyth soon eased into Wycombe's culture of all-for-one-and-one-for-all. 'Nobody allowed you to feel down here. There was a time I felt useless. It was killing me not being in the team. I wasn't depressed, I just wasn't me and I needed to talk to someone.

'Big Bayo grabbed me in a headlock and said he needed to have a chat. I wasn't doing the right things in training. I talked with B and I felt back to normal again. He reassured me so I knew that I was coming back soon [from his foot injury] and I wasn't to give up.

'Bayo was a celebrity. I knew players like him who didn't like to mix with the fans, but it was as if they gave him more energy. What you saw on his Instagram on a daily basis was what you got at training: he was happy, fun, buzzing, just a loveable guy.

'He weighed two of me, which was crazy, and still played League One at 37, which was frightening. He reminded me of Billy [Kee], but Billy could shift a bit more and he obviously wasn't as strong as Bayo. Billy liked to hold up play, win headers, to fight. I played off him and was happy to do the nippy running in behind, which was the way I liked to play with Bayo.

'I fell in love with this club the minute I walked through the door because I felt so comfortable. I was into the banter straight away.'

But there would be a decision to be made at the end of the season – whether or not to return to his parent club QPR. 'I suppose I'd need to go back to reality.'

What form that reality might take in the future was the question to which no one had the answer. The players went their various ways. The collaborative was placed to one side, each had his particular needs, desires and families to protect. A team sport had become a series of individual case studies, each human doing what he believed best to look after his health and, in many cases, wealth, as a pay cut – at the very least a deferral of wages – was surely on the way.

Each player drove home with a myriad of thoughts swirling. Should the season be screwed up and thrown into the bin? Should it be completed no matter what and how long it took? Should matches be played behind closed doors to protect the new 'social-distancing' rules to which some of the public were adhering, though you could hardly social distance *on* the pitch? Certainly not if you were Curtis Thompson.

* * *

Most clubs in the EFL lived a precipitous existence, with some more hell bent on suicide than others. Rick Parry, who had been appointed league chairman in September 2019, revealed the average Championship club spent 107 per cent of its income on wages, the economics of the nuthouse.

The most incredibly reckless club was the one nearest to Wycombe geographically, Reading. For the 2018/19 season their income:wages ratio was 226 per cent (i.e. for every £1 generated, they spent £2.26 on salaries). The average weekly pay packet was £19,000, ten times greater than Wycombe's.

Of the three clubs relegated to League One at the end of the previous season (Bolton, Ipswich and Rotherham) the latter paid the lowest average weekly wage, just over £3,500. Their income:wage ratio was 56 per cent, which was as close to sanity as it got.

These horrifying figures did not deter Rob Couhig. He wanted that place in the Championship, regardless of its death-rattle finances. The American had come to the club to inspire a hope of survival and nine months on had caught the whiff of something that could define him in the history of a place he hadn't set eyes before he was 70.

The week before the coronavirus spread became truly horrifying, we had sat in a cluttered office at Adams Park to piece together his journey to club ownership and how he perceived its evolution. In one corner rested a safe of disproportionate hugeness to the club's noted poverty.

'It doesn't have any money in it,' said the new Wycombe boss. I asked if he'd like to be referred to as Mr Chairman. 'I'm not big on titles. That's much more of an English deal. I'm Rob.'

Rob's perception was that 'our customers, clients and fans were more my boss than I was theirs because if they didn't show up tomorrow what the heck was I going to do the next day? When we were down looking at Yeovil the chairman there was all excited by his title. It was wild. But I suppose any mark of respect at this stage of my life I accepted.'

The takeover Couhig assumed would take six weeks dragged on for three months before everyone was satisfied with the paperwork. Since the travesty of 'screwball' Steve Dale at Bury, the EFL was supremely cautious about the next mug (discerning new owner) to offer to stick his head above the parapet.

'I suspect the management of the league felt that this [Bury] could never happen again, which was probably why I was the first victim of understandable caution.

'I didn't have enough of a case study to know how the league worked. They treated me with respect. I was struck by the fact that there were no rules on what you could do with the club when you owned it. In the US you couldn't borrow more than 40 per cent against total assets and that was a responsible rule. Here everything seemed so disparate and I sensed the league struggled with that.'

His first move once in control was an extraordinarily unusual one. There weren't many new chairmen who recruited a former chairman as a consultant before they had wiped the dust from their shoes. Couhig had kept tabs on Andrew Howard, who ran the trust from 2014 to 2017, before he became Wycombe's sporting director, delivering real focus and purpose.

Howard told Phil Catchpole's *Ringing The Blues* podcast in the autumn that he was owed substantial sums by Wycombe, 'though I've never asked for anything out of it,' and that if the wrong people had taken over, 'brutally I'd call my money in tomorrow. I didn't want to be involved with anyone who was going to stiff the club.

'There was always a vibe at Wycombe. It was a cool place to work even if you felt you were at debtor's door every 30 seconds.' Howard said his mentality was, 'Let's fight them all, let's take them all on.' He could provide Couhig with a very interesting ally.

'Andrew understood the game much better than I did. His wife said we had different approaches but were the same in many ways, though I wasn't a confrontationalist. I didn't get a great deal of joy out of negotiating. Andrew enjoyed it.

'You could say, "I thought you were a lawyer who tried cases for a living?" The reason I tried a lot of cases was that I was never very good at negotiation. I would much rather try the case where one of us was right, one of us was wrong, and I was pretty sure the guy who was right was with me.

'My nephew Pete would ultimately be the negotiating guy at Wycombe, but he was new to England, to agents and the industry so if we could both learn from Andrew why wouldn't we? I think he liked that I was focussed off the pitch, which was the way to grow the situation on the pitch rather than vice versa. That was the mistake a lot of people made.'

* * *

Gareth Ainsworth and Richard Dobson accepted new contracts, the telling fact of which was they were tied as a double act rather than single entities. Why sign Rodgers if you hadn't nailed down Hammerstein? One came with the other.

'I remember last fall when Lincoln came knocking and my first thought was, "Oh man what am I going to do?"' Couhig said. 'I didn't have any authority to keep them. Somewhere at that time Gareth and I had a discussion. I said, "I can get you some money now," which meant me underwriting more. We began to establish a pretty good working relationship and over Christmas I said I wanted it to be a lasting relationship.

'I told him that the day after I took over we'd agree a new contract and discuss its parameters. We both knew sports. If Man City came in tomorrow afternoon he'd be gone; if he went 0-27 in results he'd be gone.

'There were two things about him I admired, one personally and the other institutionally. Personally, he was a mature guy and that wasn't always found in sports. He had an ego but he could sublimate that to the benefit of the organisation, he loved the community and what he was building. He had also done what I'd asked him to do.

'Right away I said, "What do you need squad-wise so I don't have a heart attack in April?" He told me and I gave it to him. We established our relationship that day. He was as good as his word. I believe I was as good as mine.

'Institutionally, I watched what happened in the game here and everybody raced around like chickens with their heads cut off as soon as they lost two games. The best businesses had a continuity of management. That didn't mean he could go off and do something foolish and wouldn't be replaced, but the way I operated I wasn't going to look at a game or a series of games and start saying, "Are we progressing and if not why aren't we and is there anything we could have done differently?"

'We knew the things we needed to do. We needed to have a much larger squad. One of the reasons Wycombe didn't do well historically was that it wasn't deep enough. To sustain through 44 games we needed to be 24/25 competing for a position and another five or six learning to compete.

'I needed a squad of 32, that would cost money, but that was different from saying, "There's a guy at Ipswich who's the greatest striker and for a mere £4m we can bring him in." That, to me, made no sense.

'You would never get that money back. From my perspective, one player didn't change your team. Sure as hell, you'd spend that money, he'd pull a muscle and I'd have lost him for three games so I had to fill in. Athletes were very fragile assets.'

From the day he first spoke to supporters in July 2019, it was clear Couhig's twin focuses were increasing revenue and enhancing the matchday experience for those already committed to the club and anyone newly tempted to give it a try.

'People said, "If only I had a better team I'd attract more people." I believed exactly the opposite. I would attract more people because I provided an environment where you wanted to come, your wife wanted to come, your two kids wanted to come and in that scenario I'd have more opportunity through the gate to spend money on the players who could produce winning results.

'As an illustration, I was speaking with the Rebellion beer people about what we could do in the Frank Adams stand to put in more beers. I asked, "Can people come up here from the family stand for a beer?" They told me absolutely, but they didn't do it in case people might stay. I said, "People aren't going to cheat to stay in a seat for £4 and if they did they'd be embarrassed when they were asked to move."

Getting more people to come to Adams Park – wherever they sat – was an absolute priority. Wycombe's average attendance had risen during the season by enough to keep the chairman content but not complacent. 'We'll probably end up averaging around 5,600, which is 600 more than last season. Next year I'd expect 6,800 in League One and if we were in the Championship closer to 8,000.

'I think we could sell it out every time, which would obviously give a different dimension to everything we wanted to do.'

* * *

Rob Couhig began his career in the law in 1975 in an office of 13 workers. By the time he closed the door on full-time legal practice it had grown to 275. His primary trial work focused on commercial, casualty and product liability litigation. All a bit dry perhaps, but all very lucrative if you were successful. He *was* successful.

The New Orleans native had grown to become a member of Louisiana, Texas, Colorado and District of Columbia Bars and had also been admitted to federal courts to handle matters in Tennessee, Alabama, Mississippi, Pennsylvania and California. He had a wide sphere of influence.

'Within three years in my job I was selected by insurance companies to try some of the biggest cases in the state, and by the fifth I was involved in multi-million dollar suits. I was successful enough to end up with a relatively large national practice and at the same time was intrigued by the business of law firms and very much into my politics.

'My father was in the pest control business and lost his job. I helped him buy a company, he spun that out and from it we developed into the largest of its kind in Louisiana. It all came back to the same principle: the Couhig family loved the commercialisation of things and how did we take a losing proposition and turn it into a winning one? Most people may not have thought of me as a particularly competitive person but here was my take, "Could I make Wycombe succeed?"

'The challenge was to build a financially sustainable model in the midst of a world in which nobody seemed to care that this was an imperative.'

The corner shop philosophy was not something foreign to Wycombe. The club had long had to operate on the basic values of watching the pennies. By the time the virus struck, Couhig had the bottom line more or less where he wanted it.

'The deal was always the deal, it probably cost me more in legal fees than anticipated but I was a lawyer so I had a fair idea of those costs, the accounting fees and consulting charges. From a financial standpoint it hadn't cost me as much but from a societal standpoint it had.'

On specifics, he said, 'I have already lent the club £250,000. I was prepared to put up another £750,000 and after that things were going to squeeze. We were looking to change the entire stadium digitally, increase the build out of the stadium, which was probably £3m/£4m before it was over, but I didn't count that because I was building an asset I knew I could get my money out of.

'On the other hand if I went out to hire a winger and spent £1m that money was gone, I'd never get it back and so that wasn't happening.'

'My plan was to build a fan base so that every year I went to Gareth or whoever the manager was and said, "Here is your budget and don't come back to me. I'm not getting involved any more after this. If you think you'll need some money in January, I'd husband a few bucks if I was you."

'The manager will not be my best friend and I ain't his. We are business acquaintances who get along because we understand each other. If he walked in one day and said he was going to

Tottenham, then tell them they owed me money. If he lost 22 games in a row because his team was galivanting around and he didn't have any control, it would be "goodbye see ya later".'

Was Couhig aware that Howard had said in the build-up to the 2015 League Two play-off final that Wycombe might be better off missing out as it was financially ill-equipped to handle the turbulence promotion would generate.

'Andrew gave me the same kind of statement this season but I said that, on that, we'd have to disagree. I know what I'm doing and the idea that we could somehow put this off for a year, well I didn't know when the opportunity might come by again.

'If we're going to do it, we ought to do it whenever we got our chance. I don't read much social media but I do know some of these people say it'd be better for us if we don't go up, so let's lose. I don't understand that philosophy.

'I'm trying a different model. We've called it the Worldwide Wycombe Phenomenon and that's going to be so important because I fully expect that our merchandise sales will be four times what they are now within a year and we'll able through the impetus from our exposure on iFollow to double or triple them again the year after that.

'We need to build the club everywhere. The office is getting cleaned up. When you walked through a month ago, it was a sty. We're not having that anymore. We need to have a level of professionalism off the pitch, we have a team getting paid in a mid-to-low League One level, we have a staff that is young but they have been League Two because they haven't had the assets given to them. This is a profession and you can rise in your profession.'

* * *

Matt Bloomfield's mother Jackie had run the Marwyn School of Dance for the best part of 40 years, teaching ballet and tap. By the middle of March, the doors had been shut and she was inconsolable. 'Mum didn't know if all of her pupils would return.

She'd expended blood, sweat and tears for all those years. It was always more than just a job to her.'

One day Blooms's daughters Mollie and Rosie might have graduated there, but for now he was learning how to be a house daddy knowing his contract came to an end on 30 June, he was 37 next birthday and might not always be Peter Pan.

Not only that, he knew that the rest of the squad looked to him for sense and sensibility at a time of unparalleled concern. At every twist of the coronavirus story, he'd have to be abreast of his lads' needs and wants. It was an onerous burden, but if anyone could cope with it he could.

The pandemic caught the nation looking elsewhere and the light it held to the national game was an unflattering one. Blooms was selected among a group of six captains from the League One and Two clubs and asked to find common ground and collaboration through a maelstrom of concerns about wage deferrals, furloughs, cuts, possible extensions to the season and potential abandonment.

As chuffed as he was to get the call, the realisation of what he was being asked to do represented a challenge even more troubling than that of his daughters wanting to cut his irritatingly neat hairstyle as a lockdown laugh.

Rob Couhig had agreed that the Wycombe players should be furloughed, taking advantage of the scheme through which 80 per cent of wages were paid for by the government and the other 20 by the club. It was a situation to which Blooms was personally familiar.

'My brother Dan has a business providing coaches in schools for breakfast clubs, PE lessons and holiday camps. My dad, sister and brother-in-law are all employed by my brother's business. They were already resigned to having to lay off 70 permanent, part-time and casual staff. He hoped to have saved 12 jobs. Keeping schools open for vulnerable children and those who work on the front line of the emergency services has been a lifeline for them.'

A fitness freak at the best of times, his condition would matter as much if not more to the Wycombe captain as incarceration bit. The gymnastic rings and resistance bands that passed as a home gym required topping up, so he bought a stand-alone punchbag and a couple of kettlebells to give the Amazon delivery man a work-out. He needed to re-create as best he could the conditions at the training ground.

'I'd worked too hard over the past nine months to lose the strength I'd built up during the season. I needed to find a way to preserve muscle mass, create an enjoyable session and have my exercise fix.'

He had left his trainers behind at the club in the rush to get home and would have gone back for them only that was another £30 for the diesel. The slightly cheaper alternative was buying a new pair. 'It was a tough decision to spend on new footwear because I'd a family to support and we watched what we spent. I was out of contract in three months and there was no guarantee of future earnings.'

The emotional tear for a player like Bloomfield between expense and staying strong was as much as the one confronting him as an individual working for the whole in his PFA role – the need for Wycombe to have a chance to secure promotion properly and his desire for as many clubs as possible to survive this grotesque attack.

'The captains knew it was likely to get worse before it got better,' he said, three weeks after the publication of the EFL's initial letter to the clubs which advised that training could not commence until 16 May at the earliest.

At its estimation the leagues would require 56 days to complete outstanding matches, including the play-offs. The 'working assumption' was that matches would be staged behind closed doors mindful of the need to 'mitigate the costs of this to clubs as best we can'. It was a scenario that sent shudders down most lower league clubs, for whom gate revenue was the aortic valve.

Bloomfield and I spoke on the day the National League put its season to bed. The players' contracts there expired on 2 May rather than 30 June, so calling a halt was the most sensible of its lack of options. The first brick had been removed from the wall and many more would likely crumble before anyone saw a team run out of a tunnel for real and in person.

'In the Premier League, I think players can afford to give up "x" amount and if they don't get it back it won't bankrupt them. Can players in our situation afford to give up? Can they afford to defer? If it protected the long-term future of their current club then great, but there were players out of contact in two months. That was the situation facing me personally.

'If we were playing in July, who paid the wages of the players? Was it the responsibility of the clubs already under terrific financial strain, did the PFA step in, or did the players play for free?

'There were so many different issues to sort through. You ask anyone in any walk of life if they would be prepared to give up some of their income when it was possible they might not have any in the future. That was very difficult.'

Blooms's wife Mads had lost her income from a cleaning job. It took her and the children a few days to get used to having a man about the house on a regular basis. His girls would ask if he'd be there for breakfast because his normal routine would be to help put them to bed and be gone by the time they woke up, for his football work in Wycombe.

The captain's new daily routine was: 6.30am wake up; 7.15am girls' breakfast with mum as dad was in the garden for a strength workout, or on his bike for a 28km ride; 9am Joe Wicks's PE workout on TV; 10am crafts, puzzles, spelling, colouring; 12 noon lunch; 1pm playing in garden, bikes, scooters, trampoline, games, a walk later in the afternoon; 5pm tea; 6pm bath time; 7.30pm girls asleep, so either TV, catch up with emails, WhatsApp, texts, and then the imperative of catching up with the PFA developments.

Bloomfield had been on a Zoom call that day with Couhig (who was stranded in Louisiana, a state with initially one of the worst infection rates in the US), his fellow generals Adebayo Akinfenwa, Dominic Gape and Joe Jacobson and the manager to mull the implications as the lockdown pertained specifically to Wycombe.

'From my limited knowledge of the finances, whether we'd have got to this point without the Couhigs was one thing. The timing of their arrival enabled us to have the season we've had and now protecting livelihoods was as important as sporting achievement.

'Without them I wouldn't have been able to play any more for the club I love and the gaffer and Dobbo wouldn't be on this romantic journey.

'Has there been a worse time to take over a football club, a month before a pandemic? This must be so hard to navigate through but their conception of running the club has been life saving for Wycombe hasn't it?

'I'm not sure this [the suspension of football] is something that could be sustained indefinitely, but the message we got was that there were no deferrals at this point, to let the lads know they would be paid 100 per cent of their money. We discussed the furlough and how it would be possible to move the club forward, but Rob remained committed to topping up our money and we wouldn't go short.

'I personally thanked him for that, it's an incredible gesture from someone who has just come into the running of the club. We're very appreciative, we have mortgages and kids to support, we're normal working families as League One footballers. The call was a reassurance but also what they may need to do if we can move forward.

'None of us know how deep their pockets were and how much they were prepared to put in and what the club would be like in the future. He honoured our wages for this month when we haven't kicked a ball for him. He's been a massive figure in our history and probably didn't realise how important he would become when he first flew over to have a look around.'

* * *

The suicide rate in Britain had become an insidious spin-off of helplessness in the face of the pandemic. Young men were most at risk. Richard Dobson, in tandem with psychologist Misia Gervis, had come up with a handful of 'dos and don'ts' to send to the players.

'Misia worked up a set of three-minute videos, how to deal with isolation and the need for purposeful behaviour to work towards what you were looking to come back to. It was about being mindful, while they were at home, of what they are and who they are.

'Of course some of the boys were getting down because they wanted a date and to know what they were going to be aiming for.

'You could worry yourself sick thinking about that. I was trying not to get bogged down with dates, because every time we were given one it was pushed back.'

It was going to be vital to keep minds occupied and accentuate the practical and progressive as much as possible. Matt Bloomfield had suffered familial heartbreak when Stuart Hedley, a cousin who had lived not far from his Suffolk home growing up, took his own life in his 30s without anyone realising how much trouble he was in.

'Stuart and I were really close as kids. I had no idea at all that he was suffering. Would I be quite so empathetic with the players if I hadn't had that experience? I tried to life-learn from it and be on the front foot. I tried to be as close to as many of the players as I could be.

'My days were non-stop but not everyone was in the situation where they had kids to take their minds of things. Sat in a flat on your own, what did you do when you had time on your hands: you thought, you worried, you could be tempted to have a few beers and what was to prevent you from considering the worst-case scenario.

'I'd had a massive awareness and my eyes were opened. I spoke to Micky Bennett, the PFA's welfare officer, and Ben Purkiss, the chairman, to make sure that as a union we were getting the message out to players by whatever means that services were available. Footballers were no different to anyone else, with fears and anxieties about work and the effect on their income.

'I wasn't questioning what had been done before, but there was never a more important time to have regard for player welfare. We couldn't pick up the phone to every single one of them but we needed to make sure we put it into their heads as often as possible that there was help out there.'

Gareth Ainsworth asked Josh Hart to trawl through the season match-by-match and assemble a three-minute clip of his best moments for each member of the squad. 'We pulled them out randomly. Every day a different one went out via the players' group, to connect the lads with what they'd done this season. It gave that one person a real boost that day, there was anticipation and excitement.

'The other lads would send texts which further boosted that player's ego. These were the little techniques used to keep everyone connected. We would have everyone sent their clips in the time frame before we were due back to training on 16 May.'

Though Ainsworth had been given the idea by a Championship manager, his embracing of it knowing the sense of community it would enhance was further illustration of the creativity with which Wycombe were becoming the envy of the league.

Dobbo told the lads a week before lockdown that other clubs were eager to unearth the secret behind the Chairboys' culture and use it for their own benefit. He encouraged them to stay a step ahead and placed a new board in the canteen on which he wanted the players to write the titles of books, audios or films that enhanced positive thinking.

The list had just started to grow when the room was declared out of bounds.

* * *

Andrew Howard had come back to the training ground the day before the lockdown to re-introduce himself to those who had been at the club in his period as chairman and greet the recent arrivals. He looked and spoke like the kind of man who loathed pussyfooters.

The players were called into a huddle in the gym. Howard told them a bit of his background, urged them to hold their nerve when the bad news started to fly, and, above all, be the last team standing when it was all over.

Then we said our goodbyes.

Fasts, Philosophies and Variables

TIME passed. But how to pass the time? Monotony cuts through a footballer's soul. They are not programmed for chair-bound activity but live for the strain of combat, the smell of the horse oils, the scent of the grass, the rousing inspiration of a crowd's acclaim, the rush of a victory, the crush of a loss.

As moving as lockdown images were from Jack Grimmer's landscapes of Scottish mountains, Adebayo Akinfenwa's new off-the-shoulder Beast Mode vests (soon dripping wet), Jason McCarthy's gospel Q&As, Alex Pattison's 100m dashes with a parachute attached to his midriff and Josh Parker's sea-moss smoothies, we yearned to see the lads back playing in club quarters. How long would this take?

The reach of coronavirus was incalculable both in depth and breadth so the papers were filled with 'what if?' scenarios that shifted from one to another from one edition to the next. They were all agreed that the national sport would emerge from this scourge very different from the self-satisfied way it had entered it.

The season might be decided by dint of the completion of the outstanding matches – Wycombe had ten to fit in remember

– but as the days dragged on this looked an increasingly reckless, financially crippling policy. Of the formulae being touted as a means of clearing the mess with fewest legal entanglements, a model called PPG (points per game which divided the points accumulated thus far by matches played) had Wycombe finishing third.

On Twitter, @ad_1879v2 said, 'If Wycombe are somehow promoted to the Championship it will be the greatest act of shit-housery of all time.'

The deliberations pummelled the senses as if one was strapped to the rigging of a boat rounding Cape Horn. If and when football emerged through the storm, what would the prevailing landscape look like?

On Tuesday, 5 May Rick Parry, the chairman of the EFL, appeared before the House of Commons Select Committee for Digital, Culture, Media and Sport and delivered a withering assessment of the state of the game. Bearing in mind he was the initial CEO of the Premier League and had once been the keeper of Liverpool's treasure chest, his comments on saving lower league clubs generated a number of arched eyebrows.

The fact that Parry was on a blurred video-link from Chester did not lessen the transformative impact of his answers. 'We need a re-structuring and a re-thinking in the EFL. We need to address the long-term situation because we can't be back here in three years' time. We need hope. We need a plan. We need clarity. We can't go from one bailout to another.'

Parry described the Premier League's parachute payments that so distorted the playing fields of the lower leagues in favour of those who qualified for them as 'an evil that needs to be eradicated.'

The chairman said that the EFL season had to be completed by the end of July – 'if it went beyond that it would be a total mess. There are 1,400 players coming out of contract [on 30 June]. That is a train coming down the tunnel very quickly.' He feared for the future of several clubs in the short to medium term.

This was a stark reality. Mike Keegan of the *Daily Mail* had exposed the depth of the financial calamity a week prior to Parry's appearance before the politicians. A file marked 'Strictly Private and Confidential' had come into the reporter's possession and its contents proved that football below the Premier League was on suicide watch.

We didn't know which of the 15 clubs in League One had responded to an independent review as none were specifically named, but, from those who had, the report concluded that the average pay for a manager was £182,438, assistant manager £74,000, goalkeeping coach £40,000 and kit man £23,000. The average salary of the highest earners among the players was £247,185, which equated to £4,753 per week.

This was somewhere-over-the-rainbow economics to Wycombe Wanderers.

* * *

Pete Couhig remained in heart-breaking isolation in a rented top-floor apartment with a view across the High Wycombe skyline. He had celebrated his 48th birthday alone in the flat in April with his wife and three kids back in a state that had endured Hurricane Katrina in 2005 and knew all about coping with disasters. 'I might get whiskey drunk tonight,' he said.

At the start of the season he had offered to stick around to see the first phase of the family's charm offensive through to what became an emphatic takeover success. Now he was marooned in the town trying to work out how much of the club he hadn't heard of a year earlier might be left to pick over at the end of this epidemic.

'Did anybody buy a football club in 1939?' he said with a touching self-deprecation Americans weren't always the best at. If Covid-19 clung on as long as World War Two there would be no places left on the merry-go-round.

Pete knew the implications. He didn't go in for unnecessary prophecy even if he had begun to resemble Rasputin – wild, wispy beard and all. I had to ask what Wycombe's prospects were should there be a long-term lockdown. 'We can survive, but if all these whiney babies who think we should shut the economy for 24 months get their way I shudder at some of the scenarios.'

It was critical to be prepared for whatever landed at the club's door. 'I told Gareth and Rob [the chairman] that rather than consistently try to presume what the outcome might be, we needed to plan for multiple scenarios so when a decision was made we could shift gears into the right mode.'

One of those might be promotion to the Championship. Was Wycombe ready for that? 'Fuck yes, we're ready.' How? 'Because we're prepared to yo-yo.' The idea was that should Wycombe spend one season a level up they would budget for an immediate return to League One. 'But nothing is impossible. The goal would be to try to achieve survival with the lowest budget in the goddamned history of the Championship.'

Pete had the future budgets worked out dependant on an affordable wage structure in three tiers – high £5m, medium £4m and low £3.2m – with the top-five earners in category A, the next five in B and so on down the line through the 25 players they would need to properly compete.

Wycombe had 17 players signed for the 2020/21 season and seven officially out of contract on 30 June, including captain Matt Bloomfield, team totem Adebayo Akinfenwa and player-of-the-season candidate Joe Jacobson. All would be offered new terms. 'You want to hunker down with the dudes you love,' was Couhig's ode to the oldies. 'We basically signed everybody we wanted to for next year, so we're locked up ready to go.'

I mentioned Wycombe's wage levels and assumed Akinfenwa was the top earner. There was no confirmation forthcoming. 'In the US everyone knows what every athlete makes and the structures in every team. It's transparent. That makes sense to me. The English system doesn't, but I appreciate you don't want to talk about what y'all make so I have to accept that.'

Regarding Parry's comment about the 'evil' of parachute payments, Couhig said, 'If you took them away from those loser-ass clubs that fell out of the PL and spread it across Leagues One and Two, shiiiiit, all four levels of English football would be awesome. Each club would have enough money to have an academy that was a quality place.'

There was talk of curtailing this present season and playing 2020/21 behind closed doors for however long it took for the virus to be defeated. 'We have a pretty good business interruption policy which is when crazy shit happens that causes revenue losses in your business. I don't believe all clubs have it and I've spent quite a bit of time working on it. The best thing is we have it.'

How deep were Couhig's pockets and patience? 'Who the fuck knows dude. Anybody who says they know is talking bullshit.'

* * *

Josh Parker had developed a Rasputin beard as well. He had certainly built a reputation for extravagant thinking, a man not afraid to express powerful opinion and unfussed by those he upset. 'The normal procedure now is that it's a cool thing to be opposite,' he said.

'Someone will say, "Fresh blueberries that grow in the garden with nothing sprayed on them are the best thing you can ever eat." The immediate response will be, "No they're not," instead of, "That may be true."'

On one *Chairboys Live* episode filmed for the club's Youtube channel to lighten the lockdown mood and keep supporters entertained without a match to watch, a day's player selection was asked who they would most like, or dislike, to be in lockdown with.

Cameron Yates, the goalkeeper, whose appearance on screen was a cross between the karate kid and Bjorn Borg, said he would stick with Alex Pattison who shared the same club house

– 'He's crazy funny' – and Parker would be the worst because, 'He'd tell me that I'm wrong on everything.'

For the sake of balance, David Wheeler nominated Joe Jacobson as his preferred option as they could have a range of debates on a series of subjects, but that Matt Bloomfield would make him feel terribly self-conscious about his dedication to fitness.

Jacobson reciprocated on Wheeler for some agreeable disagreements and nominated Scott Kashket as the scary isolation partner because, 'it would be like having a baby. You'd have to wash him, feed him and generally take care of him.'

Instead it was Wheeler who anticipated fatherhood; his first child with wife Alice was expected in July. Parker had become a father for the third time in the last week of April, his daughter Zenzae arriving in circumstances that were true to her dad's character – different and proud to be different.

He said the lockdown hadn't fazed him football wise. When you had received death threats for wanting to fly home for a family funeral rather than play for your club – Parker had been at Red Star Belgrade and had wanted to take the weekend off that they were due to play deadly rivals Partizan – a difference of opinion on blueberries wasn't going to rock his boat.

'I said from the get-go the season wouldn't finish and they [the football authorities] would do the points per game thing. Nobody agreed with me in the group chats. The boys were, "Oh they couldn't do that," they felt there was too much money on the line and they had to finish it one way or the other. I said we wouldn't go back to football this year.

'At the minute [we talked in the first week of May] I think they're just using delaying tactics to make it easier to break to everyone. They know what's going on. The magnitude of this, it doesn't end in two or three months. It's almost as if they are dangling carrots in front of us when they know it's over.

'I haven't [retained any level of fitness]. I've been doing upper-body exercises. Walks. For the first two or three weeks

I was going at it like a madman, but if I'd carried on like that from the moment we left Wycombe I'd have done a 12-week pre-season by now. I don't have to run five kilometres every day. In four weeks of intense running, I'd be fine.

'If we did start again there would probably be a week's notice and then three weeks of pre-season. They couldn't just chuck us in at the deep end because we'd be dropping like flies.'

Parker had another year to run on his contract, one of the fortunate of his ilk, many of whom faced unparalleled fears for the future. 'I feel for those in that place. If you were smart you would have used these 12 weeks wisely, to learn something new.

'That's why, after I'd been running for a couple of weeks, I needed to imagine that football was never coming back and see what I could do for myself, my personal brand, just me as a person.'

In the midst of the upheaval, he became a father again and proved that he could be wrong: 'My partner Iekenah and I were certain we were going to have a boy. It rather consumed us. We have a son, Cairo, seven, and daughter Aieko, three, and the newborn was another girl.

'Iekenah had mentioned the name Zen and I remembered the gaffer's talk before the Blackpool match. He might think we were copying that. Zen is like the purest version of yourself. We did like it but decided it was too short. We chose Zenzae.'

The birth itself was much like a Wycombe performance, early lack of co-ordination, a lot of pushing, glimpses of precision teamwork, jostling for position, a bit messy near the end before a joyously successful delivery around the 90th minute.

'Trust us to be having a baby during the craziest time in the world. I'm a big believer in divine timing and that things happen for a reason. My missus had a notion about a home birth and it happened that Zenzae was born in the living room.

'I had been to the park with the kids and the only reason I left to come home was that my daughter needed a "number two" and said she couldn't hold it. We came back in and my missus was in the bath and said the baby was coming.

'We had the birth pool pumped up, I had to put the lining in and it wasn't full of water, the kids wanted to play with me and I was explaining to them that the baby was on the way. I asked them to help so I had Cairo holding the hose with the water and Aieko started to undress and climb into the bath during a contraction, thinking it was swimming time.

'The contractions were getting more intense. The midwife arrived, which was peace of mind, but my partner did it all herself. She pushed out the baby, cupped her out of the water and put her straight onto the breast.

'I was doing what most men do during birth – trying to help. My mum came around and I asked her to record the birth, and even though it may not have been nice to have a camera there at the time Iekenah will watch those videos over and over again in the future and appreciate how well she did. The birth was 90 minutes, no gas, no air.' (See what I meant about the resemblance to a Wycombe match?)

When he wasn't helping – or not – with domestic upheavals the vegan Parker never ceased to extol the virtues of a healthy lifestyle regime. I confess I never thought I would write one day about a footballer advocating the benefits of three days of eating only watermelon, but the game had changed from the steak-and-chip era. Parker's support for the cleansing value of fasts was picked up by people from all walks of life, fellow footballers, nurses and plasterers he gathered in a WhatsApp group for a sharing of experiences.

'I sent a detailed information pack and it was up to them if they wanted to take part. I explained my beliefs to people and they either bought into them or not. The person who may tell you that eating only watermelon for three days was bad would probably be tucking into a bacon double cheeseburger that same night.

'A watermelon is 95 per cent water and the remaining five per cent is vitamins and nutrients. One woman in our group had done her ACL, went through three operations and was in pain every day. After the watermelon fast she woke with no pain in her knees for the first time she could remember.

'Another girl lost 11lb in a week and another who suffered with dark eye circles and wrinkles on her forehead woke after the third day and they had gone. Honestly, I didn't get a bad word about it. There was a lot of sharing of positive emotion on social media. I based my opinions on personal experience. I wouldn't suggest anyone doing anything I hadn't done myself.' He was about to undertake his eighth fast, water only.

These three-day regimens would, Parker says, starve the parasites that built up in your gut and loved the nasty stuff we poured down our throats. 'When you stopped eating certain foods is when you had the cravings. It wasn't because you needed them. After day two or three, when you'd starved the parasites, they died. When that third day came, you weren't hungry any more.

'If you and I bought a bike at the same time, you rode yours every day and I rode mine once a week, whose bike was going to wear out faster? People didn't give their body a chance to rest and that's why there have been fasts for thousands of years.'

Jack Grimmer joined a three-day water fast, content that there was nothing in the world to match the crystal-clear water of the Scottish Highlands. He hadn't played football *for a filie* – since Tuesday, 26 November to be exact and epitomised the yearning of a young athlete to get back to what made his life tolerable. He was none the worse for the adventure.

Grimmer epitomised eager players with rested bodies eager to empower their careers once more. They were probably too desperate given the possible health risks. But they were athletes and not to be able to show off those skills was becoming intolerable.

Parker said, 'I can't deal with not playing because I know how good I am and that isn't arrogance. If I'm let off the leash and I can be myself I know I can do anything anyone else can do.

'I was chatting with my agent this week and we had the same sensation. I hadn't been getting games this season and I didn't know why. I was doing everything the manager asked and extra sessions on top and my agent said, "Wycombe's going to be promoted, you're going to play in the Championship next season and rip it to pieces."

'This can be a game-changer. My gut feels different when it comes to pre-empting stuff and it's never wrong. I feel it rumbling now as if it knows this is going to happen. I was thinking before that this season had to be fate – how could we have lost six out of ten or whatever it was at one stage of the season and still have been in the top two? That would never happen again in any league. You needed to appreciate a sign when it was being given to you.

'The gaffer is very loyal to the players who've been there for a while. I signed because I bought into what I'd heard about the club. I could have gone to Bristol Rovers, Blackpool, Doncaster and got double the money. For me it was about life, my family. I'm a big believer in divine timing.

'I know the team inside out, the gaffer knows what I bring in terms of my aura around the place and what I do for people. I don't need any more gelling time, no more "Can you come on the coach because we love what you bring to the squad." I'm a player. Hopefully next season there are no excuses.'

* * *

Lockdown had a strange effect on managers. One from the lower leagues got himself in a spot of bother on Instagram by conversing through direct messaging with a lady who happened to be the wife of his leading striker without knowing who she was. The players' group chat was quite illuminating for a few days.

Gareth Ainsworth's single indiscretion was to paint his face as Gene Simmons, founder, bassist and co-lead singer of KISS, the US rock phenomenon, when he hosted a lockdown quiz at his former club, Queens Park Rangers. Free of adornment, he was keeping in touch with his players as often as he could.

'My leadership is being tested in different ways. Football is so tactile, touchy, feely, you're with the boys, you feed off their energy. It's very difficult to do that remotely. It's the non-decision that's killing everyone. It's preying on all our minds.'

The greater percentage of his time in familial isolation was spent forecasting figures, talking contracts, looking at players, working through the various permutations in his head. League One? Championship? Lottery numbers. It was doing his job without having flesh and bone to work with.

He was grateful the League Managers' Association were doing a worthy and unheralded job of keeping their members' minds active. 'There have been personal phone calls from Richard Bevan, the chief executive, with twice weekly emails asking us to raise any well-being issues and offer courses online. I've been really, really impressed.

'I heard a lot about the need to go back for the integrity of the game, but what did that mean? Was it the 34 matches we had already played or clubs going out of business? The integrity of the game surely had to be that 92 clubs started next season in a healthy way. Don't finish the season if we were going to lose five clubs, that was stupidity, not integrity.

'At my level people have mortgages, they have bills to pay, I've got players ringing me asking if they should apply for a mortgage holiday. That's a serious statement. How must they be feeling inside when they ask a manager something like that?

'It's all very well for the PL to talk integrity, they are never going to go out of business. We're almost in a different sport. Integrity for me is being there for your players. It's the FA making sure there are jobs for us all next season. You look at what's happening in the world, a company like BA cutting 12,000 jobs. Wow. This is a world-changing moment.'

Ainsworth had kept a dialogue open with many fellow managers and detected a welcome sense of solidarity among them. 'There's not one who wanted to force the issue, everyone was totally sympathetic with the situation. That would have been my mantra regardless, but this pandemic had rain-checked a lot of them. The managers have all been calm, it's nice because I didn't know that was out there. The human side of people is coming out which is really good.'

'I've endured chaos as a manager but nothing on this scale. You have to deal with it. There are people who've reached the top of their trade in various positions of power and now we have to wait and see if they're good enough to be in those positions with the decisions they make.

'I almost don't want to be talking about playing football at the moment with so many deaths on a daily basis, and I don't want it back if it would put people's lives at risk. Darius Charles lives with his grandmother and how are we expecting him to train, mix with all the people around the club and then go home to his grandmother?

'He's being super vigilant of course, and at the other end of the spectrum we have players with very young kids, some a year old. As the manager, I'll stand up and say what's not right. We won't be bowing to any pressure until we know it [playing again] is the right thing to do.'

Even so, he couldn't delay the players' contract discussions *ad infinitum*. There was much to take into consideration. 'I know what Bayo means to us with his ability to see what the team needs, even if he's not in the side. He's an amazing guy. I'd definitely have him as a coach when he stops playing.

'Blooms, JJ, I have the ultimate respect for them. I want to give them all new contracts. They pay for themselves as guardians of the culture and they're teaching others how special it is to keep hold of what we have here.'

* * *

Richard Dobson was helping to home educate his children, Harrison and Daisy. He said he'd ask Harrison after each lesson,

'What could you have done better?' or 'What does excellence look like?' His kids now knew what hundreds of aspiring footballers had been confronted with down the years.

'Harrison said to me, "Dad, none of my friends are having to do this." I said, "Just because no one else is doing it, it doesn't mean you shouldn't do it."

'Daisy had a piece of work which involved watching and writing about a mini-clip from one of the Harry Potter films. We'd never seen one before or read the books. By the end of the next week we'd watched seven of them. The kids have been inspired. Daisy wanted to have a Harry scar on her forehead but we stopped short of that.'

When he wasn't playing domestic professor, Dobbo was spending hour upon hour on Wyscout, the app that platformed matches from across the world, giving coaches and scouts an opportunity to seek the special gem they'd normally spend foggy Tuesday nights assessing.

As the days dragged, Wycombe's assistant manager became ever more frustrated with the quality on view. 'I watched so many players they were starting to merge into one. I had to say the defending at under-23 level was abysmal. Regularly, you would watch 20 passes sideways and backwards. I kept thinking, am I going to see something productive here or is it a sideways or backward pass. And then that's what it was.

'I did get excited watching an Italian youth international at Manchester United in the Baresi mould [Franco Baresi was a great central defender/sweeper for AC Milan and Italy in the 1980s and 90s]. When people came to get the ball, he was like a rash, all over them, giving them no time or space.

'I wondered what he'd be like in the competitive element of the game and when there were loose balls and he was cool. I thought, "I like this lad." I was watching him for 15/20 minutes and getting very excited thinking, "I've found one," and then it came to heading duels. He didn't win a single ball in the air in his first ten challenges, and I went, "Noooo."

'I watched every team in our division over and again to see if there was one out there who could come into our side from the 23s or from some of the teams in League Two. I was looking for the next loan, the next diamond. I couldn't see one.

At one stage, early in the lockdown, Dobbo was sure that his mum, who lived about three-quarters-of-a-mile from his home in the New Forest, had contracted the disease.

'She had a bit of a cough and she self-isolated. All the symptoms they talked about she got progressively: dry cough, lethargy, headaches. I suddenly thought if this ends up getting any worse I might not see her again. It was horrible. She felt lethargic but she was super positive. Fortunately she came out of the other side. It took her a few weeks. I now completely understood the "stay in, don't do anything" message.'

Coming back to work would be a wonderful lift but at the same time Dobbo recognised the pressures it would place on everyone, 'If we had to play ten matches in 40 days, imagine what a hell of a strain that would be. A couple of positive things for us were that we had 17 players under contract, which meant that all those boys would be fighting for us next season. There may be other clubs in a situation where players would be preparing to leave and how much were their hearts going to be in it?

'I also believe there will be a levelling of the playing field. Think of all those clubs who had chased the dream for years and were close to the edge, this situation might suit someone who has been really frugal over the years. We were used to surviving on a shoestring. It was what Wycombe did.'

* * *

The daily media debating chamber was enough to stir rage and confusion in many a football supporter's soul. They will, they won't, they can't, you'll be hearing from my lawyer, we'll go bust, PPG, void, iFollow, streaming, integrity, testing, Oxford's trying to pull a fast one and get themselves promoted, conspiracy theories, it was a mess.

Sam Day was a 20-year-old Wycombe supporter studying at Oxford University, putting his incisive mind to those who promoted a 'weighted' version of points-per-game to decide the table positions in the event of the season's closure. He demolished that theory – one which would see Oxford finish third in Wycombe's stead – in a manner that reminded me of the theorem behind Wycombe's victory at Rotherham.

'No solution is going to be fair on everyone,' Sam said, 'but weighted PPG is the worst because you a) extrapolate from the present to predict future results based on whether the game is home or away and b) introduce a control variable into the calculations.

'Both points are extremely important. The season must be based upon performance rather than predicting results. As soon as you are predicting results, you're making judgements about things that haven't happened. No element of prediction should come into this.

'Once you introduce controls for home/away records you have also to consider alternative variables that may have impacted those records – particularly fixture difficulty. We [Wycombe] have more away games to play which hinders us if using the weighted model because our away form is quite poor. However, apart from Coventry, we've played all of our toughest away games. Five of our six remaining away games are against teams in 12th or below.

'Likewise, our home form is fantastic but we haven't played Oxford or Rotherham at Adams Park. Without accounting for fixture difficulty, the proposed home/away weighting views Southend away as more difficult than Coventry at home. This is obviously wrong.

'If the EFL uses the weighted model, they may as well predict the rest of the season based on form, fixture congestion, injuries, weather conditions, midweek v weekend matches, suspension, anything that could influence performance.

'It would be completely wrong to decide the season on an arbitrary variable without considering other more important variables. Weighted modelling was by far the worst solution.'

I could now add 'arbitrary variables' to 'inverted trapezium', 'anyone got some jump leads?', 'that's bullshit dude' and 'top of the league' as phrases I hadn't expected to include in the season's chronicle of Wycombe Wanderers.

A Game of Integrity

'What did you do in the pandemic, Daddy?'
'I tried to persuade the public there was
integrity in football son.'

ON Friday, 15 May a meeting was held of member clubs to determine if a semblance of closure could be agreed for the EFL season. The evening before, tossing chilli flakes into the recipe, Peterborough United's owner Darragh McAnthony sent a tweet that began with the eye-catching, "***Breaking News***".

McAnthony revealed he was writing on behalf of his club and five others that nominally equated to League One's Big Six of Peterborough, Sunderland, Portsmouth, Ipswich, Oxford and Fleetwood to register their combined insistence that the season be completed.

'We have no desire for voiding, PPG scenarios or letting a computer decide our footballing fate. For the integrity of our sport we are all looking forward to completing our pending fixtures under guidance from the EFL at a time when it is deemed safe to do so.'

The message emboldened the other clubs in the group to pipe up in a similar vein. An alternative view from Accrington Stanley's Andy Holt was typically robust: 'Anyone who puts sporting integrity and football in the same sentence is deluded.

'They'd shoot their grandmothers for three points.

'It's all about money. It's a financial war, not a sporting battle. It's exactly because there is no sporting integrity that clubs are dying and football is on its arse. We cannot waste £640,000 to play the season out and pay for testing just because six clubs want to play off. We're using next season's cash already due to the EFL loan.'

There was no doubt the six were spooked by the very idea of Wycombe Wanderers being promoted by the points-per-game algorithm considering they were obviously far more worthy because they were, well, bigger. It wasn't fair that they would be consigned to another season in League One while piddling Wycombe might go up.

It was so different now. In the days when they struggled to stay in the Football League on a beggar's budget, football folk envied Wycombe's pluckiness – what a brave little bunch. When they dabbled with promotion they ought to be grateful for all the luck they had. A place in the Championship? This was an affront to decency.

My mind returned to the evening of the match against Blackpool at Adams Park in January when Gareth Ainsworth made his rousing 'zen' speech and displayed the badges of those clubs who *had* to be promoted. They were six and the same, who weren't only working for themselves but for each other. The Chairboys weren't in this particular club.

Later, on the evening of the 15th, the EFL issued a statement saying that varied views had been shared and it was, 'determined there would be a further period of reflection and consultation to understand what creative solutions could be implemented.'

That spurred Sunderland (seventh in the table, one place off the play-offs having played two matches more than Wycombe) to raise the idea of an eight-club play-off that, lo and behold, would give Ipswich a way into the fun. There was an awful lot of 'big' club 'I'll scratch your back if you scratch mine' going on. All in the cause of integrity.

Phil Parkinson decided to enter the fray. 'If it's not possible to finish the fixtures, another solution would be an extended play-off scenario, a mini tournament to determine the play-off places,' Sunderland's manager told the *Newcastle Chronicle*.

'League Two has decided to adopt the play-off places as they stand but that only happened because Port Vale and Bradford City magnanimously decided they weren't going to be involved in that [obviously Sunderland hadn't mastered magnanimity].

'In League One it's been so tight all season and when you look at ourselves and Wycombe not only do we believe we can get into the play offs but we have to believe we could still finish in the top two because so much can happen in the last eight to ten games of the season.'

McAnthony indulged in more cage rattling, threatening all and sundry with legal action if the season was either voided or 'unweighted' PPG was used to determine either the end of the season or places in a prospective play-off. In the latter instance, his club would finish seventh and one out of the desired spots.

He told Peterborough's podcast, *The Yellow Block*, 'The plan with Ivan Toney [his highly-regarded striker] was for us to win promotion, offer him a much better contract, watch him score 20 goals in a Championship season and then he'd be worth £20m to £25m. That could be taken away from us without kicking another football.

'We don't have to sell him if we don't go up, but he wants Championship football and it would be hard to deny him that chance. It could be he's played his last game for us. There isn't going to be much money floating around in football after this is all over, but it doesn't mean we're going to sell him on the cheap either.

'This business has worn me down but I'm fighting on. My lawyer tells me we have the blockbuster of a case. We will take action against the EFL and the other clubs if they deny us the chance to have a go at promotion.'

The EFL board met on Wednesday, 20 May to discuss their position and put it to the vote two days later. Two days prior to that gathering, Nigel Clough relinquished his position as manager of Burton Albion along with brother Simon, the chief scout, and assistant manager Gary Crosby.

'We hope that by stepping away it helps the club with the financial pressures in these unprecedented times and that it will also help the club secure the jobs of as many of the staff as possible going forward,' Nigel said. I could envisage a heavenly body giving a two-thumbed salute to that.

The League Two curtain had been lowered, though, with an indicative vote that would require formal ratification, especially as it wanted Stevenage, bottom of the table, to be spared relegation to the National League. The plight was eloquently outlined by the owner of Port Vale, for whom Ainsworth remained the most expensive signing (£500,000 from Lincoln in September 1997) and most expensive outgoing (£2m to Wimbledon 13 months later).

Carole Shanahan had gone into the league meeting with every intention of voting to complete the season. Three hours later her opinion had shifted to the good of the game first and Vale's needs second.

'We're eighth. We had every reason to believe that if we carried on we would have a good chance of the play-offs or even above that. I couldn't see any reason to vote for anything else. When I listened to everybody and to what people would have to go through to continue the season I realised actually being a part of League Two and what was right for the league was more important than the hurt Port Vale would feel.

'It felt horrible to have to tell the manager [John Askey] that all the work he'd done was to no avail this year. To take that message to the fans was not easy. It was the right thing to do. It sits easily with me that we did it. It just shows that eighth is the worst position in the league.'

Wycombe were eighth in League One.

* * *

Amid the vast correspondence to and from the EFL's Preston headquarters as the coronavirus strengthened its grip was a letter from Wycombe Wanderers' head of medical Cian O'Doherty. The Irishman was a meticulous man with a demeanour that brooked no argument. His haircut alone was as sharp as a scalpel.

Very often at the training ground you'd find O'Doherty with one knee pressed into some extreme corner of an unfortunate player's anatomy to try to coax it back to full power. Even the blaring music could not completely blot out the moans from those whose muscles he was unknotting. All in a good cause though, I often reassured myself.

What wouldn't those same players give now to be clenching their fists in agony as O'Doherty trampled all over them?

The medical boss's determination was to make sure that if his boys were sent back out to play and complete the season, they were truly safe and protected. His note to EFL chiefs outlined his concerns about a lack of proper medical protocols and how a rush to re-start could have serious detrimental effects on player health, both physical and mental.

O'Doherty was furloughed during the epidemic and thus could not reach out to speak to the players on whose fitness and demeanour he kept such a forensic daily check. To tell a man who spent all his life 'hands-on' that he had to be 'hands-off' was a tough one to accept.

The concerns about infecting anyone or being infected with Covid-19 was clearly atop the priorities, but O'Doherty feared that not enough consideration was being given to the non-pandemic-related issue of the short and long-term perils of pushing athletes out to perform before their bodies were properly in sync.

He had no idea what each individual player had been up to in the previous nine weeks. 'Coming back into training is going to be a very slow progression, it will be about dealing with injury prevention to begin with, seeing where the boys are at, what their fitness levels are. They're going to be at different stages, some will have done loads, others will have done a little bit, others may have been very relaxed about things.

'We have to think about how we screen them in a safe manner. The protocols received so far from EFL definitely would be very restrictive as to how I could assess the players and the likelihood is that we wouldn't be able to do that properly and to understand where their bodies are at.

'Unless the players come in with a specific injury, we're pretty much told not to touch them or go near them. If they picked up an injury in training, we're going to have to be able to treat and assess them within a short time frame, wearing full PPE if we can get our hands on any. But we're not allowed to do the routine screening we do before training every day, and that's where the risk is.

'What is the time frame for returning to matches going to be? It looks like we might have three weeks to prepare the boys. And we haven't played for so long; are there going to be friendly games with the risk of injury? Any player picking up an injury before or when we resume, we'd have to consider the mental health elements because they're going to be pressuring themselves to make sure they're ready.

'If we're going to rush back, there's a very high injury risk, and with ten games to play in a short period of time, recovery time is reduced, particularly with our squad numbers. In playing a lot of intense football very quickly, the risk grows of chronic overload injuries that can take six to 12 months to sort out. I'd be very concerned about that.

'There's game sharpness as well. Is your timing going to be 100 per cent? You might be a second off making a tackle or getting away from a player. What is your landing technique like after a header? Everything is going to lack that edge.'

The only one who couldn't let his guard down for a minute was O'Doherty himself. We discussed the prospect of a player going down with a head injury. 'The first thing you did was use your hands to support their neck and you were pretty much on top of the player. If we were using government guidance that would mean me running on with a full face mask wearing plastic apron and gloves. I'd look like a spaceman.'

The new and most frightening element to all of this was the virus itself, the unseen enemy that had so far ridden every tackle and kept coming back for more. 'Think if someone came in with symptoms, they would have to isolate for seven days, if a household member came down with symptoms, then you were gone for 14 days. You could have a full squad one week and 50 per cent the next.

'The signs were there could be another peak in a few weeks and that's what we had to be mindful of. This hadn't gone away, it was still out there, there was no cure and no vaccine. Treatments were adapting and hopefully we could start to contain it but it remained a very infectious disease with a high mortality rate. As it attacked the respiratory system, we had to be especially careful of any player who suffered from asthma. And we had to be sure from a cardiac perspective that any exposure couldn't damage players' hearts.

'Were the players going to be tested before each training session, before and after every game, what were quarantine requirements? How much was it all going to cost? It was going to be both risky and scary from our perspective. The last thing I wanted to do was be infected and bring anything home to my wife and kids.

'We had to bear in mind all the time that it hadn't gone, people might have been getting bored at home and wanting to get back to normal but the reality of the situation was we didn't want to end up back to square one.'

* * *

It was on Thursday, 21 May that the EFL issued a statement that shook the game to its core. It was a declaration of intent that the resumption of the season was the preferred option but they had to plan for that to happen in stages and maybe not at all.

The decree was that 'unweighted' PPG should be used to decide divisional placings, meaning Wycombe would leap from eighth to third, promotion and relegation should be retained and play-offs would be played 'in all circumstances' but should not be extended beyond four teams.

The EFL said that if the play-offs could not be played the board would 'determine the appropriate course of action'. It considered that a majority required to curtail the season in any division should be 51 per cent. In that case, 12 of the 22 teams in League One would have to vote to complete the season for the matches to be played, at a probable cost of £500,000 per club.

Darragh McAnthony melodramatically altered his Twitter profile to, 'Owner of Peterborough United "not allowed to play football" Club.' Fan forums turned nasty, most notably at Oxford United, whose contributor 'holdsteady' wrote, 'Ainsworth will have Wycombe players running around hospitals to catch coronavirus [which] won't even be the most negative tactic he's used this season.'

McAnthony – an Irish entrepreneur who had become Peterborough's owner at the age of 30 in 2006 – then began to backtrack and insist he hadn't threatened his fellow clubs with legal action. He said he had no desire to cause a rift, only to have a nice chat about what the future held.

'We spoke to a lot of other clubs and to those Coventry and Rotherham fans who are upset about it [wanting to complete the season] and we tried Wycombe. The Wycombe owner emailed me a few weeks ago and we tried to get him on. The bottom line is we wanted it transparent that we wanted football back on, it wasn't us versus them as some people took it. That wasn't the intention. For that I can apologise.'

On Friday, 22 May Gareth Ainsworth and Fleetwood manager Joey Barton appeared on Sky Sports to discuss the implications with host David Jones and regular analysts Gary Neville (the co-owner of League Two Salford City) and Jamie Carragher, who warmly engaged with his fellow Liverpudlian Barton and remained strangely subdued during the Ainsworth segment.

The backdrop to the 'should we/shouldn't we play on?' debate, the daily outpourings of outrage from Peterborough who might not go up and Tranmere who might well go down, was that coronavirus fatalities were registering in heart-shattering numbers on a daily basis. Ainsworth used the word 'death'. That particular day's toll was just short of the accumulated number of four Hillsborough disasters.

The point was stressed to Wycombe's manager that his club had made no public comment during the lockdown and hadn't joined the 'posh elite' of the six so vocal in their desire to push on with the season.

'We believe that everything should be done in-house, privately, my owner is big on that, he's a lawyer from the US who only took over two weeks before the lockdown. He believes in keeping your cards close to your chest.

'There are some huge decisions to be made. This is life and death and that is pressure for people. We didn't think putting added pressure on them was the right thing to do. We're happy with our position on that.

'Look at the Bury and Bolton situations this season. Clubs have been spending more than they've been earning. We're still tight with the pennies at Wycombe. We have to look after the sport. I understand playing on is the right thing but you can't do it when people are dying and clubs may go out of business. You mention integrity but does that mean knowing clubs might go to the wall and yet forcing them to play?'

Jones asked if Wycombe were going to vote to complete the campaign. 'My owner will make that decision. He will look at the finances and what it will cost to finish the season, but staging the play-offs would cost too. We'll have to have testing, training, taking the players off furlough, there is all sorts of expense involved.'

Barton talked as the manager of the side with the healthiest League One record at the start of 2020. 'We had one defeat in 17, we've been away to every side with a chance to win the league, we felt we had a right shot at the automatic spots and were two points behind Rotherham with them to play at home.

'I appreciate the reluctance of clubs who don't have an ambition to play on because they've nothing to play for. We have seen Bury go out of business and Bolton almost the same and I understand others wanting to protect their clubs and their community.

'We started the season with the aim of playing 44 matches and we should adhere to that. Rotherham have won the lottery because they had six of the top ten to play in the final period. But this is a global pandemic and we have to resolve it one or the other for the sanctimony [*sic*] of the competition.

'The players will be tested twice coming into training, have their temperatures taken before and after and be tested twice more in the build-up to games. There won't be a safer place to do any job than a professional footballer. We want jobs after [the pandemic]. We have to get the game back moving as safely as we can for morale and to save the industry we've all been very fortunate to earn a few quid from.

'The ethos of our club is to play on because we think we can get to the automatic places. We'd be a bit gutted if it went to play-offs but we're lucky to be able to play for our future. It could be a last-chance scenario for our boys to play in the Championship. We don't have the budget of these bigger clubs. Ours is three million and theirs is 12, 14, 15 million. It's right we get a chance to go up because we've earned it.'

Ainsworth, whose playing budget for the season was initially set at £1.1m, said, 'we had a good chance of getting one of the automatic spots. We had ten games, seven against clubs in the bottom half, we'd been in the top two longer than any other club, 20 weeks in total, and we dropped from third because we had Bury scheduled the week before the lockdown so everyone passed us. We still had plenty to play for.'

* * *

Dominic Gape moved home a few days before the virus struck. We were now three weeks on from when the season had been scheduled to finish. Gapey had a paint roller in his hand and white flecks festooned his purple top. He had almost grown a moustache and his hair was distinctly wavy. There was a bit of Errol Flynn about him.

He had socially distanced from deep conversation this whole time. Even on the player Zoom calls he was quieter than usual. We shot the breeze for an hour. There were so many elements to the current story that disquieted him. His sister was a nurse on the front line in Bristol but NHS confidentiality clauses meant he wasn't able to discuss what she had gone through as the Covid-19 cases multiplied, but it did lend him a sense of authority on the subject.

'I feel weird about being at home and taking a wage,' he said. 'That doesn't seem right but I have to do what's necessary. I'm in my own little bubble here with my fiancée and it's time we may not have again. I've tried to switch off from everything that's going on. It's too much to take in.'

Gape had purchased a road bike and persuaded Matt Bloomfield to do the same, not that he needed much persuading. When Dave Wates called and the pair went running and riding together, the head of sport science – a very fit guy himself – was left in Gape's wake. When the races had been run the midfielder informed his knackered companion he'd done the same regimen for the last 14 days on the trot.

Here was a man who would be ready for when the time came to play again and was certain the same applied to his teammates. He understood their character, that they were mature and self-sufficient and would quickly get their heads around any situation.

We talked about a potential play-off against Fleetwood, which was the way the fortune cookie would possibly crumble. Gape mentioned the distance between the two clubs, how would it be possible to travel together as a team, where four players sat across tables on the coach, and there were never more than half a dozen empty seats? Hotels were shut. Would the players be expected to drive 300 miles on the day of such a critical match, get out of their cars, pull on their kit and go out and play with what was at stake?

He had reason to believe Wycombe would be the best of the League One bunch through recent exposure to adversity. Then he imagined a week before a match if one player tested positive, what would happen to the rest? How could this be fair? He mentioned that Paul Smyth was an asthmatic. This was a virus that attacked the lungs. He surely couldn't be risked, which put Wycombe at a significant disadvantage.

All of this was going through his head as he tried to make sure he was painting the right room with the right colour. In this whirligig of emotions, how could professional football possibly be played and maintain the integrity everyone kept going on about? 'There is so much that doesn't make sense,' he said.

Peterborough's manager Darren Ferguson – for whom Ainsworth had a ton of respect – was gathering his thoughts on the subject and told his local paper, 'I feel for my players who constantly ask me what's happening, and for our fans who for the first time in a while had a real positivity about us winning promotion.

'We are ready to play again but it doesn't look as if things are going to go our way and that's a shame because I felt we'd get into the top two. We've emerged from a bad spell to win seven out of nine and beat good sides convincingly.

'If we don't play again this season we'll have to be ready for the next one. We have a plan in place should we still be in League One.'

* * *

In the *Yorkshire Post* of Monday, 25 May Rotherham United's chairman Tony Stewart estimated it would cost each League One club between £500,000 and £1m to play out the season. 'There's a strong sense the clubs want to abandon and call it a day and then pick up the cudgels next season. The weight of the money outweighs trying to fulfil the season.

'If you are seventh-from-bottom or ninth-from-top you might be saying, "Hang on, what do I get out of this?" The answer is debt. The EFL is being bombarded. I think there has been a little bit of bitterness, more than expected in League One.'

Rob Couhig had kept out of the frenzy on purpose. He was rising at 4am each day in St Francisville, some 120 miles north west of New Orleans, to discuss the business menu with the team at Adams Park. 'Zoom has been a life-saver but I've always preferred to look people straight in the eye,' he said.

He had dialled into the protracted discussions with the EFL where Rick Parry, the chairman, and Jez Moxey, the chief executive of Burton Albion, assumed the lion's share of the conversation. 'The meetings are collegiate and a chance for owners to talk between themselves, which I perceived they didn't ordinarily do.

'From the start it was decided everything would be confidential and if I agree to something like that I follow the rules. Less altruistically, who were those speaking out trying to appeal to? Remember what I do for a living, I'm a trial lawyer and I don't wonder too much what people in the audience or the other lawyers think, just the 12 people in the box. Our approach from day one was that we wouldn't conduct our business in public.'

That was in direct contrast to the Tranmere owner Mark Palios, a former chief executive of the FA and once an insolvency practitioner at PricewaterhouseCoopers. Tranmere were going to be relegated under unweighted PPG and the club cried foul, long and loud. They were 21st in the league, three points from the side above them, AFC Wimbledon, with a game in hand.

Palios told the *Daily Mail,* 'There are clubs who genuinely don't want to re-start because of cost and are voting to improve their own financial position at our expense. It is grossly unfair, a return to the days when decisions were made in smoke-filled rooms. I thought we were done with them.'

Couhig was unaware of any such chicanery and wouldn't have got involved if he had been. This was too big a deal. He had been caught up in the appalling blight of Hurricane Katrina in 2005 that picked off people and cities and caused $70bn worth of damage without once pausing to ask if anyone preferred unweighted PPG to obliteration.

'My entire city of New Orleans was wiped out, we weren't allowed back in our homes for six months. It taught me a lot of lessons. Number one was I'm the luckiest human on earth because in the month before Katrina we had closed on several deals that gave us the financial wherewithal to weather the storm and keep all my people employed. That took the blooms off the rose of financial stability for a while but we were able to do it.

'You can't do anything about what you can't do anything about. There's no point in sitting around saying "oh woe is us". It's how do we get from here to there and proceed forward. When I look at this pandemic and us getting to the other side, I know we have to take whatever steps necessary as prudently as possible.

'Having been through various traumas I know life isn't fair, nothing that's happened with this virus is fair, so the "it's not fair" argument doesn't go very far with me. We do what's best for everybody as best we can and try to get ourselves back on board. If we were just talking about cost savings, we would have ended this two months ago and said, "See you in September."'

'The first six weeks of the lockdown cost us nearly £800,000. May will cost us another £400,000 to £500,000 with an average burn rate for the next four to five months of £350,000. We're doing all we can to ameliorate the situation but the club will be between £2.5m to £3m upside-down by the time October rolls around. That's a huge hit.

'We're working constantly to try to figure out what we can do. We'll get there. I'm not that big on decisions being made by boards of directors, but it was important for me to talk through the status every Monday with Missy, Pete and David Smith and David Cook from the trust.

'The trust is a 25 per cent stakeholder, it could be subject to a huge cash call and if that happens it could diminish or eliminate its ownership. I told them in the early days I would never try to put them in that position and we're working around it. Don't let the apparent calm in my voice serve as a sense that I'm not anxious. I'm not the richest guy in the league and we have to take care of ourselves and be good stewards of the piece.

'My goal from day one was financial sustainability. We weren't getting into wild goose chases over players. One of the reasons I was so attracted to the club was they were already well on the course. You are going to see more clubs, out of necessity, adopting our programme. Rules will change and there will be hard days ahead.

'I don't tend to look at other people's finances but I had the opportunity before buying this club to look at the books of half a dozen others and without revenue I don't see how they're going to pay their June bills. They will get through May – June will become very difficult. It will be difficult for us, we're going to have to dip into our own pockets. We can do it but it's nobody's idea of a good time.

'Originally I thought people would acknowledge that the cost was so ferocious that the only rational plan was to shut it down and to put all of our energy into preserving resources and a commitment to starting the new season in September.

'That seemed to go by the wayside, there was the idea promoted in public of trying to play on. I don't see where you could possibly get half the clubs to say "let me go out and commit financial suicide". Then there was the expanded play-off idea someone came up with. They had their right to push it.

'Even knowing everything now we would still have done this [bought the club]. It has been a remarkable opportunity to meet some very good people, to try out our business skillset in the toughest of times and see where it goes. We will get there. I don't expend a lot of energy thinking about how I might have expected this to be done. Those days are over. You can only deal with the future.'

Three days later, Couhig issued an official statement confirming the figures from our conversation. It was chilling in its clarity. 'We have informed all our non-football staff presently on furlough that their pay will be limited to that which we receive from the furlough plan. Through 31 May everyone received 100 per cent of their pay. The club made up the difference.

'Going forward, these furloughed employees will receive 80 per cent of their salary with the maximum payment of £2,500 per month. We are also recommending that they begin the search for alternative employment once furlough ends.

'I have also informed our manager that the club will be without the services of Jason McCarthy. Jason is a wonderful player and a terrific guy. He was on loan to us from Millwall.

'While they and he were willing to extend the agreement through the remainder of the season and he would unquestionably be helpful if play resumes in any circumstances, we simply cannot afford him. I am confident the remainder of the team can achieve success when we are allowed to return.'

On Monday, 8 June, the day before the EFL announced the result of the League One ballot for its preferred option to end the season, Darragh McAnthony – pre-empting what he presumed would be the outcome – returned to the airwaves on a podcast called *Hard Truth*. 'When we come back, we have to come back with absolute passion and desire. We have to drive over the injustice. We have the largest chip you've ever seen on our shoulder. For me it's about vengeance.'

Three weeks earlier he had said it was about integrity.

The Fourth Quarter

THERE were no parents waving their kids off, no ruffling of hair, no consoling hankies to wipe away tears or empty snot-filled noses, but in every other respect Monday, 8 June was first day back at a Wycombe primary school.

The pupils were shown to a designated space in the playground. They had arrived in their uniforms, except big boy Bayo who forgot his. The new one-way system for entry and exit was pointed out by Kelly the headmistress and an orderly queue with two metres of space formed for an inspection by nurse Aly before their footwear was collected from Steve the caretaker.

Numbered water bottles were set apart on a table and each boy had a meticulously measured area on the artificial pitch only they could occupy. That rascal Fred asked if the new changing room had been disinfected. He got one of the headmistress's looks.

Head boy Cian's arms were folded menacingly and one felt any minute he would be checking the boys for nits. On the playing field were gathered PE teachers Dobbo and Dave with bib boy Josh and form-master Gareth, whose tresses were tied back in an extravagant ponytail. A few of the boys pointed but daren't take the piss.

Some of their own hairstyles had become unruly though the scissors had been taken to cheeky lad Paul from Northern Ireland. Alex from Teesside was blow-me-away toned, David from Leeds drew admiring glances for his physique, as did Nnamdi the south London kid. Scott from Essex had found his way to school despite his absence for a lengthy spell of the previous term.

Rocky the Brummie began to throw himself this way and that on the grass and was sick. His personal tutor Andy paused momentarily before the lesson re-commenced.

Cian reappeared with a mask across his mouth and nose because prefect Blooms, who sat at the front of the class, needed tape attaching to his feet. Blooms could have been mistaken for a first year was it not for the odd fleck of grey in his hair.

Josh announced it was time for PE and the boys jumped, ran up and down and twirled their legs into interesting positions. Dave needed his balls sterilising and we all thought that was a jolly wheeze. The lads told stories about what they did during the holidays. They were all sad Jason had left and probably wouldn't come back.

The brown-bag school dinners arrived in a special van. I hoped the delivery driver had remembered the special posh ones for Josh P and Darius C with all those lovely nutrients. Then it was time to go home.

* * *

Wycombe's players were back to work and the club were picking up the entire tab. The furlough period was over. I imagined Rob Couhig back home in Louisiana shaking his dime tin in the hope there were enough coins inside to produce a rattle.

A lot of new plans were being put into place but it was hard to design for the unknown regardless of how smart you were. The EFL meeting to decide League One fates had been postponed time and again and was scheduled for the day after training resumed.

Wycombe's management were met by a player group eager to resume careers and yet side-tracked, mortified and empowered by the turn of events many miles from home. A horrific image from Minneapolis of a black man George Floyd having life drained from him when a white police officer kept a knee across his throat for almost nine minutes shone a game-changing light on decades of black oppression.

The world recoiled. Adebayo Akinfenwa, Darius Charles, Anthony Stewart, Nnamdi Ofoborh, Nick Freeman and Josh Parker posed in the throng at a Black Lives Matter rally in Parliament Square. Jacob Gardiner-Smith, the son of a politician, held a placard that read, 'White Silence is Violence.'

Akinfenwa's second-eldest son Jai had celebrated his tenth birthday in the week and Bayo posted a picture of father and boy kneeling in the back garden with right arms raised and fists clenched. For those of us whose memories stretched back to the black power demonstrations at the 1968 Mexico Olympics, this carried immense resonance.

Bayo had five children aged from five to 13. He was engaged in profound discussions with the elder siblings. 'I'm very hands on, they see my life, they know what it entails. We have conversations and watch the news together. They ask why people protest because they can't fathom it. When you're young, you're pure. They ask why and often I can't give them an answer. Why are people racist? I tell them the world isn't perfect. It can be beautiful and it can be scary and that's the balancing act as a parent.

'This can't be explained in a way I can understand. We can have conversations where we differ, perhaps on football or style. I get that there are different viewpoints. I'm fine if you dislike me because I'm a dickhead. But if you have never heard the way someone speaks or listened to his views and have a hatred simply for the colour of his skin, I swear to you it baffles me.'

Darius Charles spoke unscripted words of a man who weathered so much, worked so hard, played so well and now hurt so bad. Football offered him the platform to speak out and if he didn't kick another ball this season or anytime soon, he needed to be heard.

He said that when anger was running high it was important to pause and reflect. The time for reflection had passed. His message came in three parts. 'The [George Floyd] video is a visual representation of what systemic racism looks like. It's about being born black with a foot or a knee on your neck, laid on your stomach with hands cuffed behind your back being told to act normal as a decent law-abiding citizen when your basic human rights aren't adhered to.

'It's [about] white people sitting comfortably at home with their hands in their pockets showing such disregard or care for a race that is going through a genocide. It's not using that white privilege to combat the prejudices we face as a race.

'The second part is directed specifically to my people. We come from different backgrounds and classes. We are all black, though, and I don't like how we fight amongst each other even though I understand why we do because that is part of what systemic racism has done in terms of dividing and conquering us. We didn't create the system that has made us crabs in a barrel. It is our responsibility to get out of it.

'Long gone are the days when we asked white people to take accountability for their actions. Long gone are the days when we took a plate to their table. We need to stop marginalising and ostracising our own because some people choose to be silent. Some may be scared and not feel strong or brave enough to speak up for themselves. If you have a plan or a cause exact it and action it out. Give those who don't have a platform something to join.

'Finally I believe it is time that we started to create communities by us and for us. We need to take lessons from the Jewish, the Chinese, the Indians and many other cultures that have created such communities. In our communities we need schools with pupils that look like us and teachers that educate us about our history.

'We need health care systems that cater to our needs and don't discriminate against us, that don't have black women dying at a rate of five to one to their white counterparts. We need supermarkets that cater to the diets that are best tailored to us and fuel us to allow us to function better. There's never been a better time to do something about it.

'The Great Wall of China took 2,000 years to build and is 13,170 miles long. The person who laid the first brick never saw the last one laid. We are the first bricks. We are the generation that takes our race five steps forward. The generation after that will take us further forward and so on and so on. That is our job. This is not our fault; it is, however, our responsibility to get us as black people on the right path to where we want our future generations to be.'

* * *

The day of the football vote arrived. Several amendments to the matter at hand had been tabled – the Tranmere Project, the Lincoln Project and the Ipswich Project were variations on a theme but it took no time for the EFL to secure PPG as the means to complete the season should it receive 51 per cent support from the clubs.

The outcome was 18-4 for curtailment. It was like a re-run of the Couhig plebiscite. Not even the Peterborough 'Big Six' all voted the same way which rather spoiled their façade of unanimity. Coventry were declared champions with Rotherham promoted. Wycombe's record of 17 wins, eight draws and nine losses equated to 59 points at 1.74 per game, which saw them leap five spots to finish third ahead of Oxford, Portsmouth and Fleetwood.

There was a boiling sense of injustice in Peterborough (PPG 1.69) who fell from sixth to seventh. Oh the anguish, vitriol, condemnation and insecurity. Barry Fry, the club's larrikin director of football said it was the worst he'd felt in 60 years in the game, so managing Southend for a few months wasn't all that bad. 'We've been betrayed,' he said.

Wycombe were everyone's favourite pantomime villain for voting to end the season knowing they would play a further two, potentially three, matches. Could any club chairman, hand on the Bible, say they would have done differently in the same position?

Gareth Ainsworth and I enjoyed a socially distanced coffee at the Blue Orchid Bakery, Wokingham's newest treasure. He was preparing to head back to work though he had barely stopped in his down time, home schooling his kids where his knowledge of inverted trapeziums had obviously helped his teaching of algebra. He had stayed fit, having transformed half of his garage into a gym and become an advocate of cycling. He had pedalled from Finchampstead to the Wycombe training ground via Marlow's Hill and lived to tell the tale.

'If I'm fit my aura is healthy and that's very important to me. I've taken it as a mental break because it will be full blast and not only for the rest of this season but next season too. That's going to be a long, long season. I'm probably the only one not bothered about their hair growing in a lockdown.' His bad ankle was a bit fucked though and he walked with a distinct limp.

The discussion turned to the vote and the vitriol that had been aimed at his club. 'At times we've been made to feel we cheated. We played three quarters of the season and using PPG we deserved to be there. I wanted to turn around to people and go "oi" but my dad once said, "You can tell a wise man by the things he doesn't say."

'The fairest way to end was playing all the games. The next fairest was taking a decision on what had happened up until now, the next was cancelling everything and the least fairest was trying to predict the future.

'My empathy was with the relegated teams more than anyone else and especially Tranmere. If the league had pulled the plug the day before the Torquay game in 2014 and decided the table on 99 per cent of the season, Wycombe would be out of the league and probably not exist now.'

That Peterborough's owner Darragh McAnthony was so bitter at the EFL's process (agreed by a decisive majority) was a paradox given the reciprocal respect between Ainsworth and Darren Ferguson, the club's manager. 'Darren's a good guy. We've had many chats down the years and he's been a big help to me. I asked him once about why he played a particular shape and he more or less poured out his coaching philosophy.

'I've never been big enough to think I know it all. I need to keep learning. Pep Guardiola [head coach of Manchester City] is one of the best in the world and he openly admits he's an ideas thief.

'I managed against Darren's dad at QPR early on. He came over to me and said, "I'm glad they've given you a chance." When I won the League Two manager of the year in 2014 I was in a VIP room at the awards dinner, went to introduce myself to Sir Alex and he said, "I know who you are." It made me feel 10ft tall.'

And that was as tall as Ainsworth was at the end of the season proper. 'I'm not taking offence at what's been said. I know why McAnthony reacted the way he did. His club wanted to be there. But we finished one place away from automatic promotion. It's crazy how close we were. I'm the proudest man in the world, Wycombe Wanderers third. How does that happen?'

* * *

It happened in decisive part because the club's faith in the manager was unswerving. His outward appearance and cultural bent may have antagonised potential suitors, but Gareth Ainsworth's life was exactly where he wanted it. If the length of his hair was the knee across his opportunity of a move up the managerial ladder, what the heck?

'I have amazing relationships with people and that's the way I am. I've always wanted people to be happy. Jealousy grates on me – those people who want what everyone else has and for others to fail. The best tacticians in the world will get so far but at some stage it will fall apart. Relationships underpin everything. I don't think there's a great secret to it, it's about being a genuine guy. That can be hard. I was on my A-licence coaching course and a very famous manager was taking it at the same time. He said it was impossible for managers to be totally honest with their players. I disagreed.

'One day it might be my downfall. People don't like delivering bad news and to do that you need to be straight. It can't be good all the time. If you build a dressing room so tight and together and you're dishonest with one player you've cheated them all because you've created a family.

'That's the key. You can't pick and choose. Don't be a hypocrite, create that togetherness and then be dishonest with one and honest with another.'

It mattered not a jot that Ainsworth had been physically separated from his players for the best part of three months. 'It is as if you have a good friend and you don't talk for a while, you see his number come up and you can't answer, but think, "I'll get back him" and you don't and then after six weeks you get back together, you hug and it's like you've never been apart.

'You don't have to rebuild relationships at Wycombe. You can talk about anything because you know everyone's there for you. Being six months apart from these boys wouldn't worry me because we'd come back together with the characters and dynamics in the right place.'

His personal life was in a loving, secure place. He put much of that down to Donna, his Venezuelan partner, and her calm resourcefulness. 'She re-set my life. Here is a woman who grew up in a home with no electricity in the evening, whose family sold everything to move to England for the chance of a better life.

'They showed great foresight to see how the country was heading under [Hugo] Chavez, the president. It was going to be grim. Eleven of them lived in a two-bedroom house in Uxbridge. I think the parents were wary of me at the start, seven years their daughter's senior, in the middle of a divorce and a footballer. Was there anything worse?

'But I've been so lucky to have found her and been able to experience such a different culture from the one I grew up in. It's good to have your eyes opened to different attitudes. She has set me straight so many times.' His children, Scarlett, 16, from his first marriage, Kane Presley, 13, and Giselle, 11, with Donna were his young lights.

Then there was his other blue-shirted family. As the last two [perhaps three] matches of a tumultuous season approached, so Ainsworth prepared to commit to some and lose others who had formed such a powerful bond. He agonised over the loss of Jason McCarthy who played two months of football on his return to Wycombe before his emergency loan from Millwall was called in.

'On the terms offered we couldn't afford him. It was as simple as that, 100 per cent. In January we were top of the league and needed a right-back to cover for Jack Grimmer. We had to pay good money to get Jason. Rob [Couhig] said he would finance it to the end of May. We just couldn't change the deal in front of us, it was a financial impossibility to keep him.'

For McCarthy himself the sadness was intense. He constantly had to clear his throat as we chatted. 'Wycombe kept paying all my wages through the lockdown and that was unbelievable credit to them. It seemed Millwall wasn't willing to budge. It sucks really. It would have been awesome to be involved in the play-offs.

'I'm left to deal with the consequences and it's tough. My faith has really helped and even though it won't be me in the play-offs, Jack [Grimmer] is coming back, he'll do a great job and I'm confident Wycombe will be promoted. I've been spending quality time with my family, my son [George] turned one during the lockdown. I have a lot to be grateful for.'

Bournemouth and QPR were more accommodating in the trying circumstances. The loan periods of Nnamdi Ofoborh,

Paul Smyth and Giles Phillips were extended to encompass the two-leg semi-final and the final, should Wycombe participate. The contracts of Sido Jombati, Jamie Mascoll and Jacob Gardiner-Smith expired on 30 June and wouldn't be renewed. Craig Mackail-Smith had returned after a season-long loan at Stevenage but was unavailable for the play-offs.

Ainsworth had to have one eye on the present and another to look beyond, but at what? The same league, a different league, no fans, a few fans, season ticket spikes or crashes, players equipped or not? This was another unprecedented test of his leadership skills. 'We should be more prepared than most clubs for anything given the traumas we've had over the years. There is a way through this.

'What I've realised is that Rob and Pete are real, genuine people. I don't know, nor need to, how wealthy a person Rob is, but in terms of a human being, he's very rich. He's got all the traits that you respect and he's there for you.

'I'm confident I'll have 17 signed for the start of next season. If we're still in League One the focus will be on staying there because we have taken a massive hit financially. If it's the Championship we'll have to work wonders.'

That was the Wycombe way. A revelation from the Football Association's 'clearing account' showed that the fees paid to agents and intermediaries by League One clubs for the year ending 31 January 2020 amounted to a gross £3,921,805. The Chairboys spent £25,868, the third least in the league.

Their semi-final opponent Fleetwood forked out seven times that much. Sunderland, condemned to a third season in the league after finishing eighth, the worst position in the club's history, lined third-party pockets to the tune of £1,346,373.

Send in the clowns. Don't bother. They're here.

* * *

For Wycombe to reach the promised land, one man had to be rolling from the off on Friday, 3 July at the Highbury Stadium.

Rocky Allsop may need to save a penalty, Jack Grimmer play as if he'd never been away, Anthony Stewart retain his immense poise, Curtis Thompson lay it all on the line, Scott Kashket unwrap a piece of genius or Fred Onyedinma accelerate away from a defence.

If all this happened and Adebayo Akinfenwa wasn't on his game, it may not be enough. The lift he gave those with him, the knockdowns, the irresistible challenges, the penalty-area presence as a blockade in defence and spearhead in attack were massive attributes.

He was neither going to run in behind a back line, nor chase down an opponent in possession, so the opposition could afford to defend high whereas his own back four often needed to remain deep when he was in the side for fear of being undone by a quickly-shifted pass and a burst of forward acceleration.

In the days preceding the trip to Fleetwood, Bayo played the last 20 minutes of the fourth and final practice match played under a burning sun at Adams Park. His right leg was significantly strapped. Ainsworth and Dobson allowed me to put my old refereeing qualifications to use so they could watch from the back row of the first tier of the Frank Adams stand.

I presumed it was because of the proximity of the matches to come that there was an edge, much finger pointing and a few 'where the fuck were you?' comments between friends. Matt Bloomfield told the boys at half-time to drop the self-defeating grizzly and argumentative attitude. 'We've got the play-offs to win and it won't happen if we're having a go at each other,' he said.

Practice matches were often a player's nightmare. Contact tended to be half-hearted and lack of total commitment could lead to mistimed tackles and potential injuries. Sharpness came frustratingly slowly or not at all. The virus remained all around us. Would a player want to push himself to the limit? What happened if he felt a twinge? Would he try to cover it up? The biggest match of most lives was but a few days away.

Alex Pattison scored a hat-trick and looked as refreshed and ready as anyone. Bayo had been told not to do anything silly in his cameo. At the training ground he was the super tanker surrounded by a flotilla of small ships, a grinding giant in isolation who was forced into bursts of intensity across a range of gym equipment under Cian O'Doherty's gaze and stopwatch.

It would take a while for anyone of Akinfenwa's size to get moving in a manner that would affect a game positively. 'There's a worry in my head because I'm a gradual starter. It takes me a long time to get up the hill and then I roll down fast. For a regular season, I don't have to be at my optimum for the first game. I know I'm not going to be at my best for the first, the second, even ten. That's my process. In the back of my mind this could be an unprecedented situation and I'm going to have to hit it [the ground] running.

'I always believe in whatever I do and I've always believed in Wycombe. When we were going through an horrendous run last season and the talk outside the changing room was we'd go down, we knew we had such a good set of people. There's a different energy in us that gives us an underlining confidence we will get this right because we will leave everything out there. If we fall short, we fall short, there's nothing we can do about that.

'Going into this season, if it clicked I knew we were a problem for anybody. It clicked until the moment we were seven points clear and those outside couldn't believe we were top and kept talking about the way we play. Ipswich has exactly the same style of play as us but the name came with a certain pedigree. We have a stigma. I would be lying if I thought we'd be top three for most of the season.

'Everyone said, "Oh they'll fall away, it can't last," and it's how we've used that outside negativity. We're so different to anybody else out there. We emulate the gaffer. He is very much his man and he does it his way. I feel we have enough to do what we set out to do and that is to get promoted.'

Akinfenwa's role as a general was one he took too naturally. He was a force but there was nothing forced about him. 'In any walk of life a pup comes along and your inclination is to pass on your experience. You say, "I was there, I went left and you need to go right." Helping people learn things quicker than I did is a must.

'Except for Blooms, when you get older you lose that something you had as a youngster. My mind can run all day but my legs can't. I feed off the energy of young players on the training ground, even if when I'm driving in as I have done for 20 years I don't feel I want to do it today. It's a give and take. There is such a pure energy in the Wycombe changing room, no egos, no big time.

'I've had conversations with every player in the squad and I've seen my words transpire from their body language off and on the pitch. I don't want to take the credit. What I'm saying is I feel that they've taken notice of what I've said but that's just one part of it.

'I have a responsibility off the pitch and on it. I have the responsibility to be Adebayo Akinfenwa to get the team up and to score my goals. Then there's an even bigger responsibility off the pitch to every single one of my team-mates. My main message is not to let football take away from your essence as a human being. Don't get it twisted. We're here for a period of time in football so you need to take out of this game everything you can. Every single person I've talked to has stepped up this season on the pitch. Me included.

'There's a certain energy I emit when I go into a building. I know that. I've said it to the gaffer and Dobbo. I know the power of my energy and how it can work for positivity and negativity. If I walk into a room and I'm in a mood, everybody knows it without me saying anything. I don't have to come into a room and eff and blind for people to know there's something off with me.

'At the same time I know there's a flip side to it. If my energy is infectious, I know when I go to places it can become a stampede and my take on that is it costs nothing to be nice. The only thing it might cost me is time I'm happy to give. Time is the one thing you can't get back so it you have something positive to give, don't waste it.

'There's nobody like me. I have my physical attributes so when people see me its an anomaly – something that goes against the grain. I looked at a video yesterday of me and my brothers dancing and thought "I'm a big boy", and that was just dancing let alone running around a football pitch.

'When you look at something that doesn't fit the mould you automatically think it shouldn't be there. I get that. Then there's a sense of "fair play to him, he's doing what we didn't think he could do". I get the abuse and the banter and I'm big enough to handle it.'

It would be easy for a player of Akinfenwa's size and (social media) spread to dominate the club, for it to become Bayo first and Wycombe second. That never had and never would happen.

Ainsworth said, 'Bayo could be more powerful than me. He could hold court in the dressing room but not once has he without acknowledging me first. He's such a character but his respect for me is huge and that's because we've both had real tough times. I've helped him through those. All the things that have happened to me in life have given me the weapons to deal with all my players. Most have young families, some have had marriage breakdowns and have kids with more than one woman. I know about that, I've been there.

'For me, it is about what Bayo delivers. You wouldn't mess with him physically so that gives him an advantage. He walks into a room and you know he's there. Which gives him power. But he never ever steps over the line of "I'm more powerful than the gaffer". He has this humility as well, he knows his fame and celebrity pushes Wycombe higher but he always stays under me.'

It was often reported that coronavirus took more of a toll on Britain's BAME population, that people of black, Asian, and ethnic minorities were more susceptible to catching

Covid-19. Akinfenwa took that as he took much else, on his considerable chin.

'I'm not scared to come back and play because I'm black. It's not as if I'm sitting in the house protecting the family and waiting for a cure. We've got to live. I want to get back into life. I'm more vigilant for everyone.

'I don't know how these games are going to go. Can I play in the Championship? There have been times when I wondered if I could finish this season. The strongest thing I have is my mind. If there was an opportunity and we got to the Championship there's no way I wouldn't want to test myself, even at 38.

'I've been in Leagues One and Two all of my career, for 20 years, so it's not as if I've earned crazy money and it's cool, I can retire.'

* * *

In the lucky dip to come, Gareth Ainsworth would make career-shaping decisions. Whatever formation he selected, a goalkeeper in form was going to be pretty crucial. It was noticeable in the Wycombe fans' forums that in the debate about preferred play-off teams most named David Stockdale ahead of Rocky Allsop.

Stockdale had returned to training in as a good a physical condition as he'd possibly ever been. The first time he entered Wycombe's gates in November 2018 it was the manner of his transport rather than his physique that caused tongues to wag. He had joined on an emergency loan from Birmingham City and drove into the training ground in a Rolls-Royce Ghost.

He took some gentle ribbing and the next day pulled up in a Volkswagen Golf. 'People thought it [change of vehicle] was because I wanted to fit in but it was more about the cost of the petrol. I'm a Yorkshireman after all. If I was coming from the Midlands to Wycombe for a decent spell it wasn't financially viable.

'I had to bring the Rolls back a couple of times because all the lads wanted to have a look. I offered the keys to any of them to drive it but nobody took me up. It was just a dream car of mine and I could afford it. I've still got it at home.'

Stockdale, then 33, had fallen out of love with football and anything was going to be an advance on kicking his heels at St Andrew's. 'I made friends straight away, it was the type of changing room where you didn't have to worry about being yourself. I played twice and the second time at Accrington we won and I had one of those nights. It was cold and windy but everything fell into place.'

'Then [chairman] Trevor Stroud and the gaffer came to me and said Birmingham were being awkward and wanted me back. I went a little nuts because I'd been promised four weeks and I was enjoying being back in a competitive changing room. I had to go back.

'This time it was a case of if Cam [Cameron Yates] got injured, they wanted a bit of competition for Rocky and I was in a situation where I needed to be out enjoying football again. I didn't know if I was going to be playing.'

Stockdale professed surprise to find himself in the first team, selected on his return. 'We had a meeting, the manager asked if I wanted to say 'owt and I said, "I'm here to help in whatever way I can, if that's on the bench I'll be 100 per cent supporting whoever plays and use my experience." The lads knew me and took that well.

'I was surprised to come in and if I'm honest it might haven been a bit too soon. I'd played half a dozen games in two years. It's amazing because you do lose contact with match fitness and people think it's about how fit you are but so much of it [goalkeeping] is about decision-making.'

Stockdale played twice, the team took three points from six, conceded three goals and Ainsworth immediately reverted to Allsop. 'You put personal feelings aside when a manager makes his choice and you get behind the team because it's a special place and if you didn't you'd get pulled up on it by a lot of individuals.

'There are support systems within the changing room and luckily I'm an age now where I've been dropped a lot of times and you deal with it in different ways. There are a lot of young lads around and if they see you take the decision and work hard to get back, they can learn from that.

'This is an honest club. If someone wasn't picking you for a certain reason you'd rather know what that was because nine times out of ten you'd work on that to improve it rather than sitting there wondering what you'd done wrong. They explain decisions here. No one is in any doubt.'

Two days before the first leg against Fleetwood, Ainsworth told Stockdale he was picking Allsop. The player turned to his manager and said that he would be there 100 per cent for his team-mate in practice and support him as never before.

* * *

On Friday, 1 July Wycombe had -£2,500 in the bank. The season ticket prices for 2020/21 had caused something of a stir but like every club involved in a play-off it had to work these out blindfolded given it may be playing one of either Norwich or Northampton twice in the months ahead. In these circumstances, the thud of resistance was relatively dull.

The expected flow of income for renewals hadn't been banked by 30 June – the end of football's financial year – thanks to red-tape bollocks that left Pete Couhig cursing at his laptop.

It had been an eye-watering few months for an American in control of an English football club's finances, made more comical that the man he was dealing with at TicketCo – motto 'event payments made easy' – went by the name of Odd. 'Weird shit,' Pete said.

Those supporters who declined the offer of a rebate on their 2019/20 season tickets – four home games had gone up in a viral cloud – did so knowing the leftovers would be ploughed into squad strengthening. The four [Mascoll, Jombati, Gardner-Smith and Mackail-Smith] not offered new contracts all wished to stay with the lads until the final ball was kicked. They took their seats on the two buses that headed north, another additional expense because everyone needed to be properly distanced.

The check-in at the Barton Grange in Preston went as smoothly as one could imagine given there were no other guests in the building. The hotel chef had been brought back from furlough to cook for the squad and the £20-per-head restriction remained in force for those who wanted to go off menu, as per regular away trips.

Jack Grimmer considered returning to reception to demand a different room when he couldn't find a bathroom. Deeper investigation and he discovered it was located behind the bookshelf he unveiled like a scene from *Poirot* when the shrewd Belgian demonstrated to the assembled throng how the killer made his getaway.

'Vous sortez le troisième livre de la gauche et le tour est voilà!'

Was there to be more magic in the chilled Lancashire air? At 5pm on match day a few souls mingled in the hotel foyer. Pete Couhig, former chairman Andrew Howard, commercial manager Neil Peters, media chief Matt Cecil and Tom Darlington, the father of Oli the 13-year-old fan who had passed away in January and was a special guest of the club, stood around. They made eye contact with Gareth Ainsworth but little was said. The manager was trying to memorise the words of the speech he was to deliver to his players.

Richard Dobson took the squad through set-piece nuances and outside the room like a nervous actor keen to deliver a command performance, he stood and waited for the call. Two lads needed the loo. He paused once more and recalled that chaplain Benedict Musola had texted him a couple of hours earlier with a simple message.

Musola was driving home from a meeting in Wycombe when he said he felt a revelation. 'This had happened to me a few times in my life. I had to pull off the road and listen again to the Holy Spirit. The message came through "It will be well." I sent that on to Gareth.'

* * *

The team Ainsworth picked flashed up on the screen. 'Right, you have all the information you need for this game. Anyone in this room who has been involved in a play-off, staff included, stand up.' There was a rustling of chairs and a decent number of people on their feet.

'I guarantee you now looking around there is more in this squad than there is in the opposition tonight. We know how to handle this. The first leg is a free hit. We get to look at them, we get to have a go at them and then they come to our place. It's going to be a different experience, there's no hiding from that. There will be mannequins, scarecrows, cardboard cut-outs, it's a wet, horrible night.

'There will be no fans but is that true? Can we be each other's fans? Can you cheer a pass, a tackle or a bit of magic that someone displays? Can we pick each other up if we need to? You'd be amazed how you can transfer energy to one another. I promise you that you can. It's the way you look at each other, the way you talk to each other, it's the body language I know you've spoken about. It's the way you do it together. That's how we're going to beat this team tonight.

'I'm in no doubt the team I've picked is good enough, 100 per cent. All you have to do is bring me your best. If your best is being on the bench and cheering somebody, you're transferring your energy. Can you give me that? My job is to ask people to do what I believe they can do. I believe in you.

'In the last three months the world has torn itself apart in so many ways. There has been a reset of values, good or bad, whatever the reasons. People have realised what's important in life. Through this time think about the people you've spoken to. It's been your families, your friends and throughout the whole of lockdown you've been speaking to each other. Not just at the start and not right at the end, but the whole way through. That just doesn't happen.

'I didn't force you to do it. You did it because you're together. You train together, practise together, work together, win together and you hurt together. You've laughed together, cried together, been injured together. You've come back to this season together. You did that. That's the band of Wycombe brothers I want tonight.

'When you go into a tackle you're saying, "I'm willing to get hurt for my team-mates." There's no bigger power than that. These moments of success can't be judged by statistics, though that's what a lot of people do. You judge success by those feelings you get that the majority of people are never able to feel.

'It's those childlike moments when you're running around on the pitch, grown men hugging each other and you lose it for a second. And you don't mind losing it because it's your mates together on that pitch.

'I want you all to close your eyes and take yourself to those moments when you are losing it and you have a moment of ecstasy the majority of people never get to feel. It may be a goal you scored, your first game, something somebody said to you? That moment no one can ever take away. Visualise it and take it out there tonight.'

Applause thundered through the room.

* * *

Wycombe's players had not competed in a professional football match since Saturday, 29 February. Some 133 days had passed, most of the time spent in their own front rooms with their wives, girlfriends and children for daily distraction. No one had been to a beach or Butlins, relished a cool beer and cleared their heads from football.

The order of all these days had been self-protection, covering up, waiting, waiting, waiting for the virus to subside, for the politics to unravel and for the chance to step out and play again. These had been, indeed, uniquely bizarre times.

Since when did a team return from such a trial and have to compete, first, in a semi-final? That was unprecedented enough and then it was away from home, in front of a sea of cardboard faces and real ones covered, nose and mouth, by masks. To expect anything other than a shell of a match was absurd. And yet before we'd settled into our seats a left footer from 25 yards by Nnamdi Ofoborh, surely the sweetest he had struck in his 20 years, gave Wycombe the lead.

Two minutes on and another phantom penalty was awarded when a linesman saw something from 25 yards away the referee didn't notice from five, and when Ched Evans equalised the theme from *Captain Pugwash* resounded around the ground.

A corner by Joe Jacobson caught the wind whipping in from the Irish Sea and marooned goalkeeper Alex Cairns. This was immediately followed by a penalty to Wycombe for a horror tackle by Lewie Coyle on Jacobson that earned a red card. Jacobson took the spot-kick but Cairns saved it low to his left.

David Wheeler scored in added time at the end of the first half and performed his usual 'driver at the wheel' celebration. Then there was Rocky Allsop's second-half free kick that Cairns dropped towards Alex Samuel, who kept his balance to score.

Late on, Paddy Madden, who had scored in both league matches and was introduced as a threatening substitute, dived under a challenge from Darius Charles, was booked, argued on, was shown red and buried his studs into an inoffensive drinks carrier.

At the end of a 4-1 victory (over a quarter of Wycombe's away goals of the season had arrived in one evening), Adebayo Akinfenwa stood in the middle of the group to deliver a highly charged rallying cry. I had Charles down as the best player by a squeak. 'I'm repaying the club the debt I owe,' he said.

On the trip home the M6 was shut at junction 14 requiring a diversion onto the A34 around Stafford and the entry slip to the M42 was coned off, forcing a detour onto the A444 past Coventry. The coaches pulled in at 4am. Would it not have been fairer for the kick-off gods to chose Oxford against Portsmouth (82 miles apart) for the later start rather than Fleetwood against Wycombe (220 miles) where the away side would be manifestly more inconvenienced?

How would the boys respond, some 60 hours and much interrupted sleep later?

* * *

Curtis Thompson had a feeling he might not play at Fleetwood, that Nnamdi Ofoborh would get the nod. He spoke with the manager and said that though these were potentially the biggest matches of his life and Championship football was a dream, whatever decision was made he'd be there, 100 per cent, for the lads. 'This is more than about one person,' he said. 'I need to do what's best for the team, not me.'

Wycombe started with the same XI in the second leg. Adams Park was bedecked in tributes and telling illustrations. A massive banner proclaiming 1.74 (the PPG average that lifted the side to third place) had pride of place on the BMI Healthcare Stand, and next to the press box were images of those who had departed this life including Mark Bird and Oli Darlington. The manager told his boys to do them all proud.

We knew Fleetwood would throw caution to the wind. There was no alternative. This lack of awareness was manifested in crisp interchangeable passing, drawing Wycombe all over the pitch, inviting crosses and enabling openings. The home side blocked, scrambled and harried. They covered for each like men possessed. Eventually a nick appeared in the dam when Danny Andrew's smasher from 20 yards reduced the aggregate by one. Wycombe clung on for half-time.

Ainsworth decided he had to introduce a destabiliser. Alex Samuel's impact had been negligible so Adebayo Akinfenwa came on for no other reason than he often drew two defenders to him. Within two minutes of the restart, Fred Onyedinma gave Harry Souttar a run for his money, the defender mistakenly tried to keep the ball alive on the by-line and succeeded only in setting Fred up with a chance he eagerly took.

By now the noise from the Fleetwood bench and its directors was in full, nauseating blast. One director began to sing 'Swing Low, Sweet Chariot', which one took to suggest Wycombe was to use rugby tactics, though the song's connotations of black oppression and slavery went decidedly deeper than that.

As Adebayo Akinfenwa was introduced at the start of the second half, someone in the Fleetwood camp was overheard using the words 'fat water buffalo.' The player didn't hear it, which was extremely lucky for if he had he said he wouldn't have been available for the final. Fleetwood was not an edifying group. Referee Darren Bond told a group of their players, 'You lot complain more than my missus.'

Bond awarded the third penalty of the tie with which Ched Evans restored Fleetwood's lead on the night and after more possession that probed rather than penetrated, Rocky Allsop's one-handed save from Evans's header ten minutes from time was perhaps his most telling stop of the season.

With two minutes of stoppage time to play, Onyedinma collected a defensive clearance, exchanged passes with Nick Freeman, took a couple of side-stepping strides and spun a right-footed shot into the bottom corner, a goal of unutterable brilliance. Wycombe was heading Wembley way.

* * *

At two o'clock on the day of the final, Gareth Ainsworth sat down at his desk at the Hilton Hotel just off Empire Way, picked up his private green book and began to write his final oration of the season. He had prepared three short videos. In the first, Laurel the cleaner, who had turned up at the training ground each day since lockdown, was asked what she thought of the lads. She said, 'Thank you for making me so welcome and feeling a part of the team. I'll be watching tonight and thinking of you all. Bye luvvies.'

'Then Jason McCarthy said he'd have given anything to be on the pitch with the boys tonight. Lastly Ben Frempah, a non-contract player who had done everything I'd asked him to do for me, played anywhere for two years and never once asked for anything in return. He said he'd be with the boys in spirit and, finally, "When you win, I win." It was so powerful.'

The manager completed his speech with the words 'right place, right time, our time'. He wrote them on the dressing-room board with emphasis on 'our time' in blue ink. As Oxford lined up in the tunnel outside they heard 'right place, right time, OUR time' in a startling crescendo. 'They must have wondered what was going on.'

Ainsworth belted out the national anthem as if it was the last song he would ever sing. 'I wanted to win the national anthem for our side. I was going to blast it out with all my heart and not be embarrassed. I couldn't ask my support players to shout for the lads all game and not do the same with the anthem.'

At half-time Wycombe led 1-0 through a mammoth far-post header by Anthony Stewart. The manager was rousing his team and noticed Matt Bloomfield on one knee in a corner. 'He was being sick, almost convulsing, and Cian gave me the sign that he couldn't play on. Everything that man worked for, his whole career, had been about reaching this point. He had given everything and couldn't give any more.'

Oxford's 57th-minute equaliser from Mark Sykes was a replica of Jason McCarthy's goal against Rochdale in January, a right-wing cross expected to move away from the goalkeeper that reverse swung across an outstretched arm. Rocky Allsop then made two telling saves with that same big-gloved hand to deny Oxford the lead before his thumping clearance was misjudged by centre-half Elliott Moore and Fred Onyedinma toe-poked it past goalkeeper Simon Eastwood, who clattered into him.

There was the longest pause before referee Robert Jones made the only decision open to him. Joe Jacobson – who had missed his attempt during Sunday's penalty practice – heard

Oxford's defenders telling Eastwood which side he'd choose but importantly recalled goalkeeping coach Andy Fairman's advice to hit it straight and true. The delivery was perfect.

'I was never prepared to get promoted,' Ainsworth said. 'I don't know whether that was my pessimistic streak. In my head, because of the Southend play-off in 2015, I was tearing myself apart. One side of me had to persuade these boys they could do anything. I had to convince myself too because the other side was preparing to say to the press, "What an achievement just to get to the final."

'Right until the final whistle when they [Oxford] had the ball I said to Dobbo, "Surely this can't happen again." That Southend match scarred me so much I thought they were going to score. Then the whistle blew and Dobbo was close to bursting into tears. He never gets emotional. He said, "What have we done Gaz, what have we done?"

What they had done was to inspire a season of such ridiculousness that neither anybody on the pitch nor those gazing upon it would ever see its like again.

At the time the last whistle blast bounced through the echo chamber, Wycombe led Oxford by two goals to one and had thus secured promotion to the Championship. It took a few seconds for that to work its way into the brain. Thereupon erupted some delirium.

The old stadium was awash with heaving bodies, great jerking movements from those in Wycombe blue collapsing under a sheer monumental emotional explosion. No one could stay upright. Matt Bloomfield, pale as a ghost, sank in a heap. Alex Samuel and Adebayo Akinfenwa were on their knees praising God. Cheap champagne washed over exhausted bodies. Medals were placed around necks.

In the director's box, those who had been in charge for years and the relative apprentices, embraced in fraternal disbelief. I turned to those players who hadn't been involved on the night seated in the box to my left. Cameron Yates, the goalkeeper, was in such an uncontrollable flood of tears I feared for the foundations around his seat. He had been told that those players not in the squad could not go down onto the pitch with their mates. Benedict Musola, the chaplain, moved over to comfort him.

Jamie Mascoll, who had tweeted 'We haven't come this far only to come this far', though he would not appear in the colours again, was being consoled by former trust chairman Trevor Stroud. It took a hell of a lot of persuading from his mates for Jamie to be pictured in a team group with the League One play-off trophy. A 133-year-old breakthrough achievement.

It was entirely fitting that a Wembley final should be the emphatic full point to what made this Wycombe side special. Through it beat a heart of lionesque commitment and unswerving belief in each other sprinkled with a little magic dust.

Jack Grimmer said he felt in the pit of his stomach on the morning of the final that Wycombe wouldn't lose. He couldn't quite explain it. When Grimmer and David Wheeler appeared on the same flank – the workaholics anonymous – the side had not lost a match. I christened them the 'right' brothers.

Wheels recalled the day he was rejected by Brighton and Hove Albion as a 16-year-old and how his father was overcome at seeing his son so demoralised. Now, in July 2020, 14 years on, he was a Championship footballer and about to become a father for the first time. The squad was riddled with such stories.

Most of this side had endured rejection in one form or another. Ainsworth and Dobson had been able to seize on that, utilise their skills both as healers and life coaches and bring the utmost from what was a professional pick and mix, much of it from the lowest shelf.

Amid the many crowning glories of the final was the performance of Anthony Stewart, the pride of Brixton and the season's one league ever present. Stewart had been 'Tools' ever since his job was to hammer in the touchline ropes at Wycombe youth matches. Against Oxford he used every tool in the box, classic interceptions, giant headers, thunderous clearances and the far-post connection that gave Wycombe their early breathing space.

His reflection was of 'the hard moments in life, not for me personally but as a club, when we survived relegation in 2014. I played in that game. We've come a long way, I know how tough it's been but the family we are, that's what makes today so special.

'It wasn't always this way. Bit by bit, since he took over, the gaffer has created this and it's beautiful to have seen how it has developed. We can meet up at any time, call at any time, be there for each other at any time. That's not normal. It shows on the pitch, the desire, how far we're willing to go for each other. I've never heard anyone talking about a bond in a side like the one we have here.

'Tonight is quite weird. At the beginning of the season I said to myself I was getting to peak age as a footballer and always wanted to play in the Championship; call that selfish if you want, but it is what I wanted to do. To achieve it with Wycombe, I've literally been crying since the final whistle [we were talking at one in the morning outside the Ship Inn in Marlow where the party had only just begun].

'Yesterday I was having to control my emotions so much. I tried to stay strong around the boys, but I went into my room in the evening and was very emotional. I was thinking that we had come this far and I didn't want to come this far to lose the game. It wasn't nerves – they haven't affected me. I'm just thinking about this now. This is life changing for all of us.

'The gaffer's man-management is incredible. He knows how to deal with players, not just on the pitch but off it as well. Life problems. When I was going to become a father last year [his daughter Sarai was now nearing nine months old] I asked him if I could miss a few days. He said I should do what's right and stay with my family. That's special because this is a business job, if he cares more about you and your family than what might be best for him, you want to give more to him every day you can.

'I owe Dobbo the world. Before I came to Wycombe, I was playing Sunday league football at 15. I was at a point when I was thinking to myself maybe football wasn't for me. I needed to start to provide for my household. My dad passed when I was just 16, and I was having to deal with that mentally as well as trying to get up and back to Wycombe – that wasn't easy.

'I felt I was losing my identity as a person. I was going to school two days a week and they probably wanted to kick me out because I was misbehaving. My agent at the time negotiated with my head teacher for me to be on day release. I went to school the first three days of the week and I was in digs with older lads at Wycombe from Thursday to Saturday. That was a major learning curve football wise. I got my scholarship and broke through as a player when I was 19.

'Dobbo has been my coach as a kid, in the youth team and then in the first team. I really can't speak highly enough of him because the job he's done for me personally has been immense. He's been through everything with me. One day I'll fully repay him.' The first goal in a Wembley final was a decent down payment.

The players didn't want to leave the field. Dominic Gape was in world of his own, looking up for a star, though the clouds didn't permit a glimpse. Jack Grimmer was face-timing his grannie in Aberdeen. In his touchline interview Akinfenwa said God made the impossible possible. 'Wycombe are in the Championship. I don't think they heard me at the back. Wycombe are in the Championship.' And we could finally believe.

Bayo's phone rang as he waited on the pavement outside Wembley. It was Jurgen Klopp offering congratulations and an invitation to join Liverpool's Premier League victory parade. Paul Pogba sent an inspirational note to Nnamdi Ofoborh saying he would always look out for him. Blooms emerged from self-imposed social media exile to say, 'All the sacrifices, injuries, proving others wrong and myself right and putting right perceived failures, came pouring out. This is why I push my mind and body to places I don't always want to go.'

* * *

For a moment, our minds went back six months. In January on Twitter @CJF_x had written, 'Wycombe in second place is like an elephant at the top of a tree – nobody really knows how the fuck it got up there but everybody knows it will fall.' Jack Grimmer said the tweet had stuck with him and remained a constant motivation. Wycombe's official Twitter account said, 'the elephant didn't fall, it climbed higher.' Those who missed out on promotion raged and ranted but their time had passed. That elephant had soared and roared.

* * *

A few miles outside Blackburn, Bill and Chris Ainsworth, their son Liam and his family were downing the contents of a second bottle of champagne in a week. They'd had one after the Adams Park leg of the Fleetwood semi-final. 'It's more stressful watching on TV than it is live,' Bill said. 'It was surreal at the end.'

So many images flashed through Bill's mind: Gareth as a bit of a timid lad, an altar boy, the pre-teenage years when he sank into his shell, the many footballing rejections, his burgeoning character, the things that players told him about his son being something more than a manager and Pete Couhig telling him what Gareth had said to the players before the Fleetwood first leg that made his whole body tremble.

'I remember Darius Charles told me when he went to see Gareth, said that he'd been advised that his career was over and couldn't help himself crying. Then he looked over and Gareth was in tears as well. When you hear stories like this I reflect on those early days of a little lad in awe of football and footballers and how much he has really grown.'

* * *

The story was over. The deed had been done. I thought of the times we had spent together with its improbable moments, tears and fears, generous and unquenchable spirit, unfathomable achievement and joys of brotherhood.

To Rocky, Jack, JJ, Gapey, Tools, Darius, Wheels, Blooms, Alex, Nnamdi, Fred, B, Curtis, Patto, Nick, Scotty, Smythy, Stocko, Josh, Giles, Sido, Jamie, Cam, C Mac, Jacob and absent friends Rizz and Jason, permanent residence in the Hall of Fame.

To Gareth with his hands thrust into the back pockets of his trendy jeans, dark-blue shirt, black-leather jacket, the slightly soiled red alligator boots, and Dobbo, the loyal assistant, always neat and trim in grey tracksuit, pen and paper in hand, the proof of management beyond compare.

To Andy, Watesy and Josh. These were my kind of football people. To Cian, Aly, Sara, Isaac and Doc Bob who showed amazing professionalism and resilience in the toughest circumstances. To Bob and Steve for oiling the wheels and to Scott for making sure they were always pointed in the right direction.

They would be starting all over again in a couple of months. There would need to be an influx of new players if Wycombe were to survive a season in the Championship. Whoever was lucky enough to be asked to play a part would enter a home fit for heroes.